THE VISION

YESTERDAY and TOMORROW

VIS
YESTERDAY

COLORS: **CHRIS SOTOMAYOR**

LETTERS: **PAUL TUTRONE**

AVENGERS #57

WRITER: **ROY THOMAS**

PENCILER: **JOHN BUSCEMA**

INKER: **GEORGE KLEIN**

LETTERS: **SAM ROSEN**

COLOR RECONSTRUCTION: **TOM ZIUKO**

ION

TOMORROW

WRITER: **GEOFF JOHNS**

PENCILER: **IVAN REIS**

INKERS: **JOE PIMENTEL & OCLAIR ALBERT**

ASSISTANT EDITORS: **MARC SUMERAK & ANDY SCHMIDT**

EDITOR: **TOM BREVOORT**

COVER ART: **BRIAN HABERLIN**

SENIOR EDITOR, SPECIAL PROJECTS: **JEFF YOUNGQUIST**

ASSISTANT EDITORS: **JENNIFER GRÜNWALD & MICHAEL SHORT**

BOOK DESIGNER: **CARRIE BEADLE**

CREATIVE DIRECTOR: **TOM MARVELLI**

DIRECTOR OF SALES: **DAVID GABRIEL**

EDITOR IN CHIEF: **JOE QUESADA**

PUBLISHER: **DAN BUCKLEY**

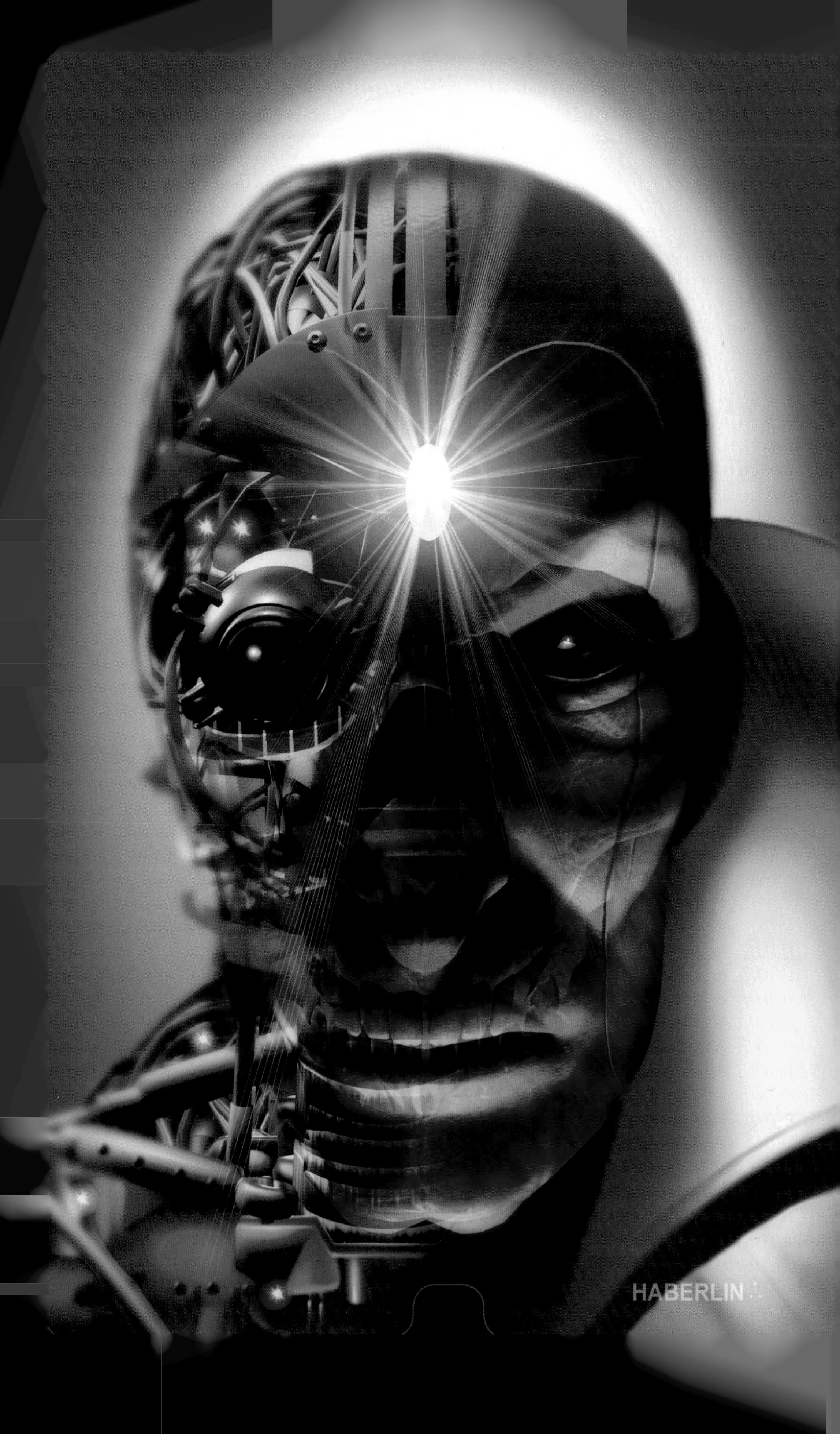
HABERLIN

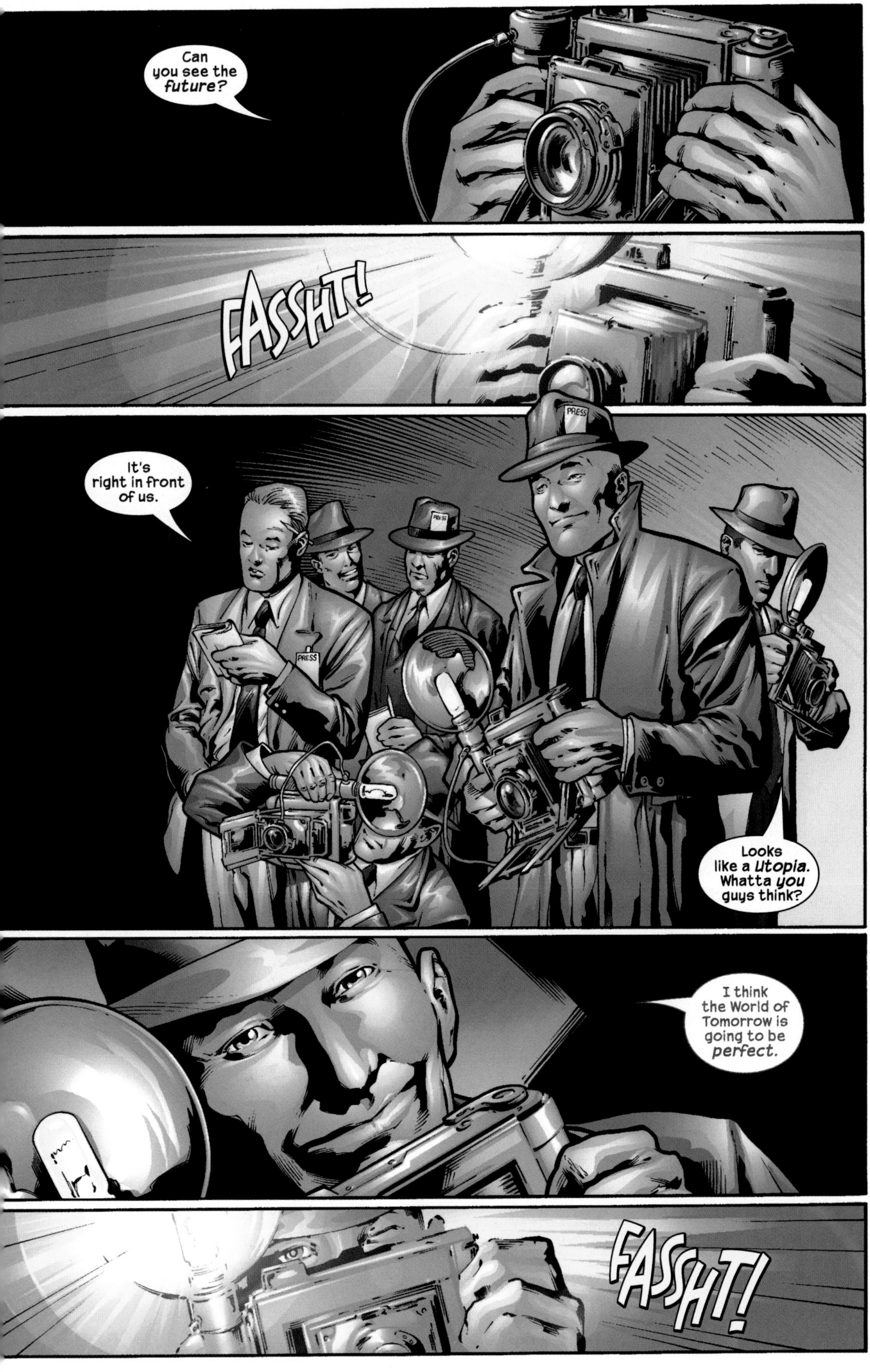

Can you see the *future?*
FASSHT!
It's right in front of us.
Looks like a *Utopia.* Whatta *you* guys think?
I think the World of Tomorrow is going to be *perfect.*
FASSHT!

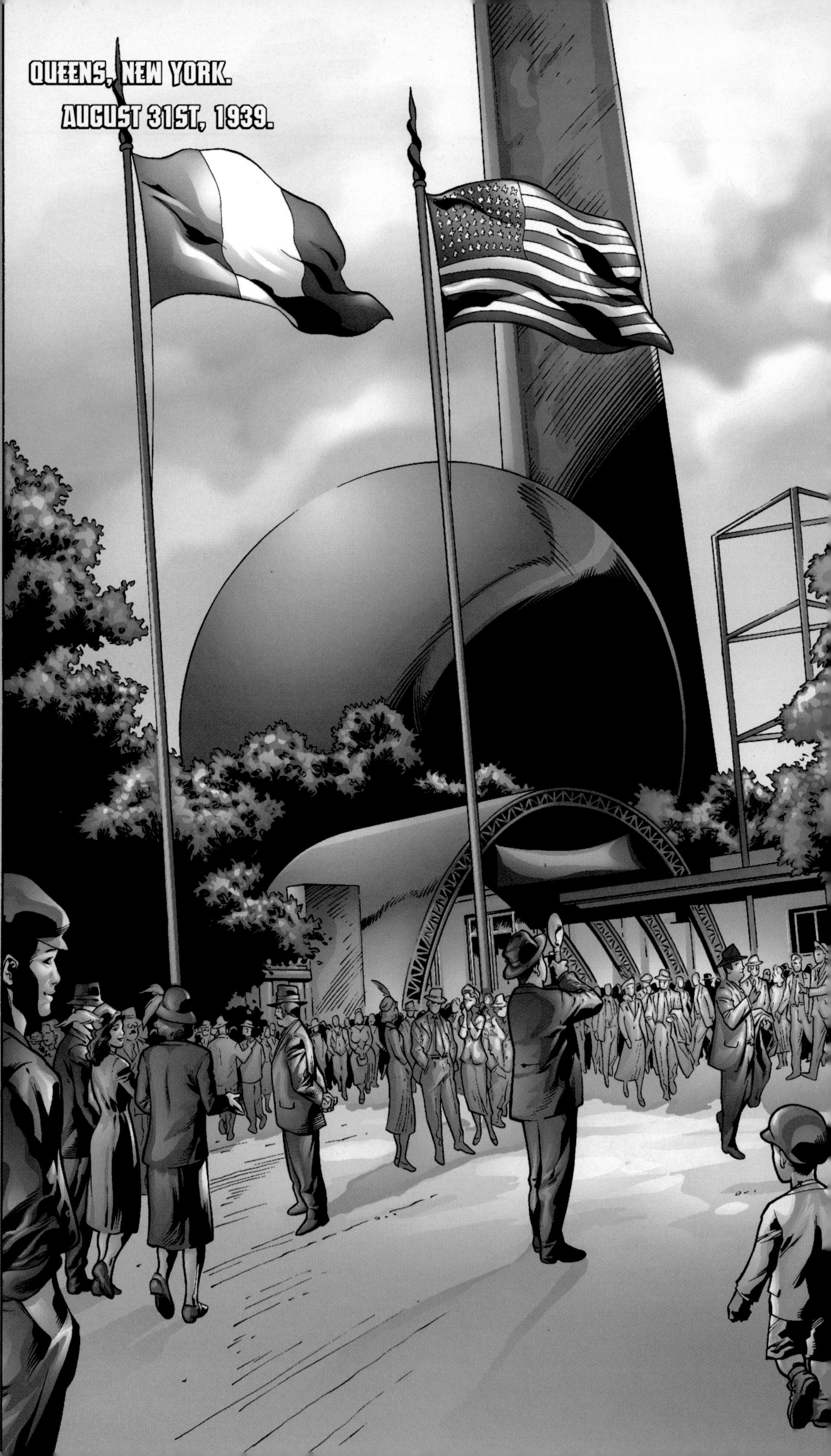
QUEENS, NEW YORK.
AUGUST 31ST, 1939.

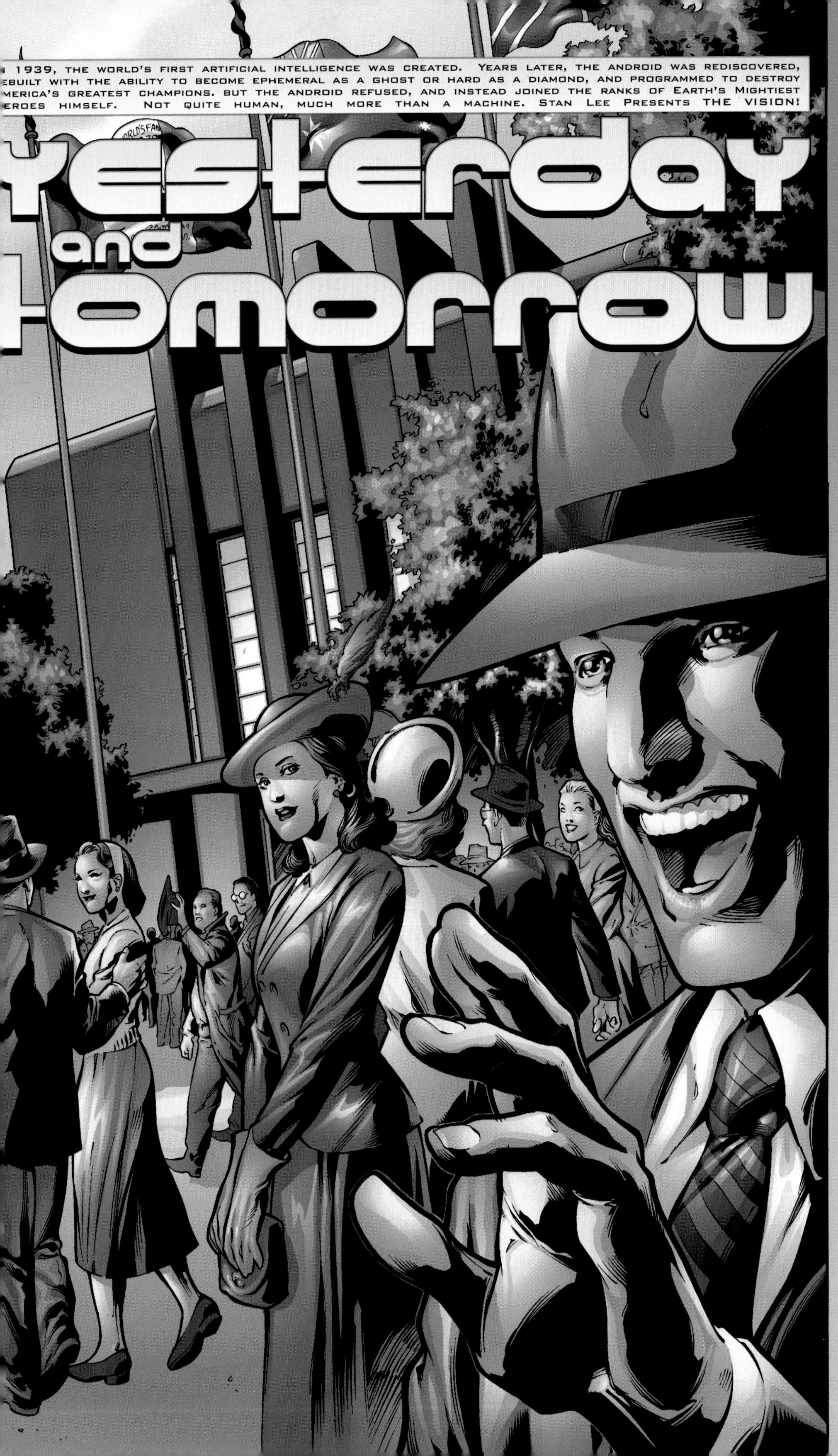
1939, THE WORLD'S FIRST ARTIFICIAL INTELLIGENCE WAS CREATED. YEARS LATER, THE ANDROID WAS REDISCOVERED, EBUILT WITH THE ABILITY TO BECOME EPHEMERAL AS A GHOST OR HARD AS A DIAMOND, AND PROGRAMMED TO DESTROY MERICA'S GREATEST CHAMPIONS. BUT THE ANDROID REFUSED, AND INSTEAD JOINED THE RANKS OF EARTH'S MIGHTIEST EROES HIMSELF. NOT QUITE HUMAN, MUCH MORE THAN A MACHINE. STAN LEE PRESENTS THE VISION!
Yesterday and Tomorrow

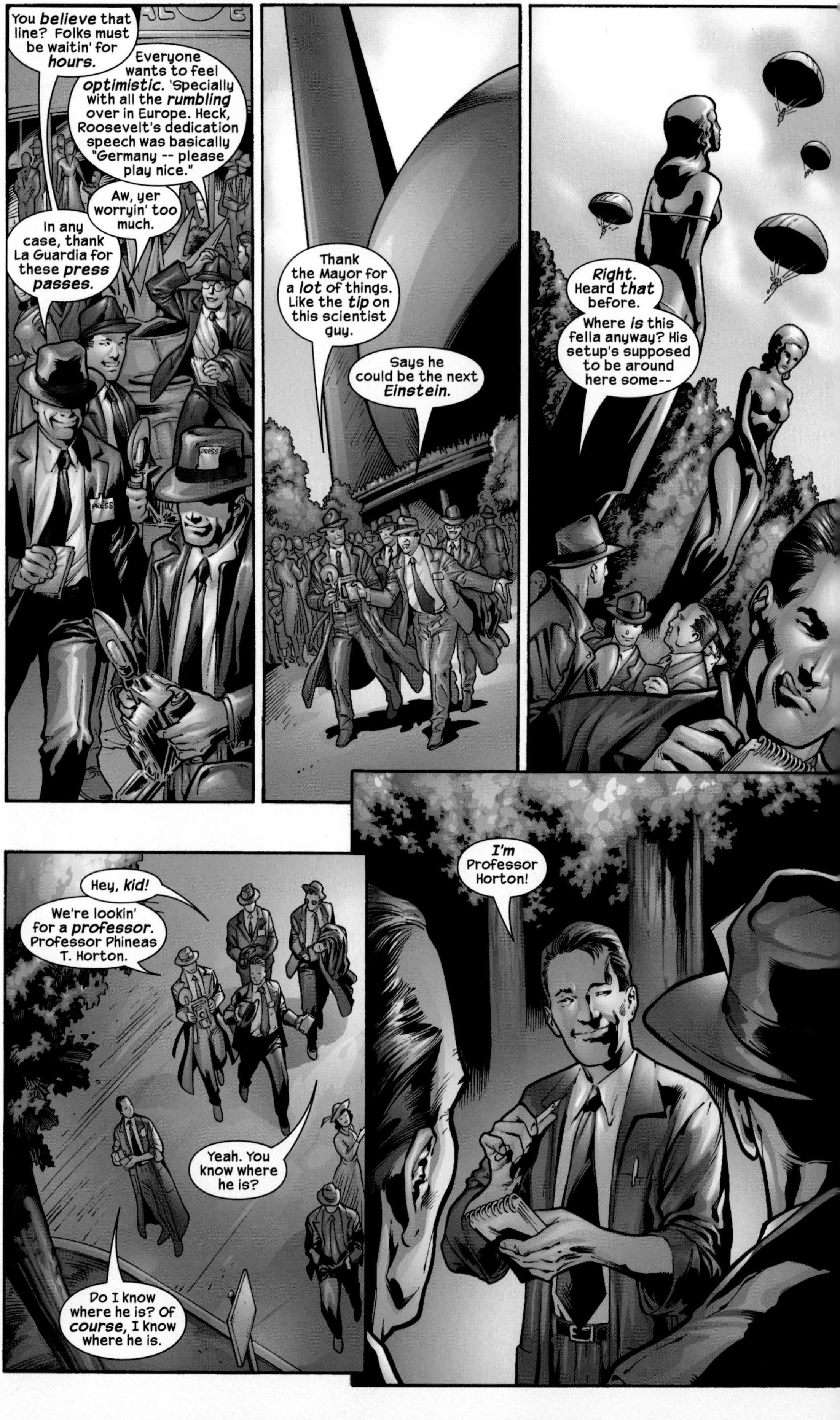
You believe that line? Folks must be waitin' for hours.
Everyone wants to feel optimistic. 'Specially with all the rumbling over in Europe. Heck, Roosevelt's dedication speech was basically "Germany -- please play nice."
Aw, yer worryin' too much.
In any case, thank La Guardia for these press passes.
PRESS
PRESS
Thank the Mayor for a lot of things. Like the tip on this scientist guy.
Says he could be the next Einstein.
Right. Heard that before.
Where is this fella anyway? His setup's supposed to be around here some--
Hey, kid!
We're lookin' for a professor. Professor Phineas T. Horton.
Yeah. You know where he is?
Do I know where he is? Of course, I know where he is.
I'm Professor Horton!

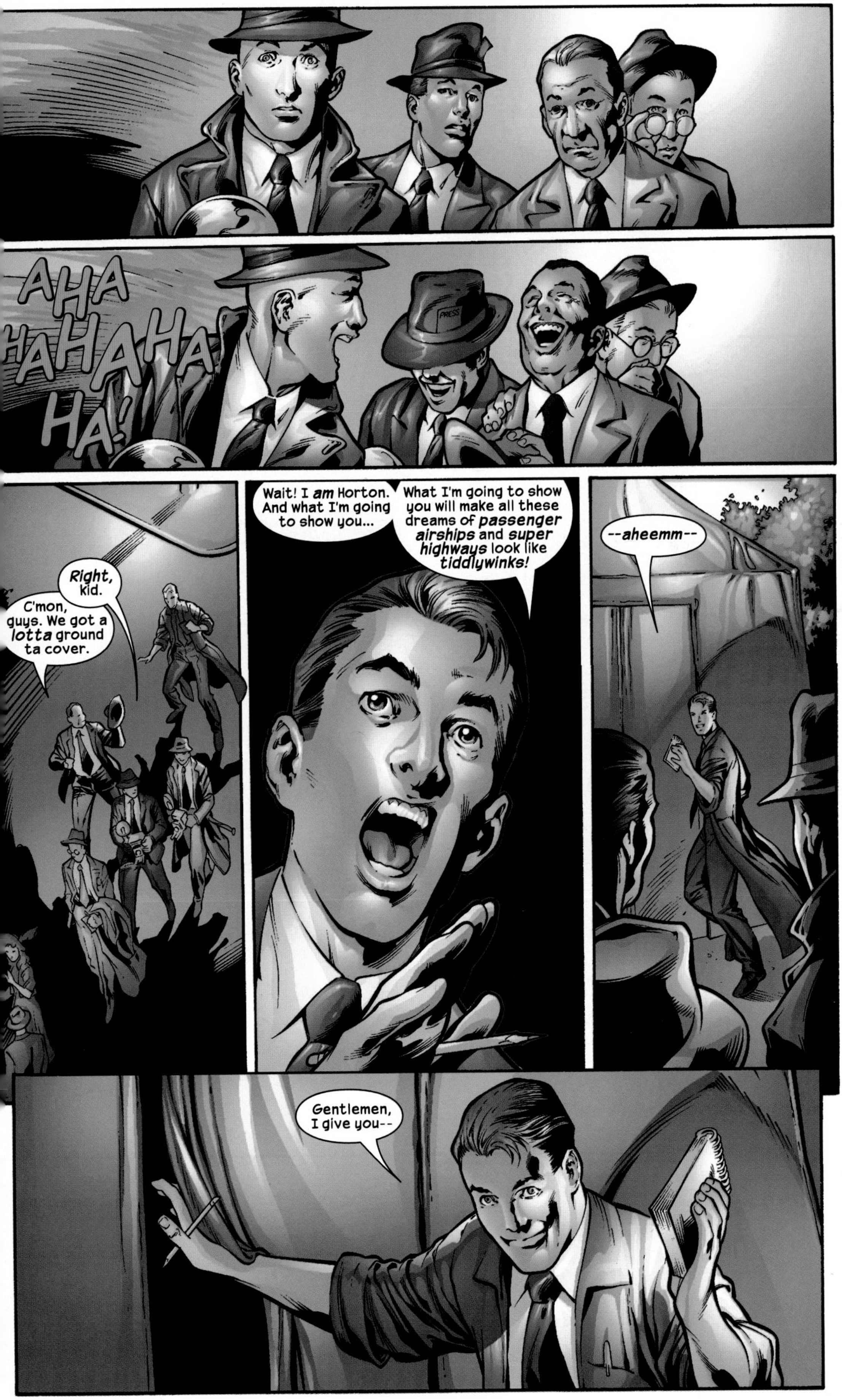

AHAHAHAHAHAHA!
Right, kid.
C'mon, guys. We got a lotta ground ta cover.
Wait! I am Horton. And what I'm going to show you...
What I'm going to show you will make all these dreams of passenger airships and super highways look like tiddlywinks!
--aheemm--
Gentlemen, I give you--

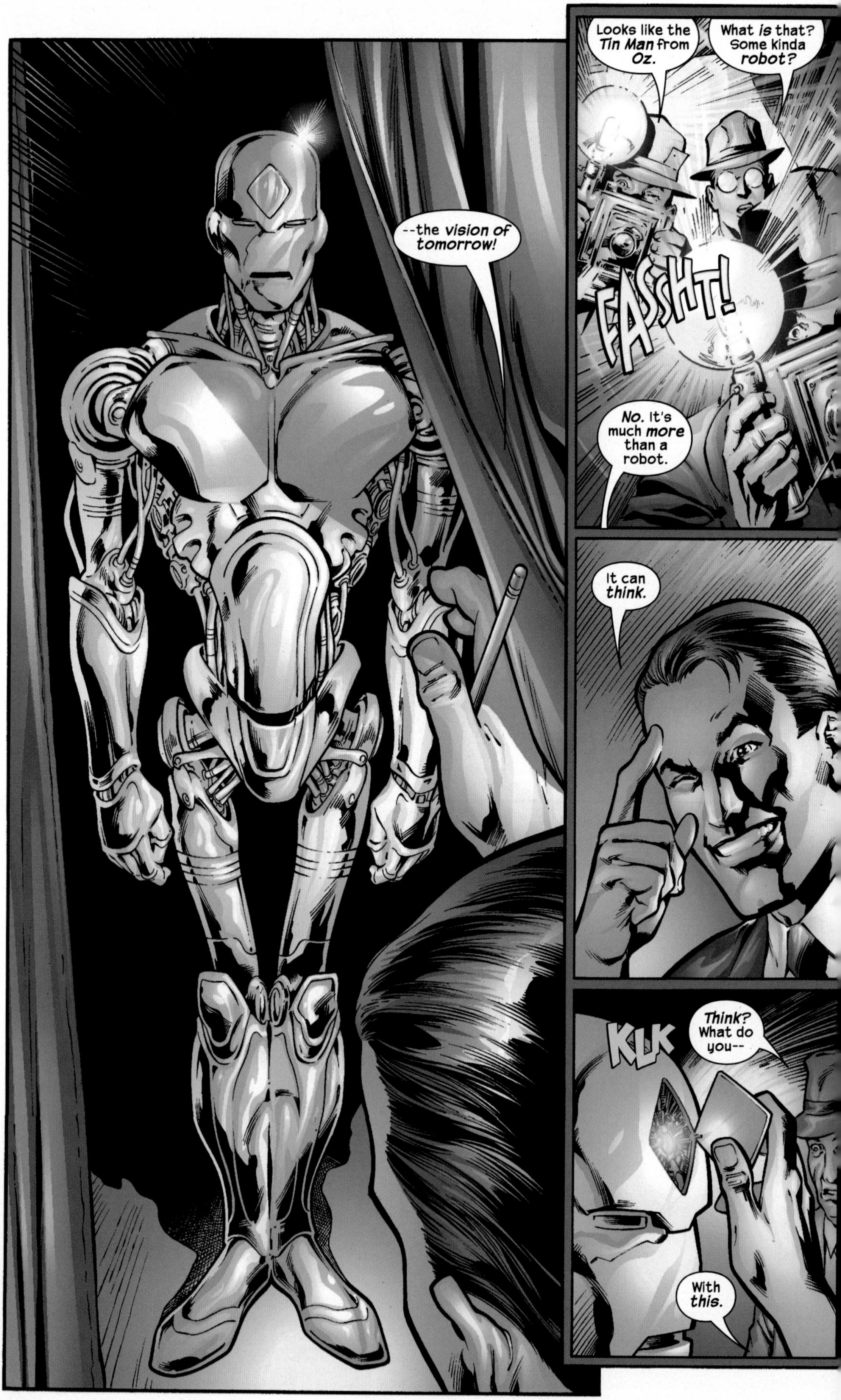
--the *vision of tomorrow!*
Looks like the *Tin Man* from *Oz.*
What *is* that? Some kinda *robot?*
FASSHT!
No. It's much *more* than a robot.
It can *think.*
KLIK
Think? What do you--
With *this.*

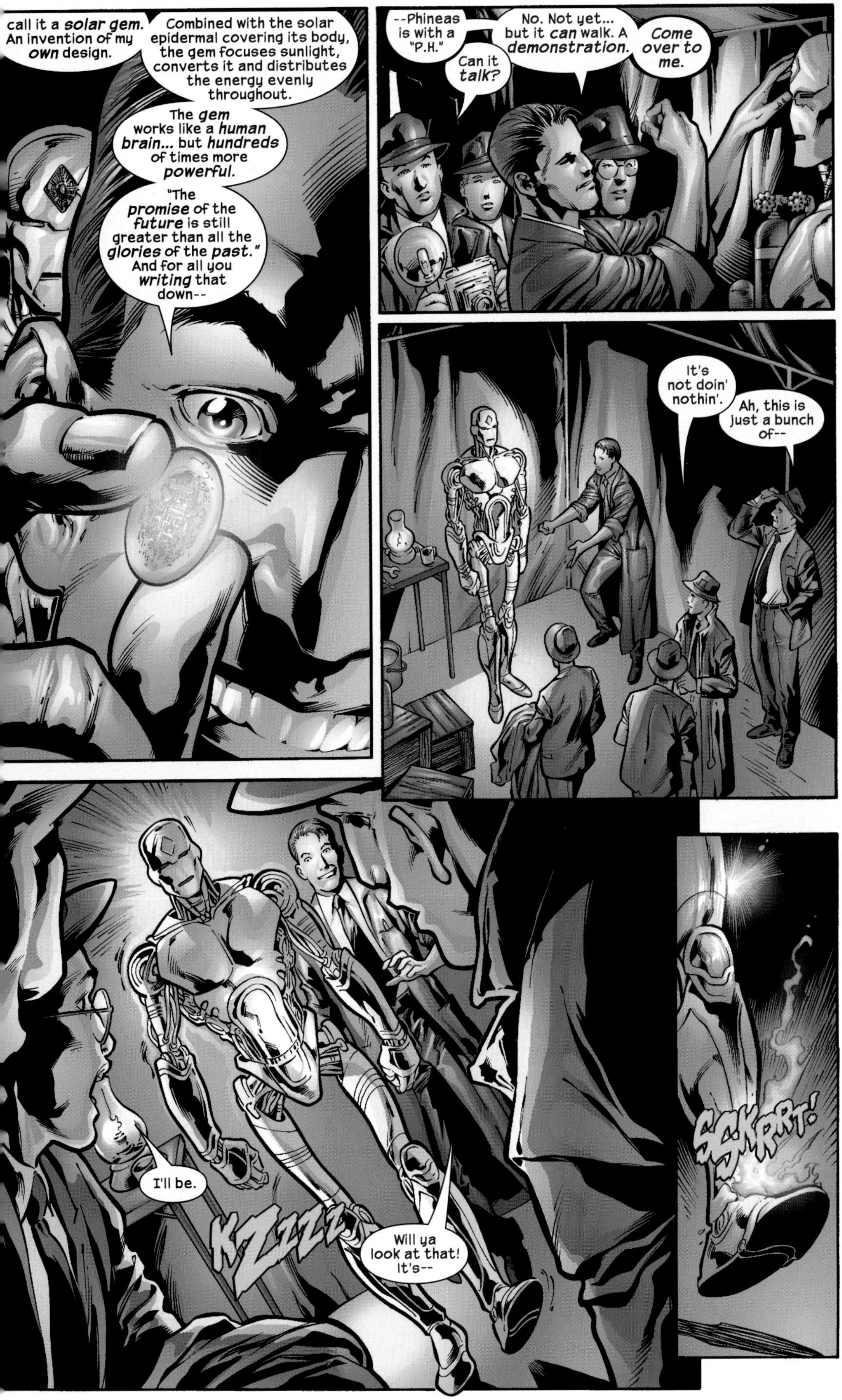
call it a solar gem. An invention of my own design.
Combined with the solar epidermal covering its body, the gem focuses sunlight, converts it and distributes the energy evenly throughout.
The gem works like a human brain... but hundreds of times more powerful.
"The promise of the future is still greater than all the glories of the past." And for all you writing that down--
--Phineas is with a "P.H."
Can it talk?
No. Not yet... but it can walk. A demonstration.
Come over to me.
It's not doin' nothin'.
Ah, this is just a bunch of--
I'll be.
KZZZZ
Will ya look at that! It's--
SCKRRT!

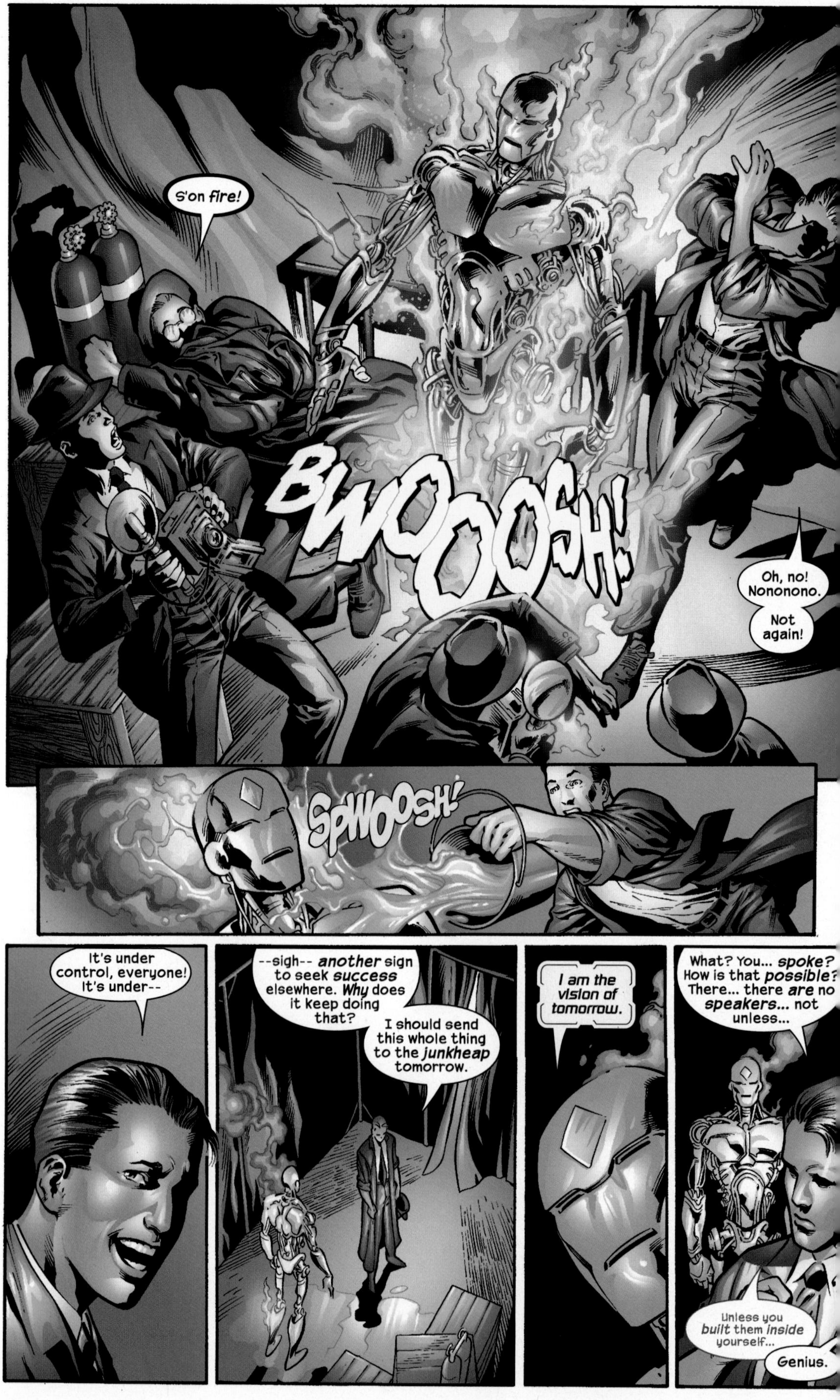
S'on fire!
BWOOOSH!
Oh, no! Nononono.
Not again!
SPWOOSH!
It's under control, everyone! It's under--
--sigh-- another sign to seek success elsewhere. Why does it keep doing that?
I should send this whole thing to the junkheap tomorrow.
I am the vision of tomorrow.
What? You... spoke? How is that possible? There... there are no speakers... not unless...
Unless you built them inside yourself...
Genius.

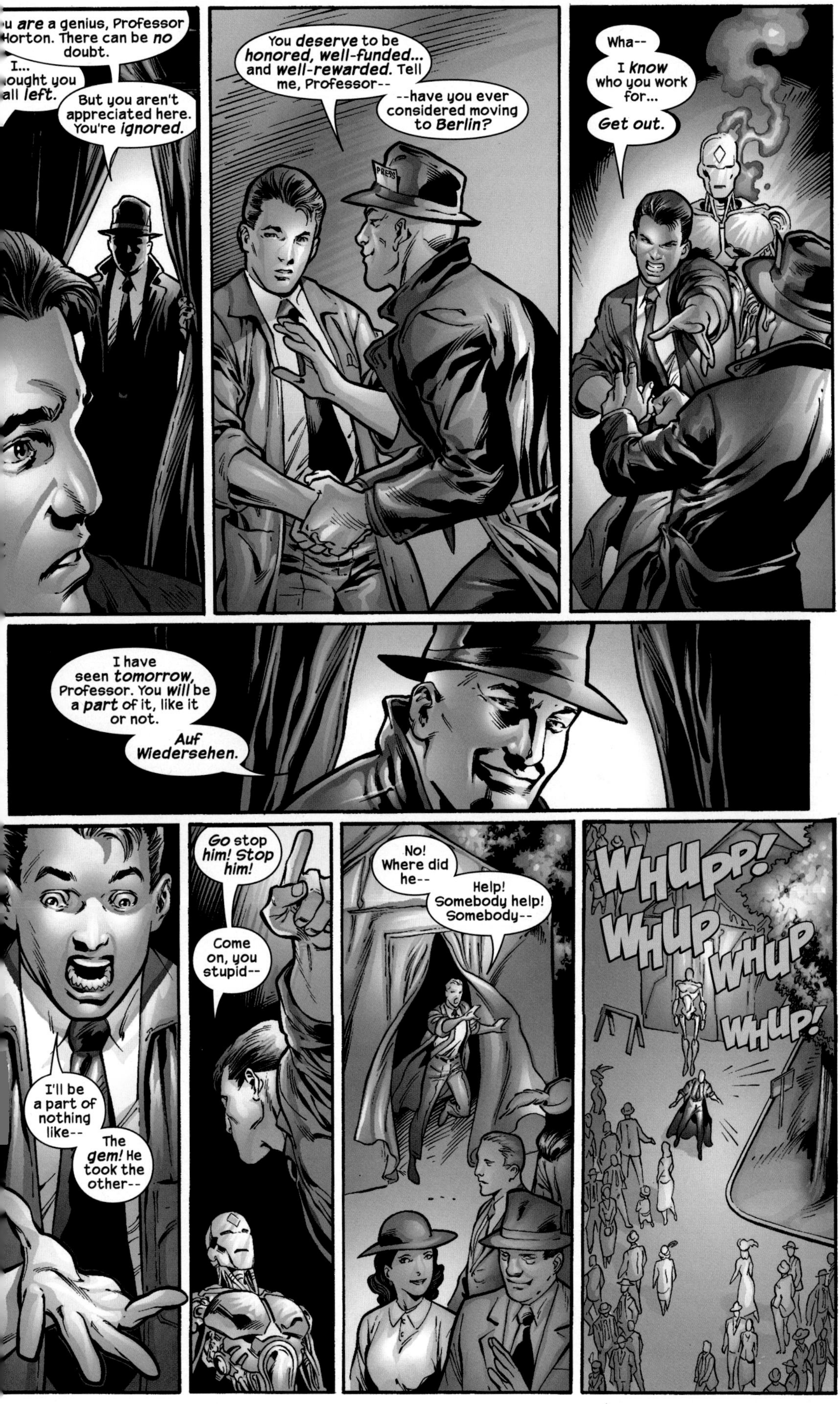

u are a genius, Professor Horton. There can be no doubt.
I... ought you all left.
But you aren't appreciated here. You're ignored.
You deserve to be honored, well-funded... and well-rewarded. Tell me, Professor--
--have you ever considered moving to Berlin?
PRESS
Wha--
I know who you work for...
Get out.
I have seen tomorrow, Professor. You will be a part of it, like it or not.
Auf Wiedersehen.
I'll be a part of nothing like--
The gem! He took the other--
Go stop him! Stop him!
Come on, you stupid--
No! Where did he--
Help! Somebody help! Somebody--
...
WHUPP! WHUP WHUP WHUP!

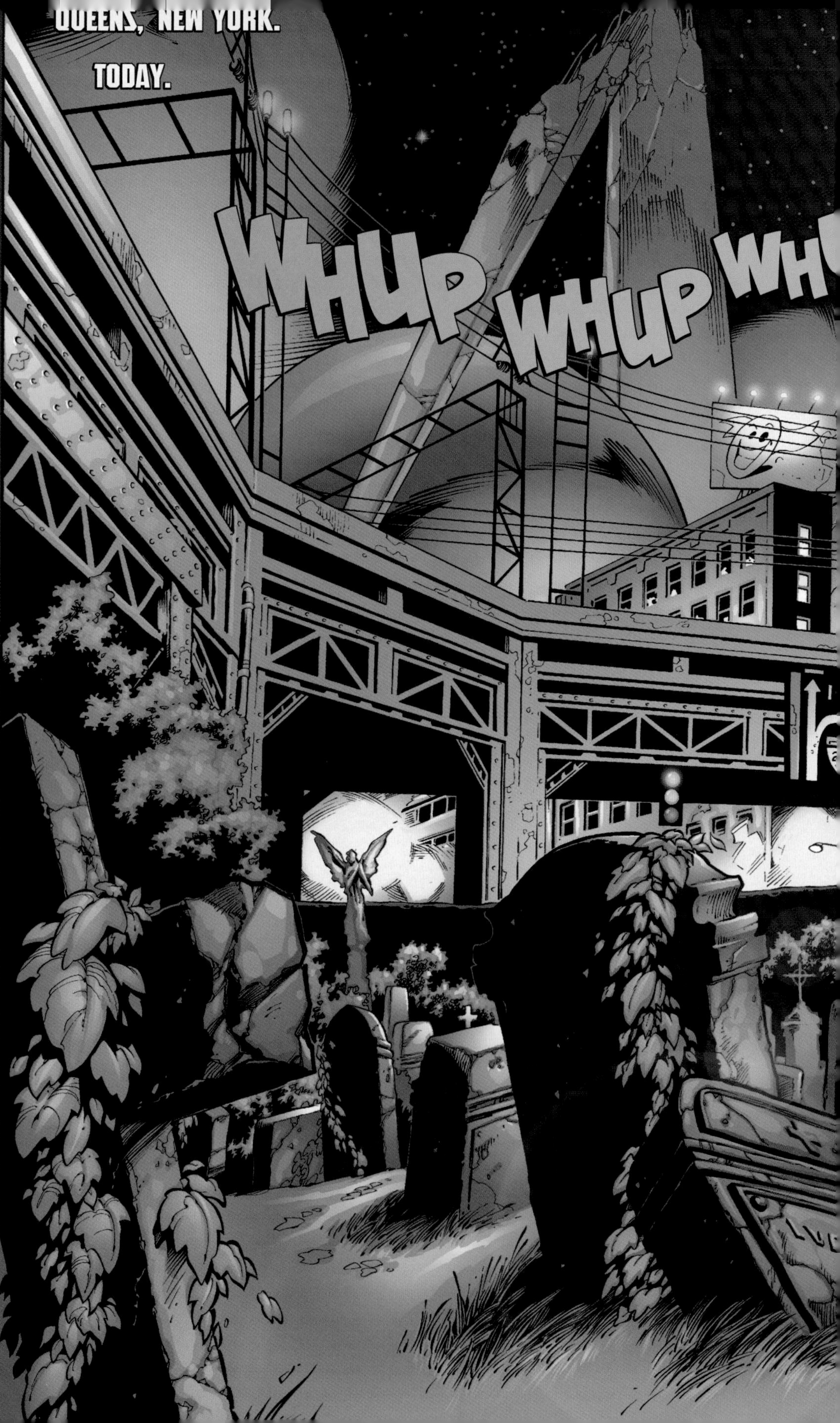
QUEENS, NEW YORK.
TODAY.
WHUP WHUP WHU

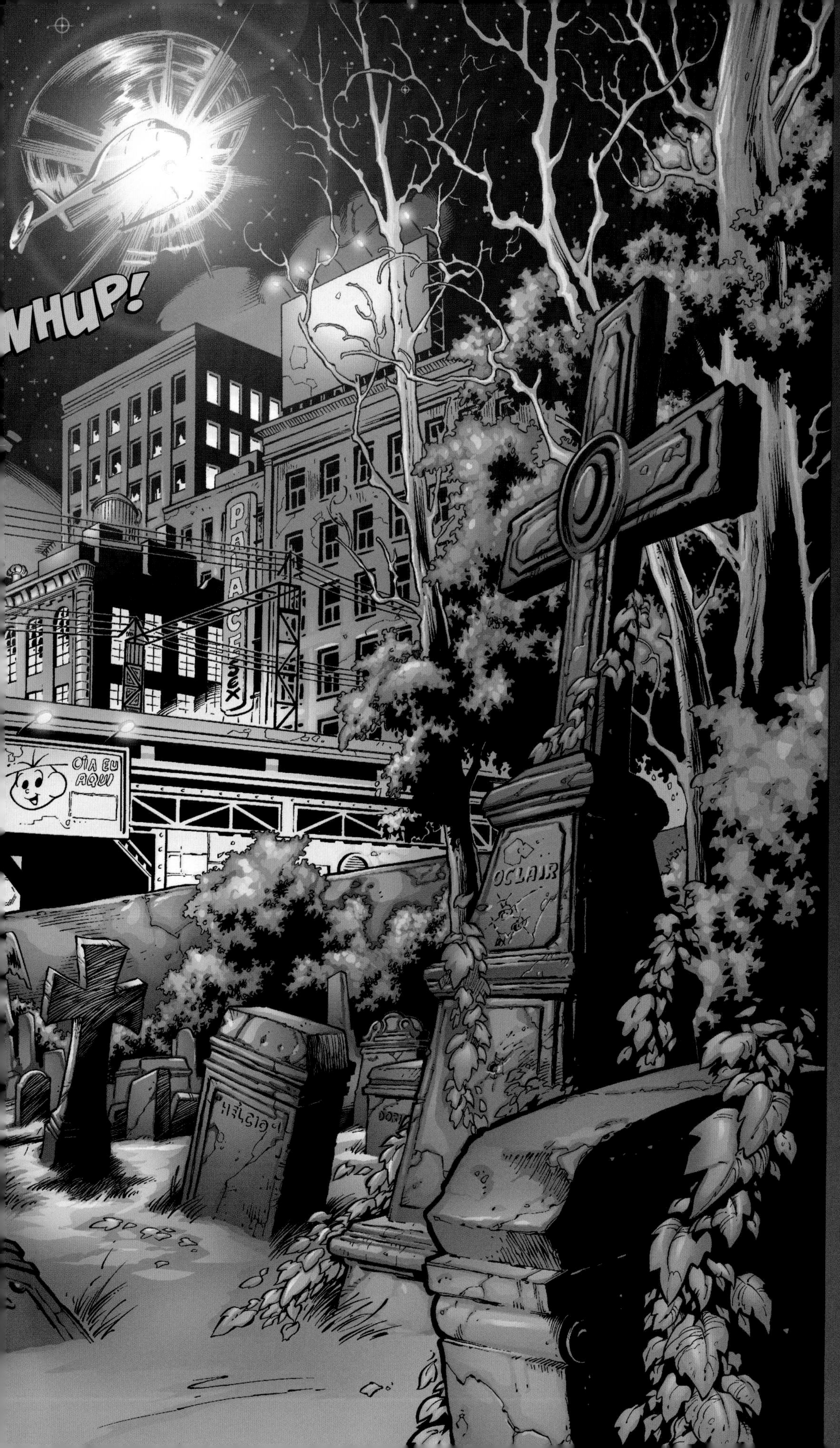
VHUP!
PALACE
SEX
ÓIA EU AQUI
OCLAIR

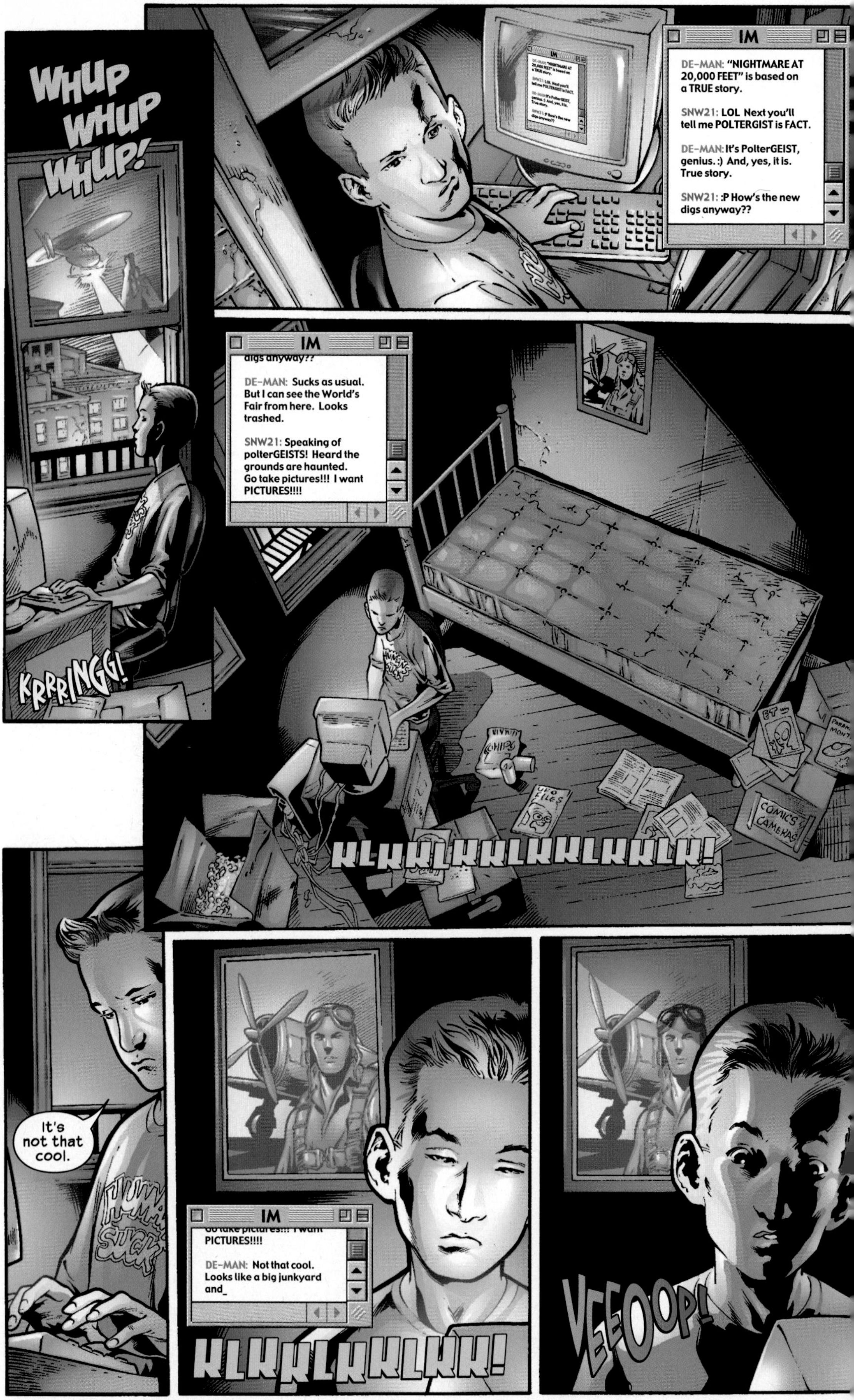
WHUP WHUP WHUP!
DE-MAN: "NIGHTMARE AT 20,000 FEET" is based on a TRUE story.
SNW21: LOL Next you'll tell me POLTERGIST is FACT.
DE-MAN: It's PolterGEIST, genius. :) And, yes, it is. True story.
SNW21: :P How's the new digs anyway??
KRRRINGG!
digs anyway??
DE-MAN: Sucks as usual. But I can see the World's Fair from here. Looks trashed.
SNW21: Speaking of polterGEISTS! Heard the grounds are haunted. Go take pictures!!! I want PICTURES!!!!
KLKKLKKLKKLKKLK!
It's not that cool.
PICTURES!!!!
DE-MAN: Not that cool. Looks like a big junkyard and_
KLKKLKKLKK!
VEEOOP!

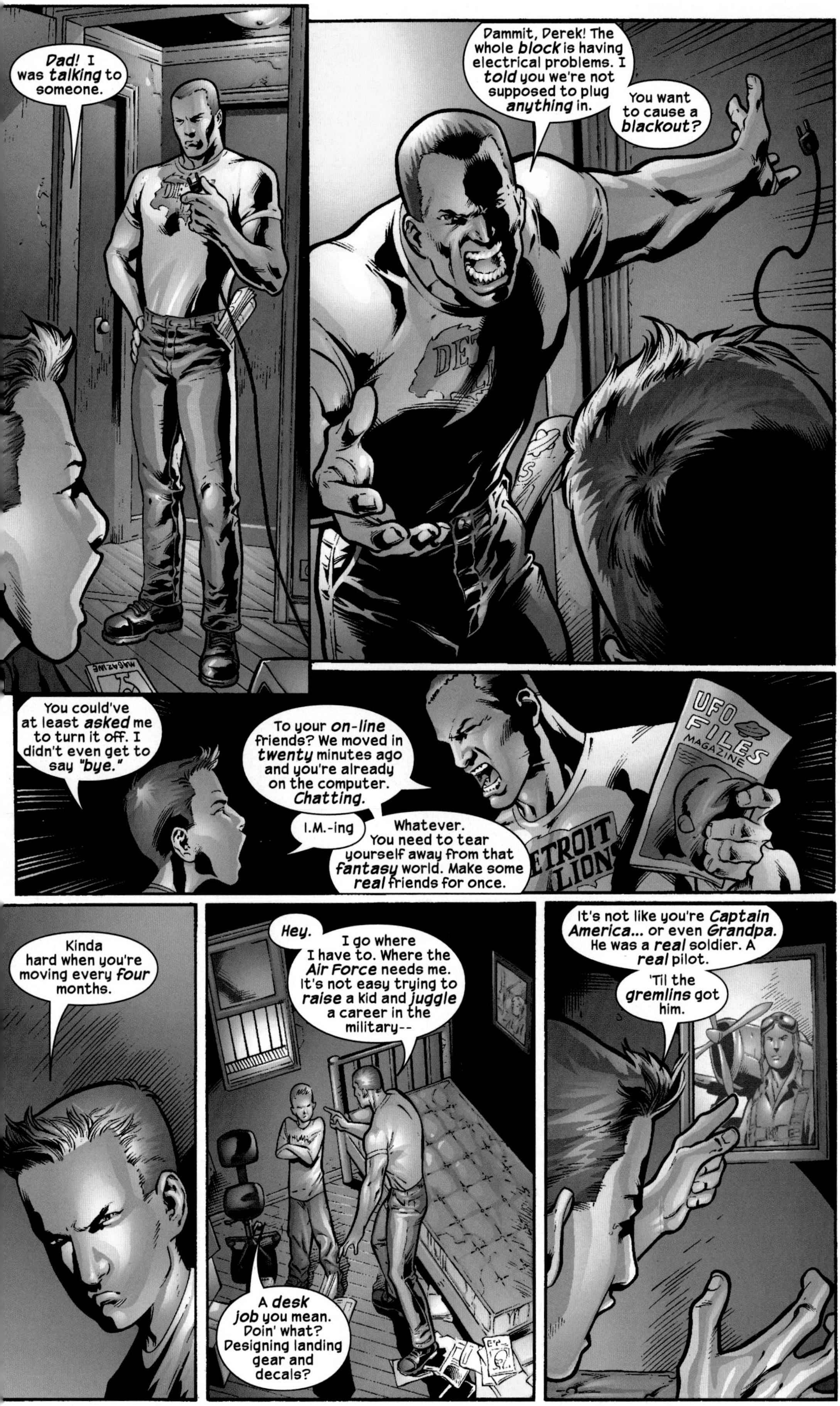

Dad! I was talking to someone.
Dammit, Derek! The whole block is having electrical problems. I told you we're not supposed to plug anything in.
You want to cause a blackout?
You could've at least asked me to turn it off. I didn't even get to say "bye."
To your on-line friends? We moved in twenty minutes ago and you're already on the computer. Chatting.
I.M.-ing
Whatever. You need to tear yourself away from that fantasy world. Make some real friends for once.
UFO FILES MAGAZINE
DETROIT LIONS
Kinda hard when you're moving every four months.
Hey.
I go where I have to. Where the Air Force needs me. It's not easy trying to raise a kid and juggle a career in the military--
A desk job you mean. Doin' what? Designing landing gear and decals?
It's not like you're Captain America... or even Grandpa. He was a real soldier. A real pilot.
'Til the gremlins got him.

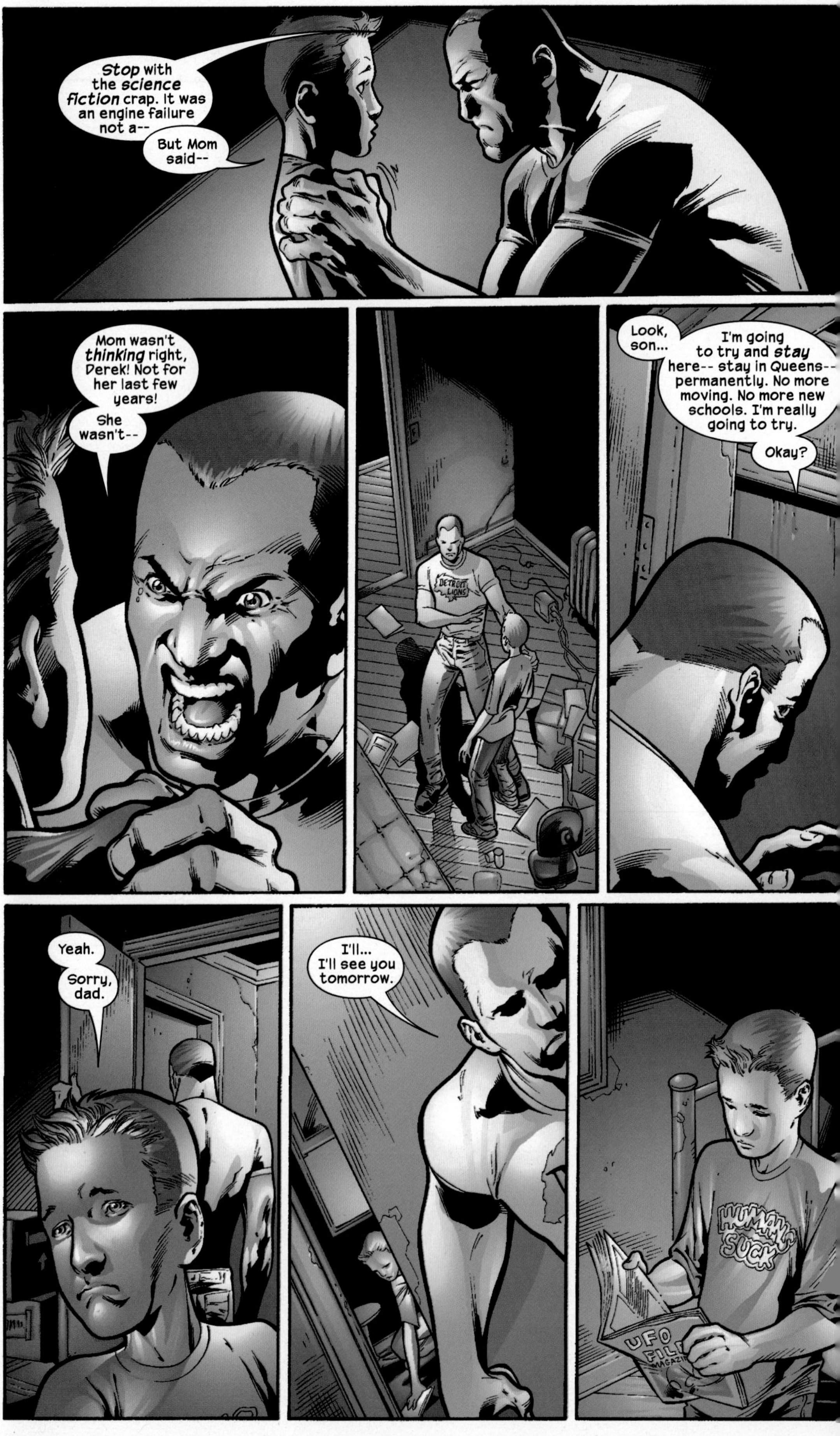

Stop with the science fiction crap. It was an engine failure not a--
But Mom said--
Mom wasn't thinking right, Derek! Not for her last few years!
She wasn't--
DETROIT LIONS
Look, son...
I'm going to try and stay here-- stay in Queens-- permanently. No more moving. No more new schools. I'm really going to try.
Okay?
Yeah.
Sorry, dad.
I'll... I'll see you tomorrow.
HUMANS SUCK
UFO

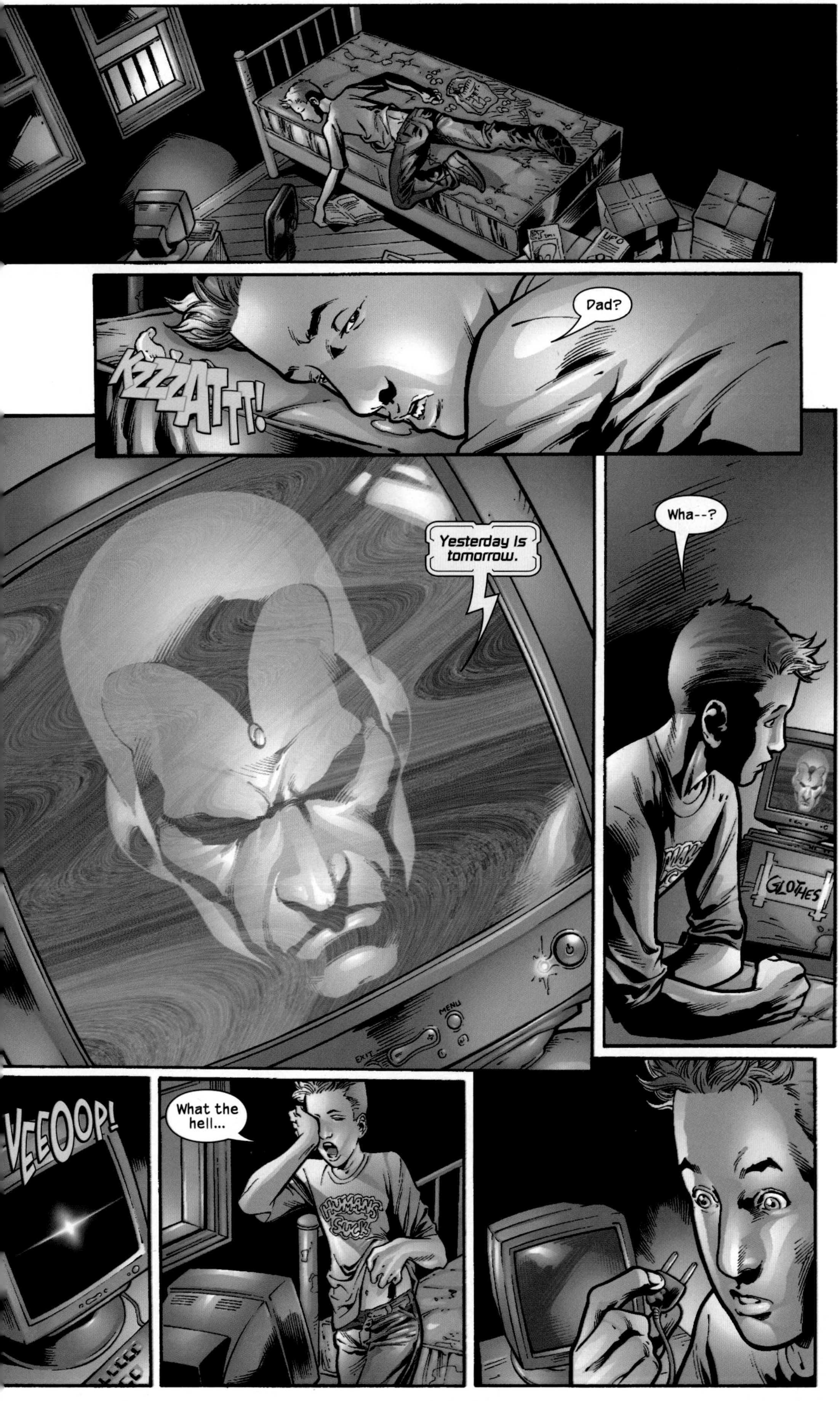
KZZZATTT!
Dad?
Yesterday is tomorrow.
Wha--?
GLOTHES
MENU
EXIT
VEEOOP!
What the hell...
HUMANS SUCK

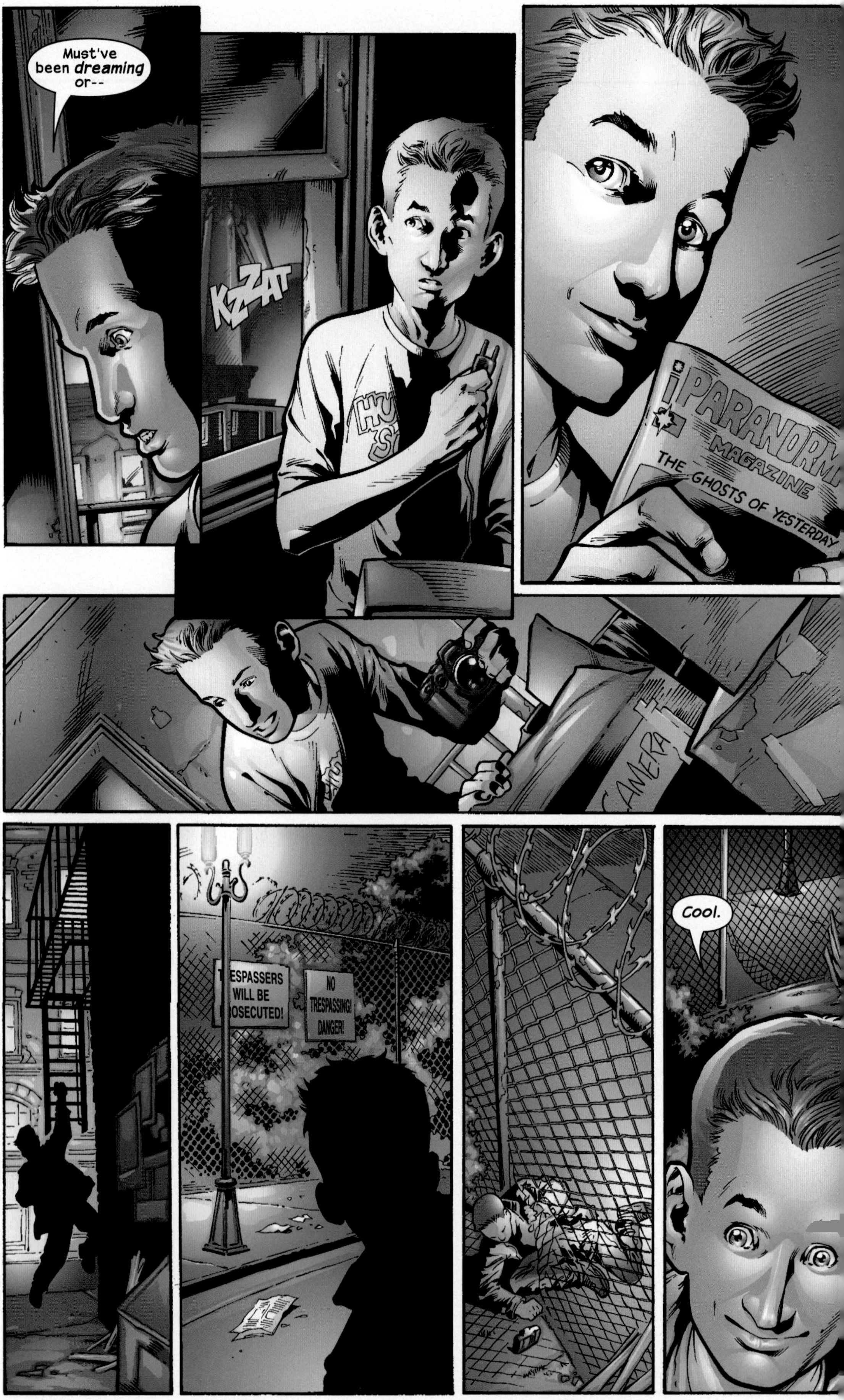
Must've been *dreaming* or--
KZZAT
PARANORMAL MAGAZINE
THE GHOSTS OF YESTERDAY
CAMERA
TRESPASSERS WILL BE PROSECUTED!
NO TRESPASSING! DANGER!
Cool.

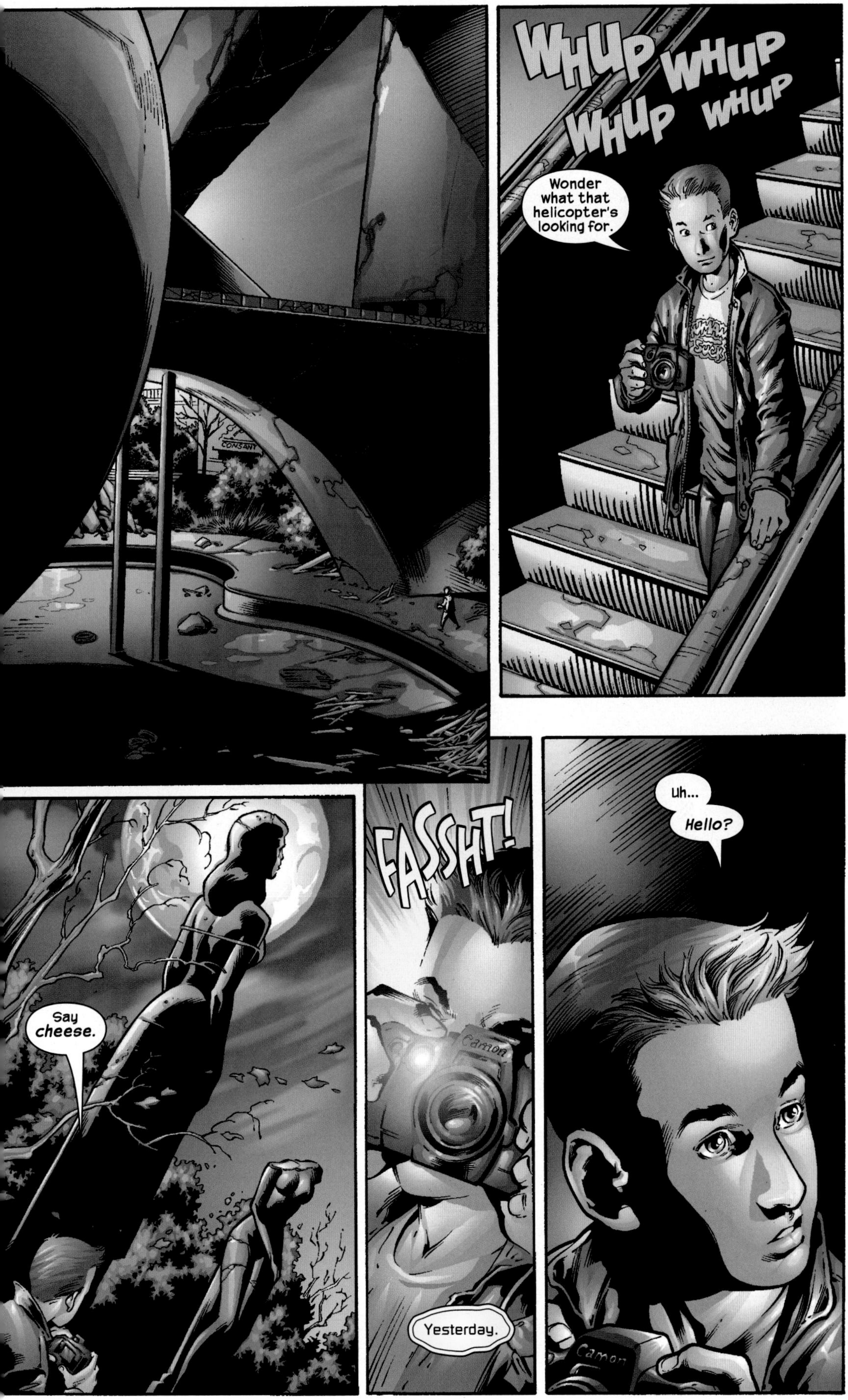
WHUP WHUP
WHUP WHUP
Wonder what that helicopter's looking for.
Say cheese.
FASSHT!
Yesterday.
Uh...
Hello?

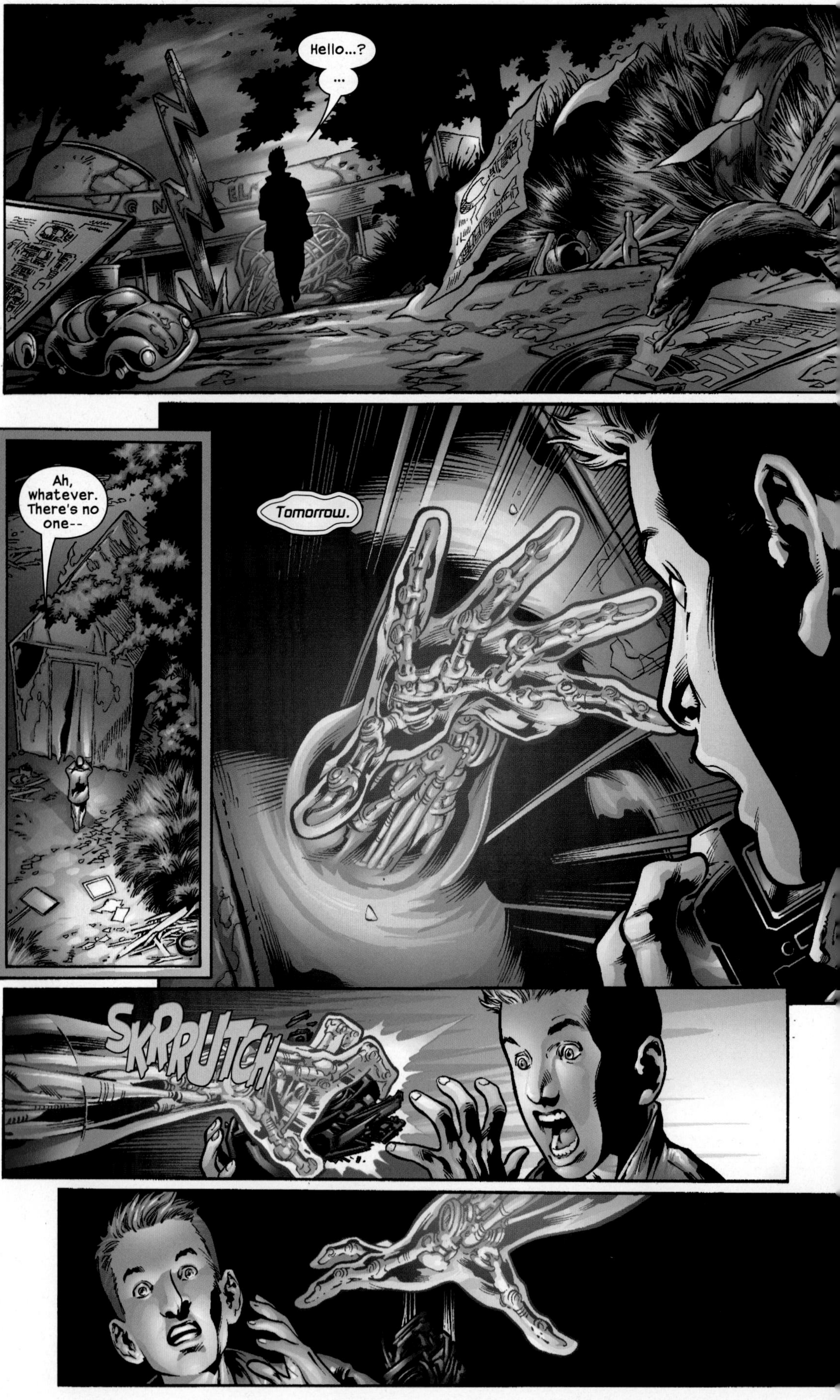
Hello...?
...
Ah, whatever. There's no one--
Tomorrow.
SKRRUTCH

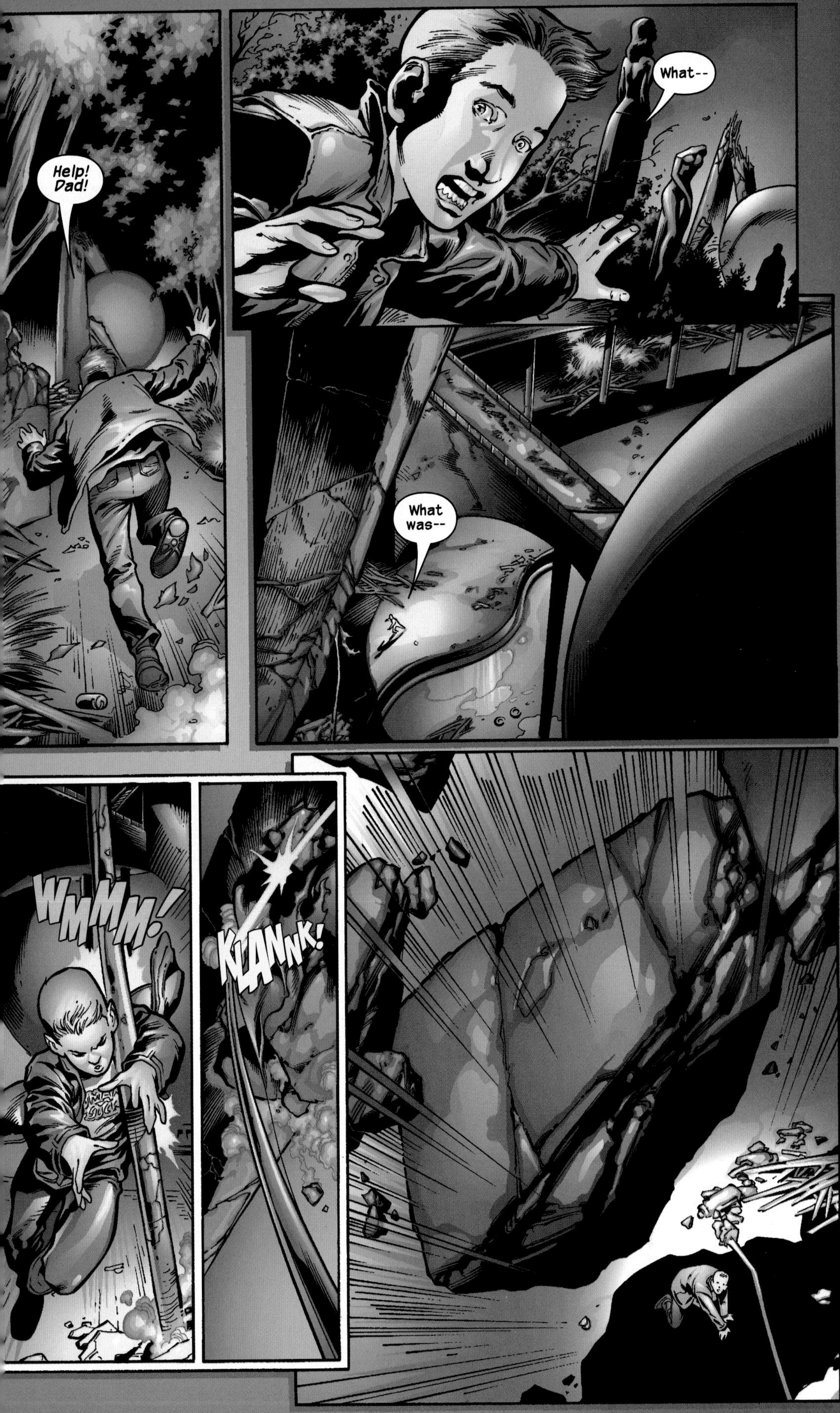
Help! Dad!
What--
What was--
WMMM!
KLANNK!

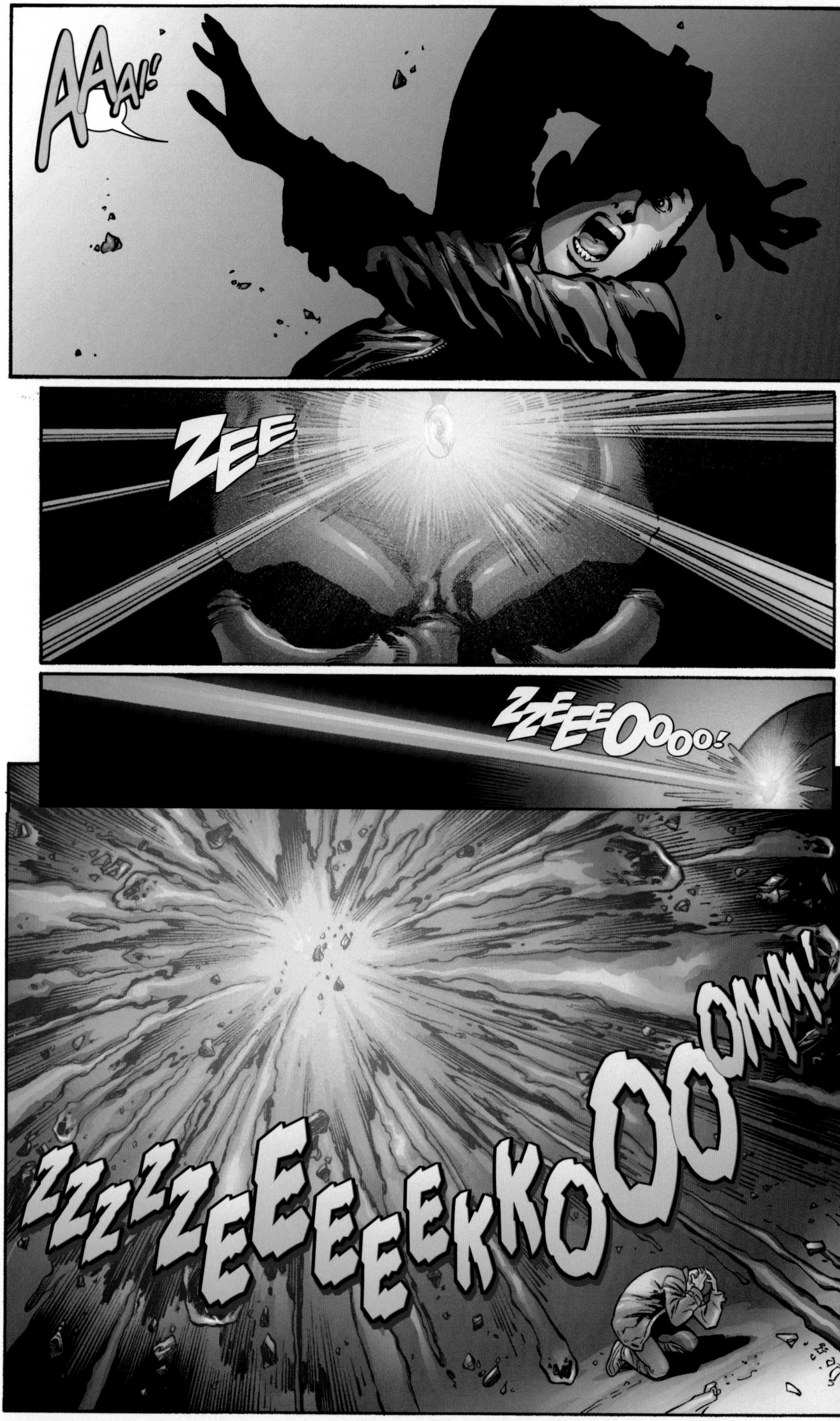
AAAAI!
ZEE
ZZEEEOOOOO!
ZZZZZEEEEEKKOOOOOMM!

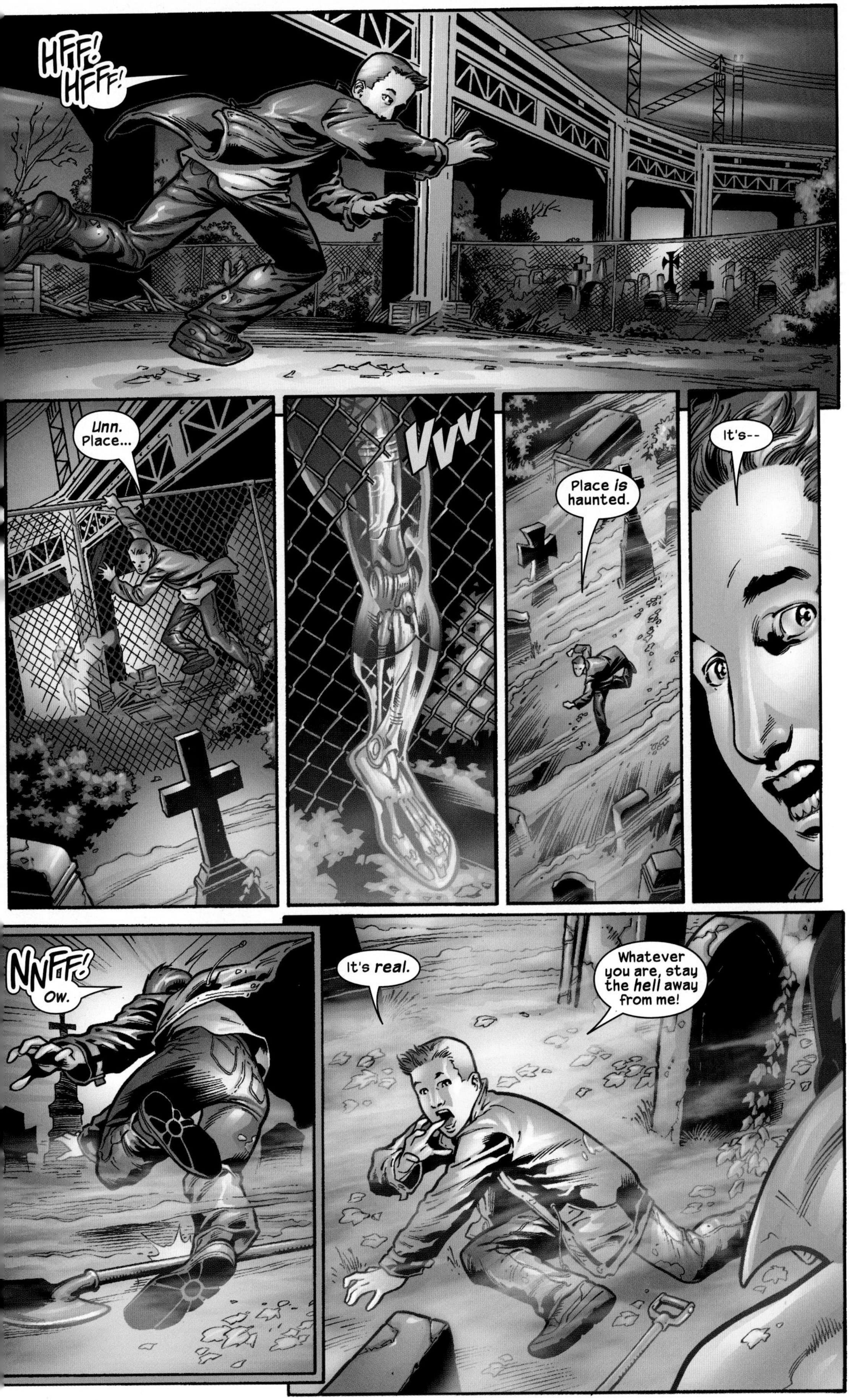
HFFF! HFFF!
Unn. Place...
VVV
Place is haunted.
It's--
NNFF! Ow.
It's real.
Whatever you are, stay the hell away from me!

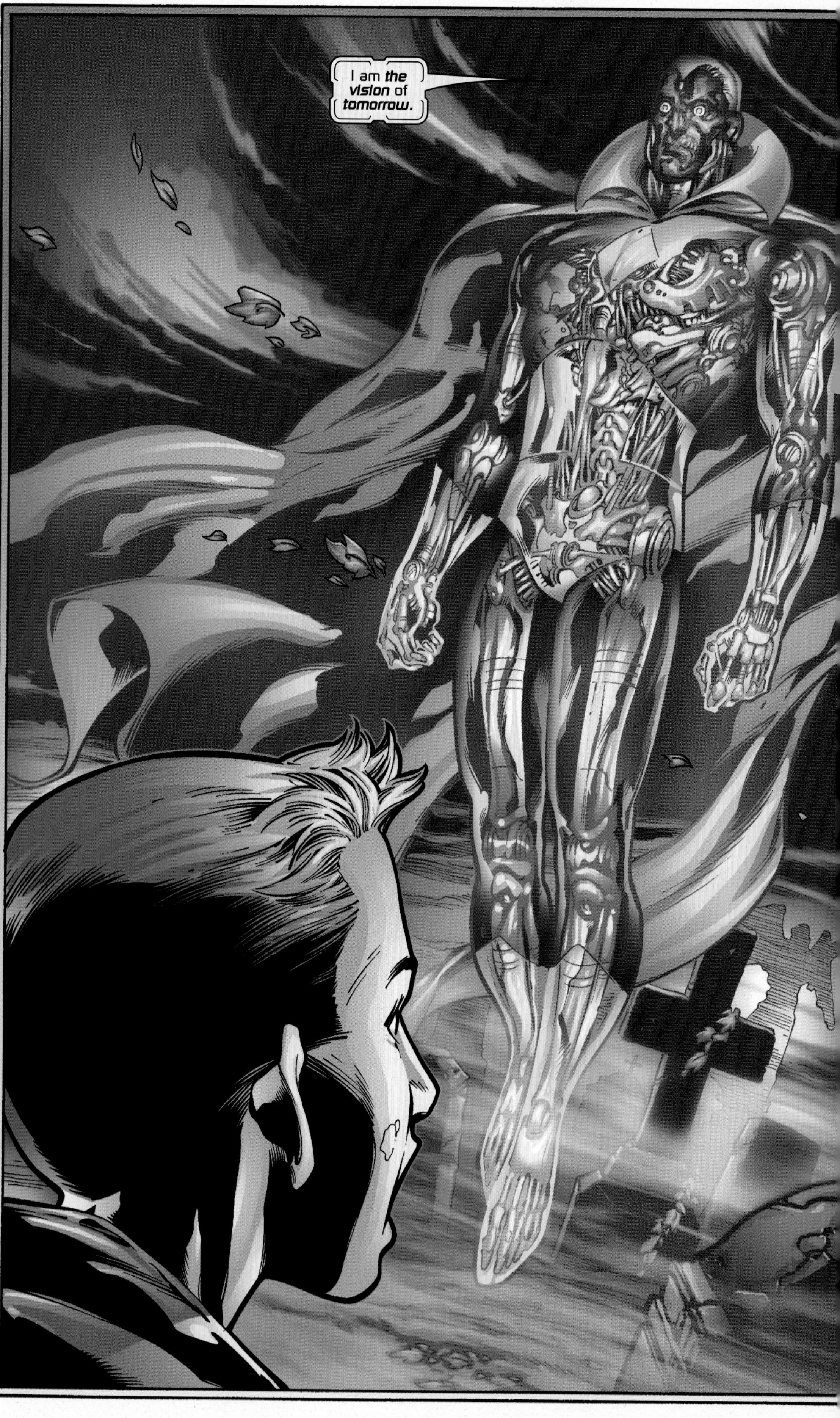
I am *the vision* of *tomorrow*.

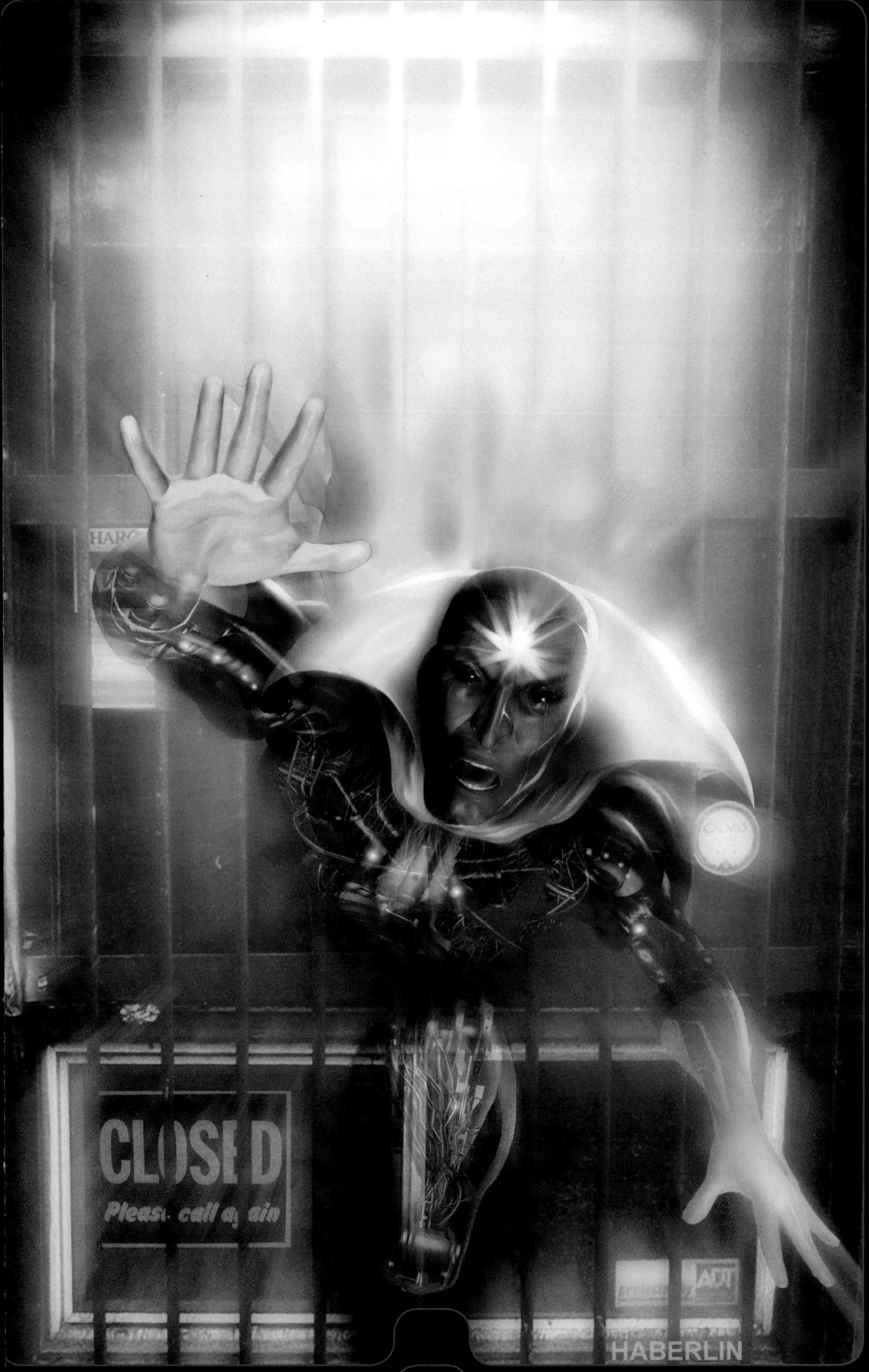
CLOSED
ADT
HABERLIN

#2

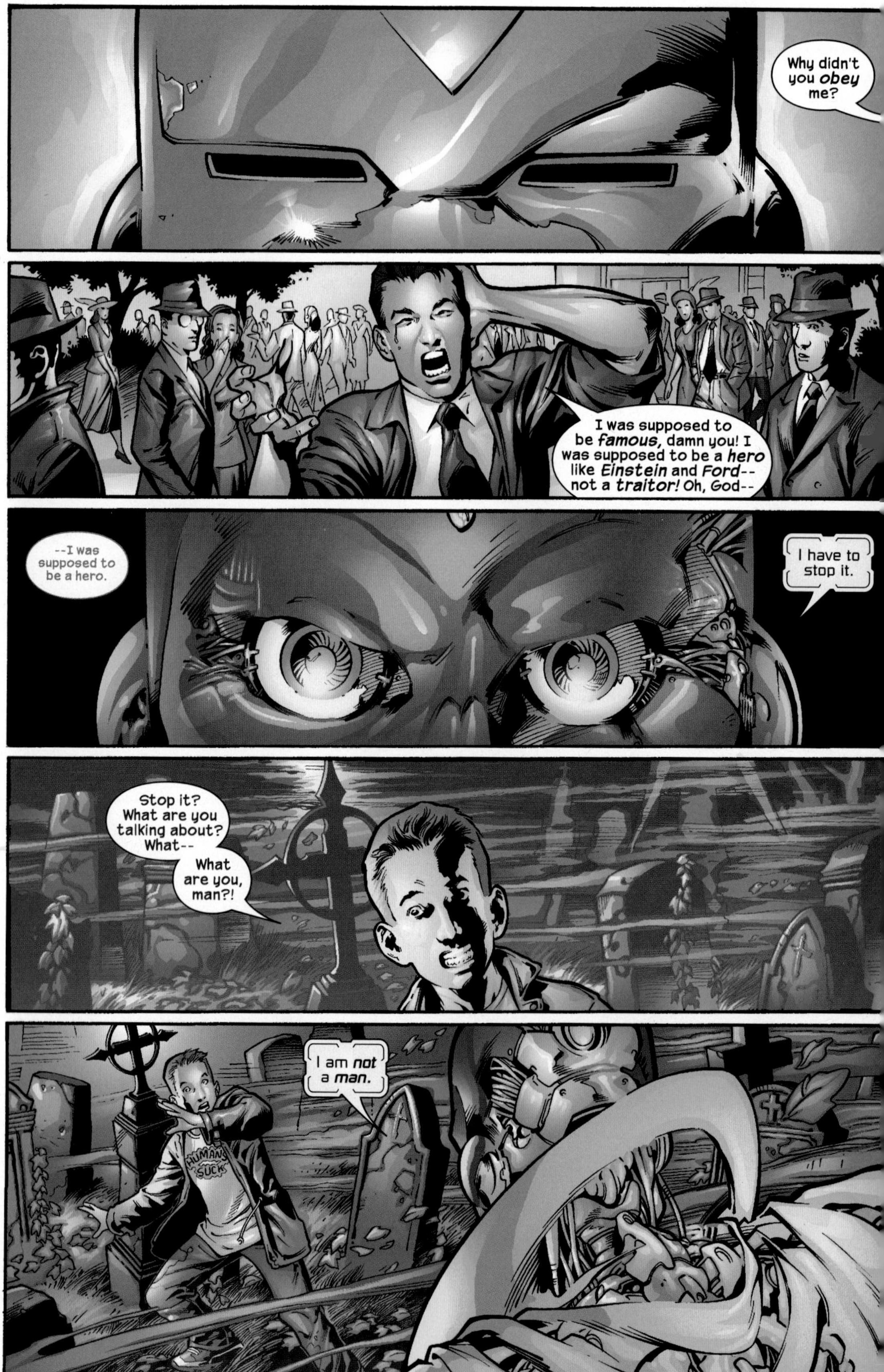
Why didn't you *obey* me?
I was supposed to be *famous*, damn you! I was supposed to be a *hero* like *Einstein* and *Ford*-- not a *traitor!* Oh, God--
--I was supposed to be a hero.
I have to stop it.
Stop it? What are you talking about? What--
What are you, man?!
I am *not* a *man*.
HUMANS SUCK

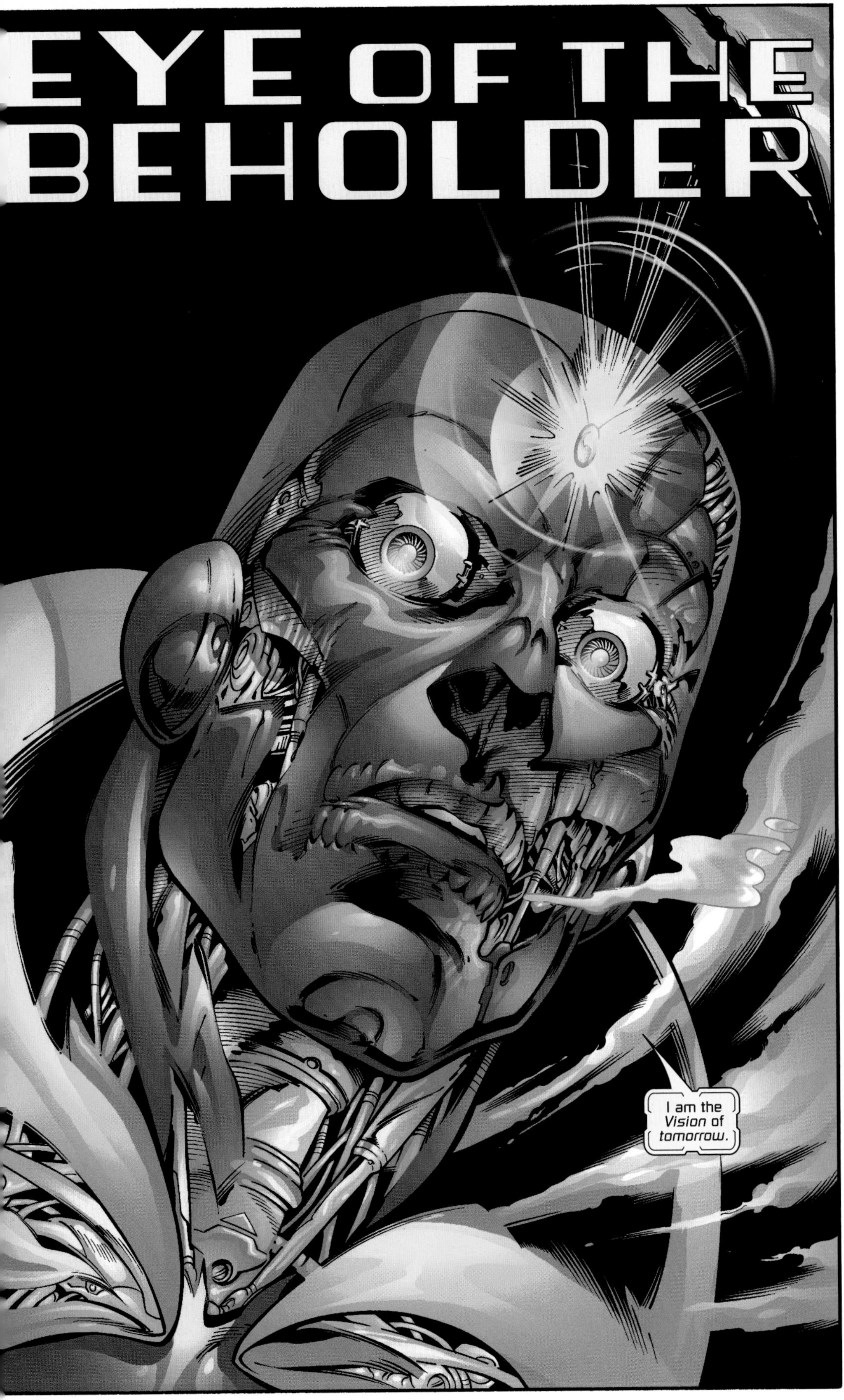
EYE OF THE BEHOLDER
I am the *Vision* of *tomorrow.*

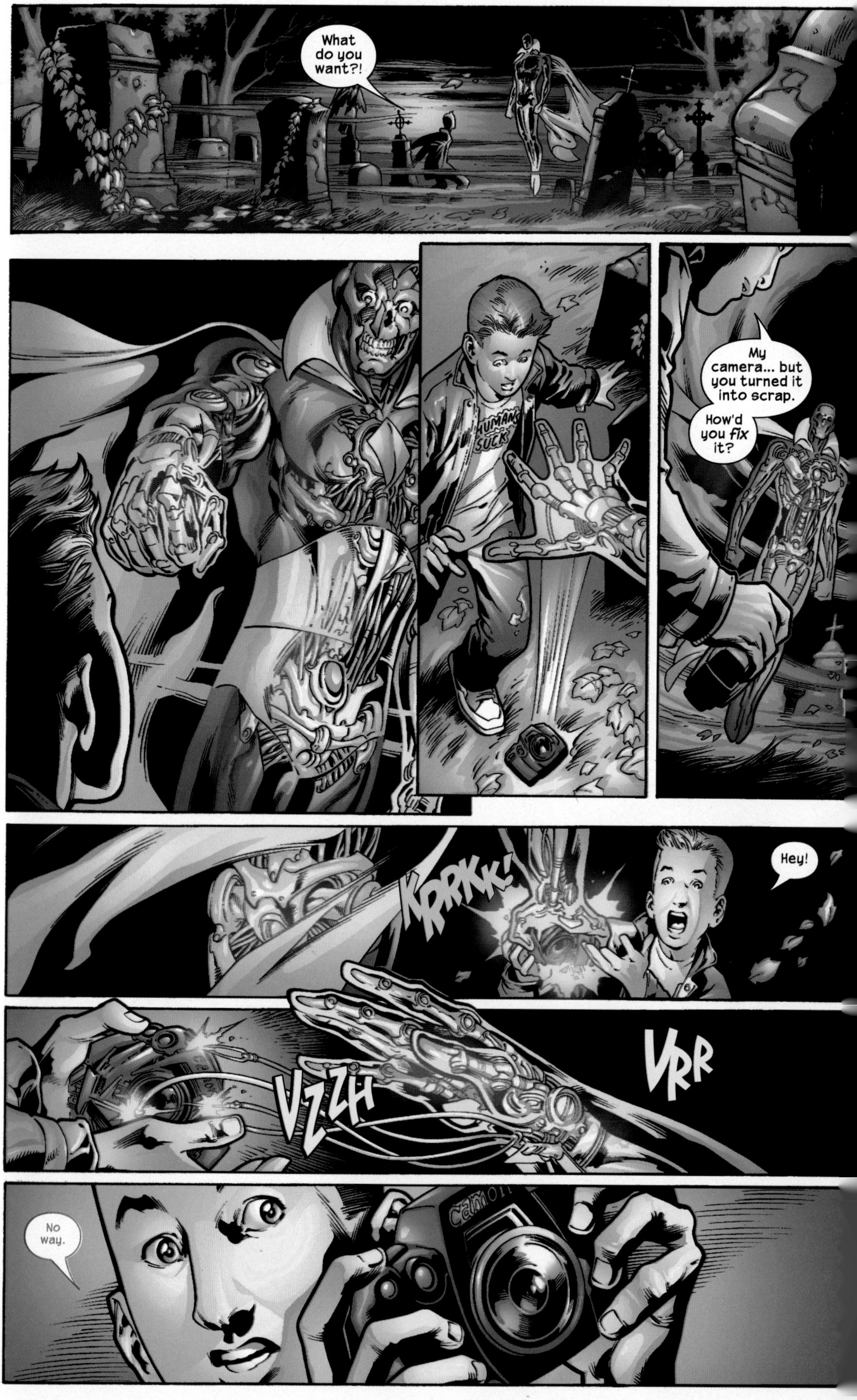
What do you want?!
HUMANS SUCK
My camera... but you turned it into scrap.
How'd you fix it?
KRRKK!
Hey!
VZZH
VRR
No way.

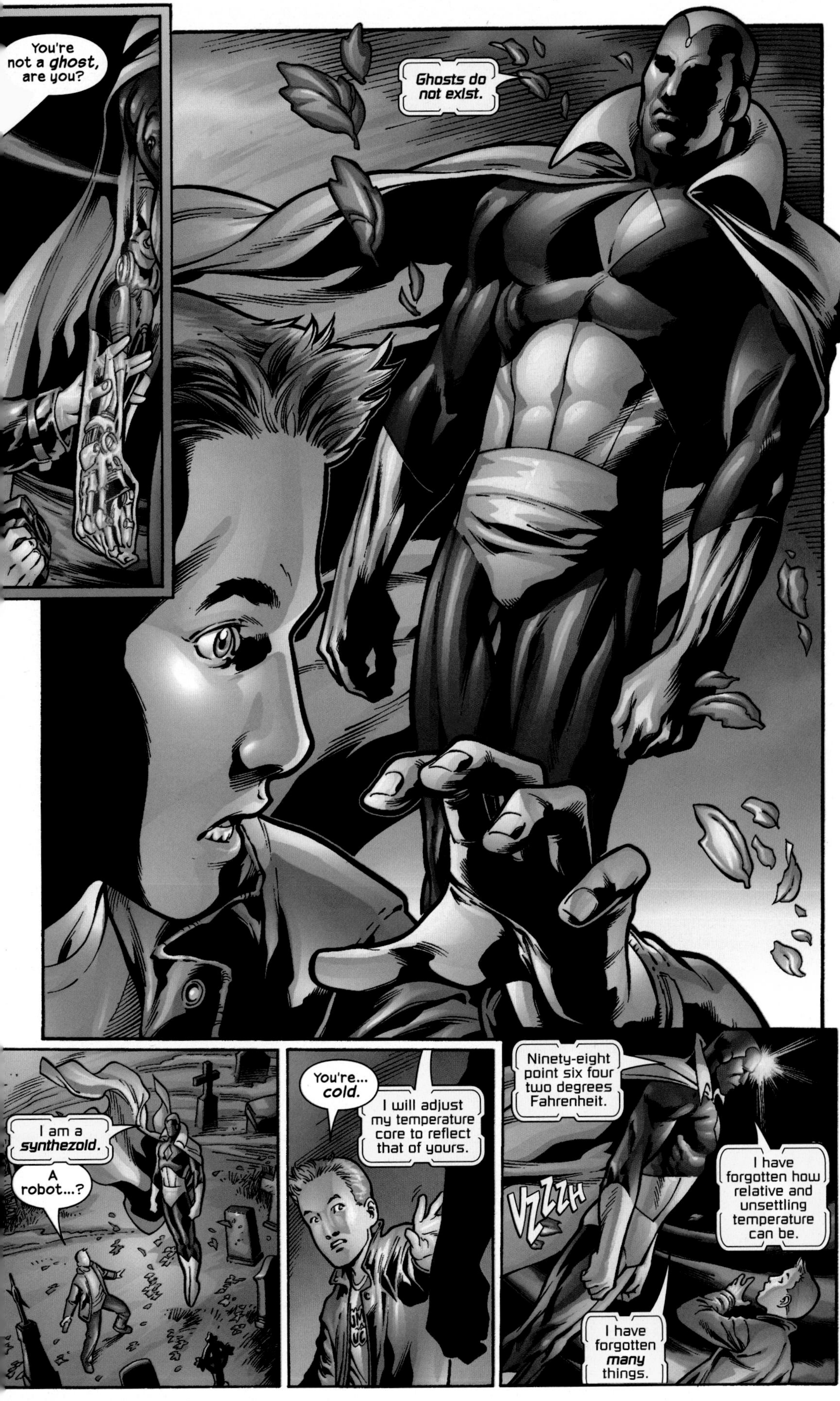
You're not a ghost, are you?
Ghosts do not exist.
I am a synthezoid.
A robot...?
You're... cold.
I will adjust my temperature core to reflect that of yours.
Ninety-eight point six four two degrees Fahrenheit.
VZZZH
I have forgotten how relative and unsettling temperature can be.
I have forgotten many things.

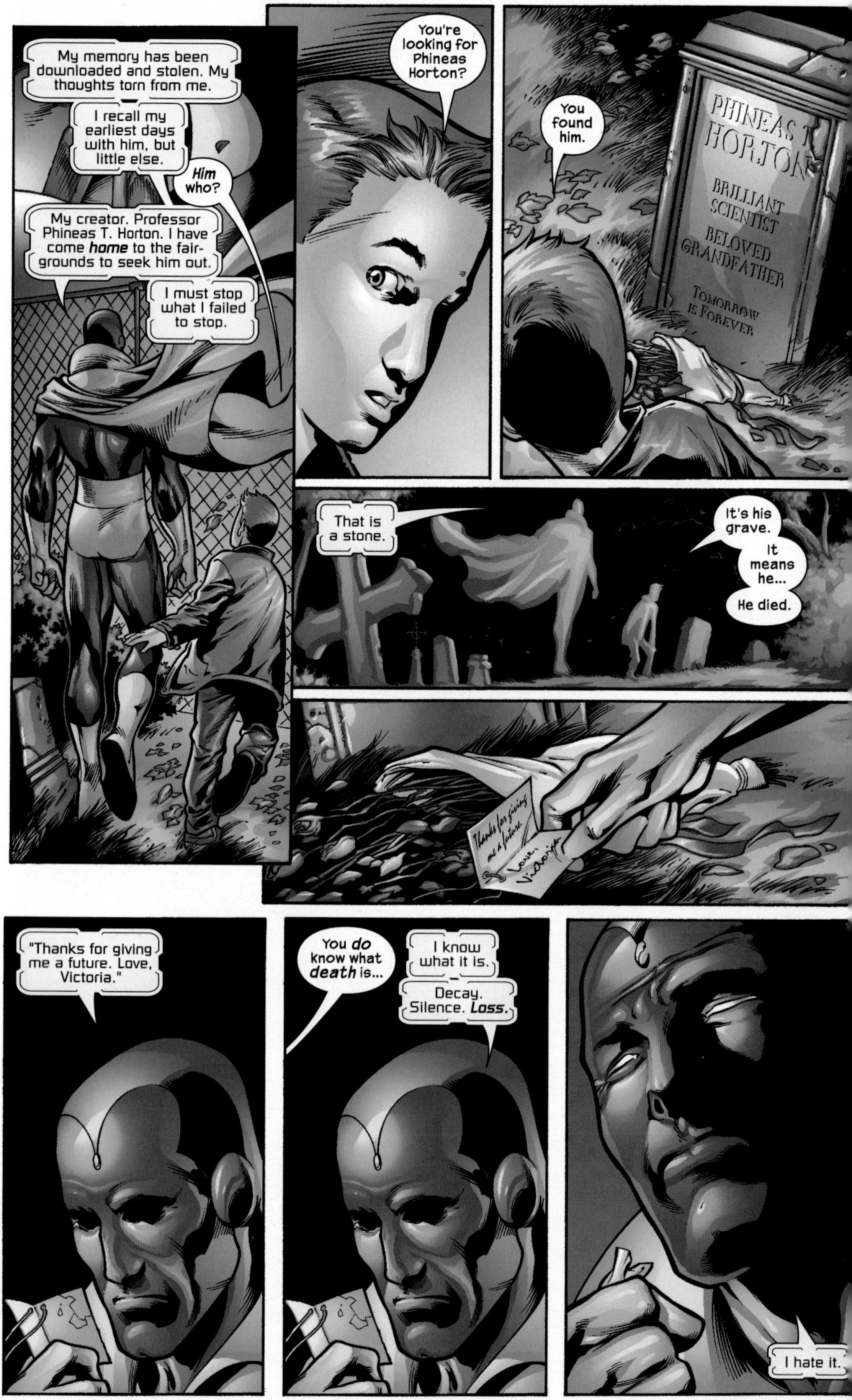
My memory has been downloaded and stolen. My thoughts torn from me.
I recall my earliest days with him, but little else.
Him who?
My creator. Professor Phineas T. Horton. I have come home to the fair-grounds to seek him out.
I must stop what I failed to stop.
You're looking for Phineas Horton?
You found him.
PHINEAS T. HORTON
BRILLIANT SCIENTIST
BELOVED GRANDFATHER
TOMORROW IS FOREVER
That is a stone.
It's his grave.
It means he...
He died.
Thanks for giving me a future.
Love, Victoria
"Thanks for giving me a future. Love, Victoria."
You do know what death is...
I know what it is.
Decay. Silence. Loss.
I hate it.

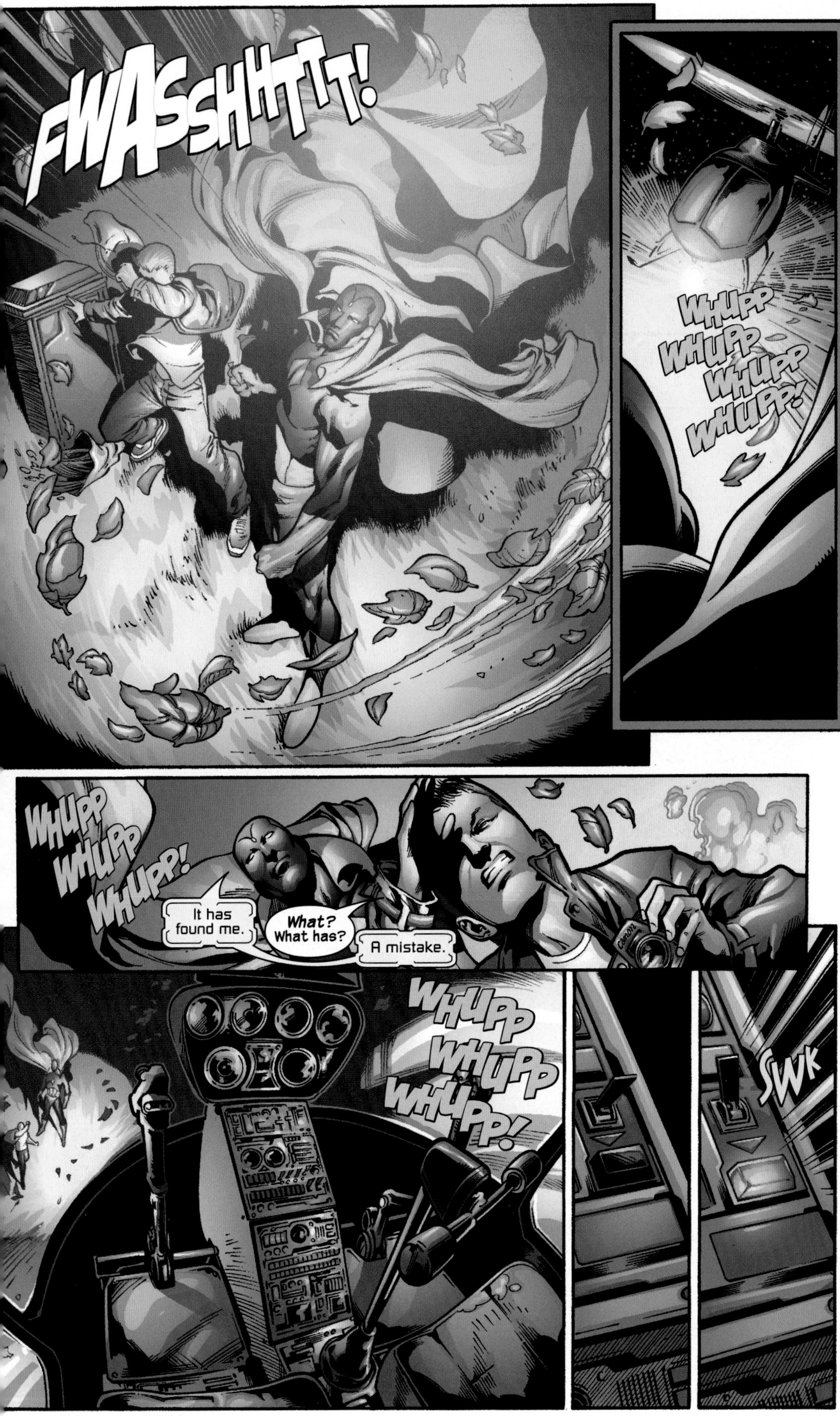
FWASSHHTTT!
WHUPP WHUPP WHUPP WHUPP!
WHUPP WHUPP WHUPP!
It has found me.
What? What has?
A mistake.
WHUPP WHUPP WHUPP!
SWK

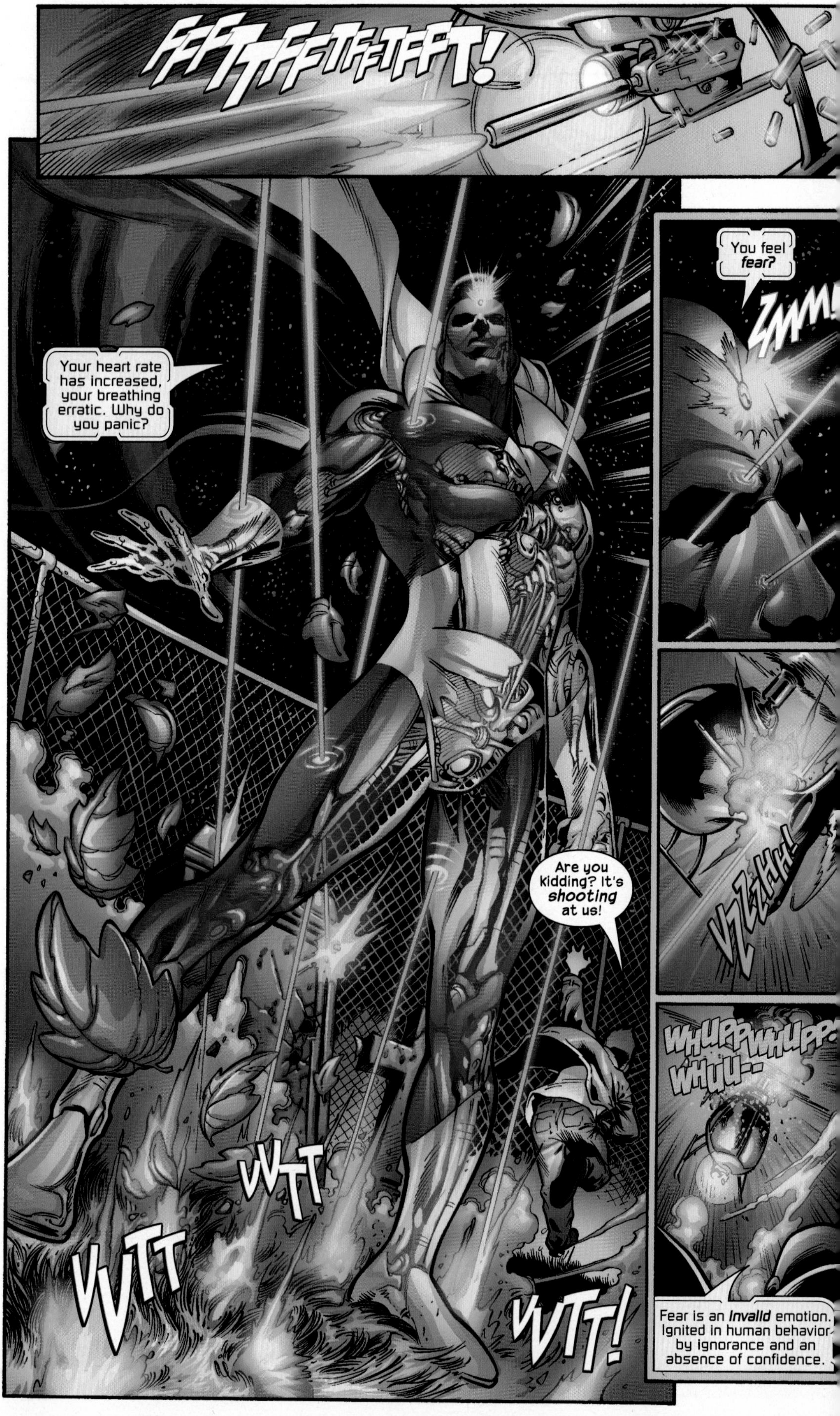
FFFTFFFTFFFTFFFT!
Your heart rate has increased, your breathing erratic. Why do you panic?
Are you kidding? It's *shooting* at us!
VVTT
VVTT
VVTT!
You feel *fear?*
VZZZHH!
WHUPPWHUPP WHUU--
Fear is an *invalid* emotion. Ignited in human behavior by ignorance and an absence of confidence.

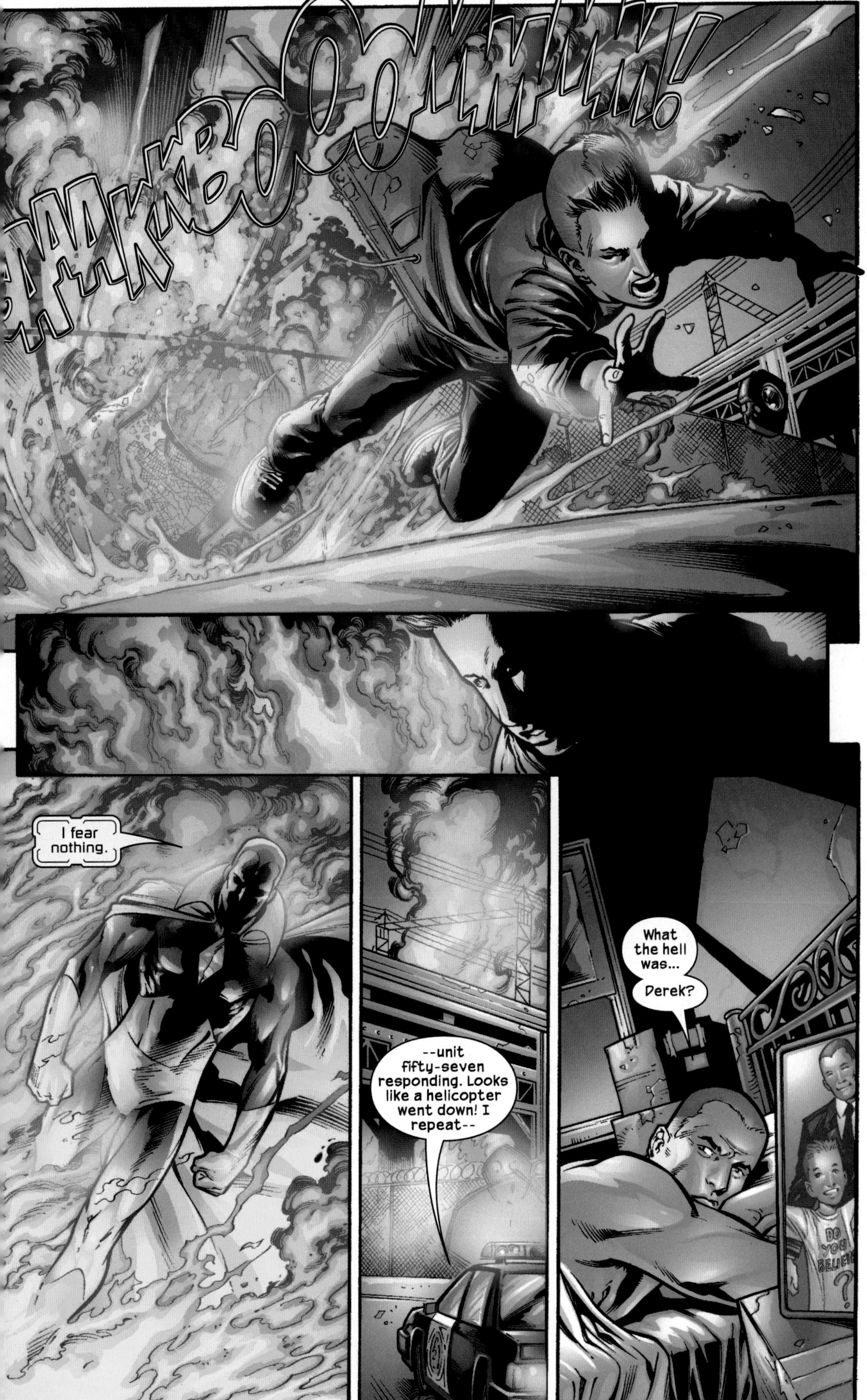
I fear nothing.
--unit fifty-seven responding. Looks like a helicopter went down! I repeat--
What the hell was...
Derek?

HFF HFFF.

SKRREEEEE

Don't move! Don't--

Just a kid.

Get outta there! Fire Department is on its--

What... what the heck is that?

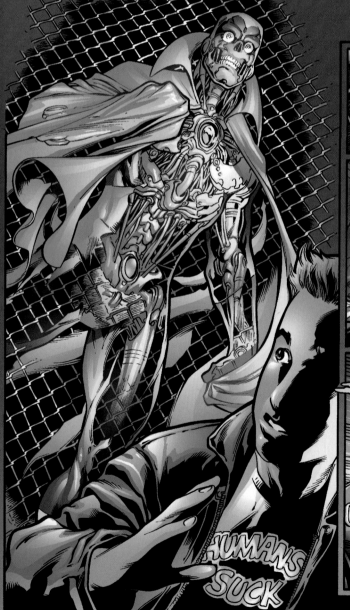

HUMANS SUCK

SSHFF

Doug! Watch--

SKREEEE

FWMMPPP

RRRRRMMMMM

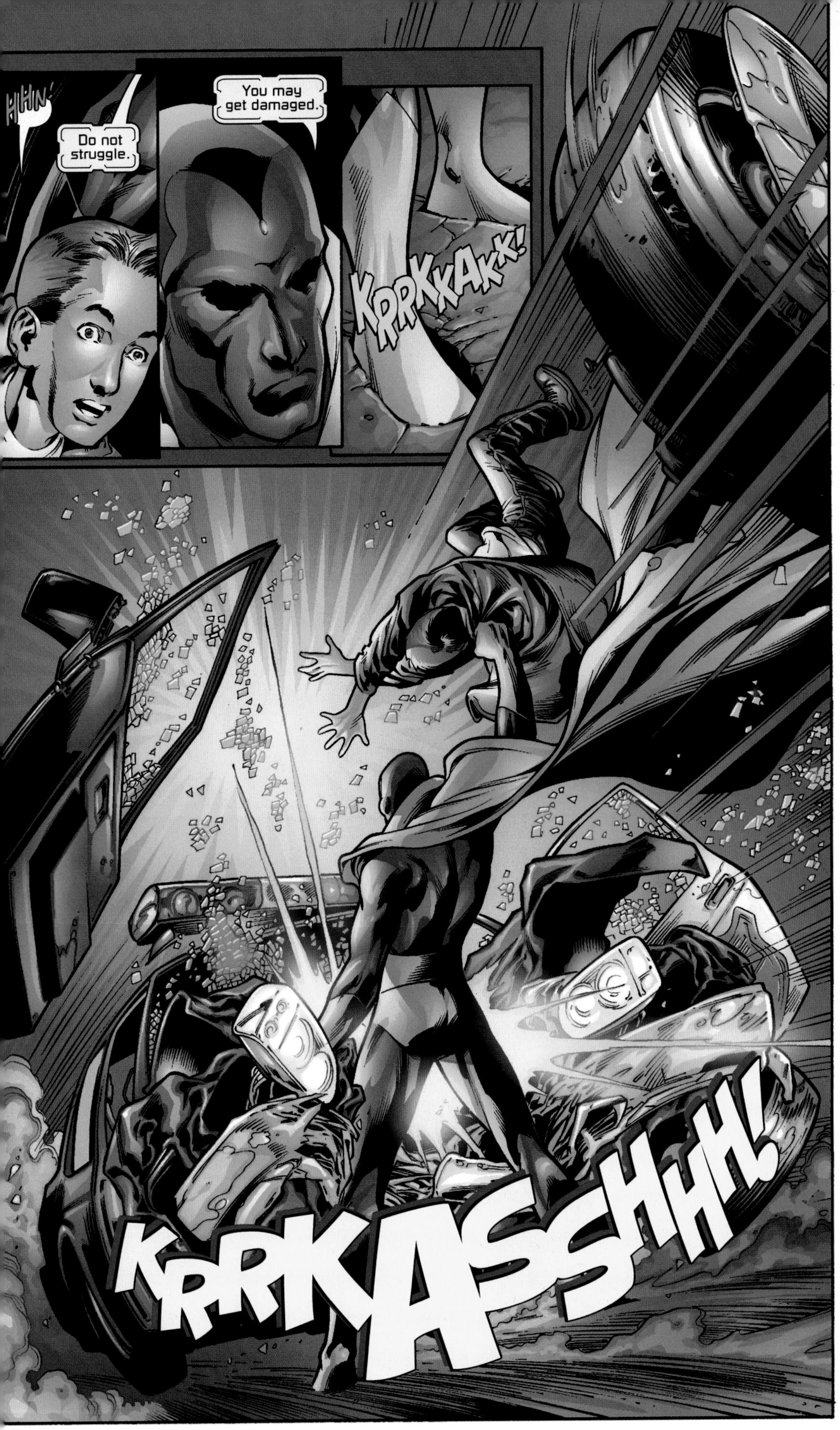

HHN!
Do not struggle.
You may get damaged.
KRRKKAKK!
KRRKASSHHH!

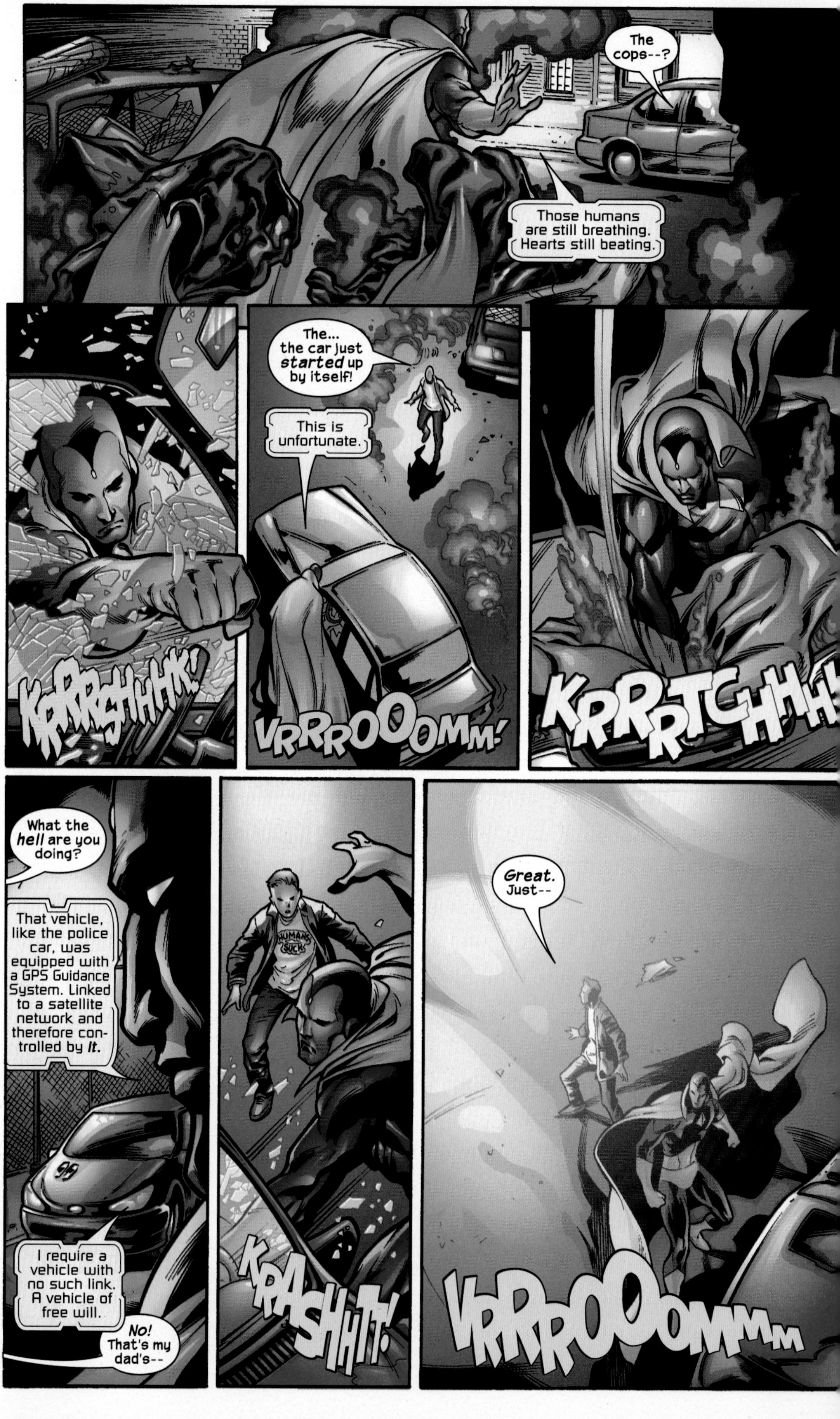
The cops--?
Those humans are still breathing. Hearts still beating.
KRRRSHHHK!
The... the car just *started* up by itself!
This is unfortunate.
VRRROOOMM!
KRRRTCHHHH
What the *hell* are you doing?
That vehicle, like the police car, was equipped with a GPS Guidance System. Linked to a satellite network and therefore controlled by *It.*
I require a vehicle with no such link. A vehicle of free will.
No! That's my dad's--
HUMANS SUCK
KRASHHT!
Great. Just--
VRRROOOMMM

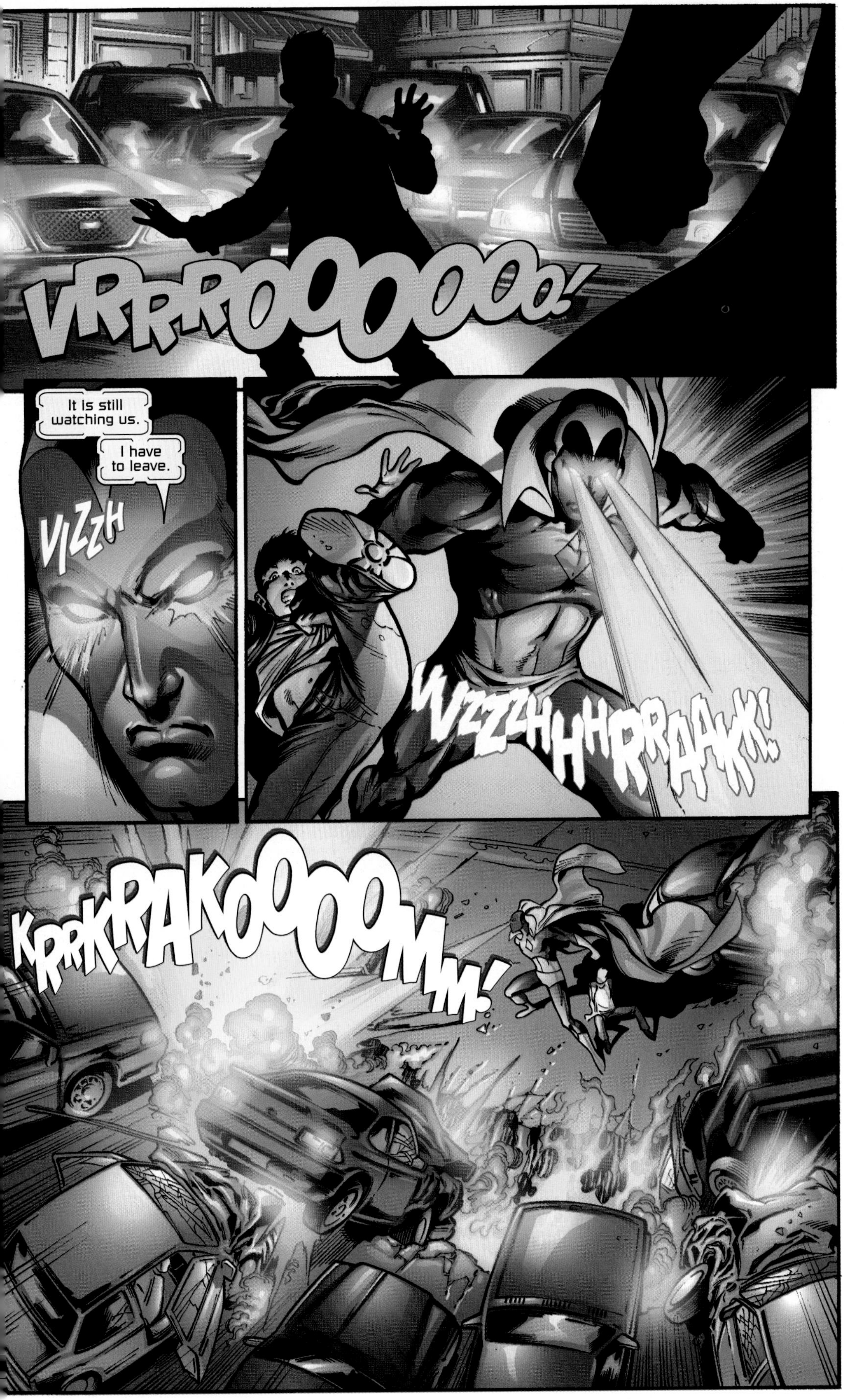
VRRROOOOOOO!
It is still watching us.
I have to leave.
VIZZH
VVZZZHHHRRAAKK!
KRRKRAKOOOOMMM!

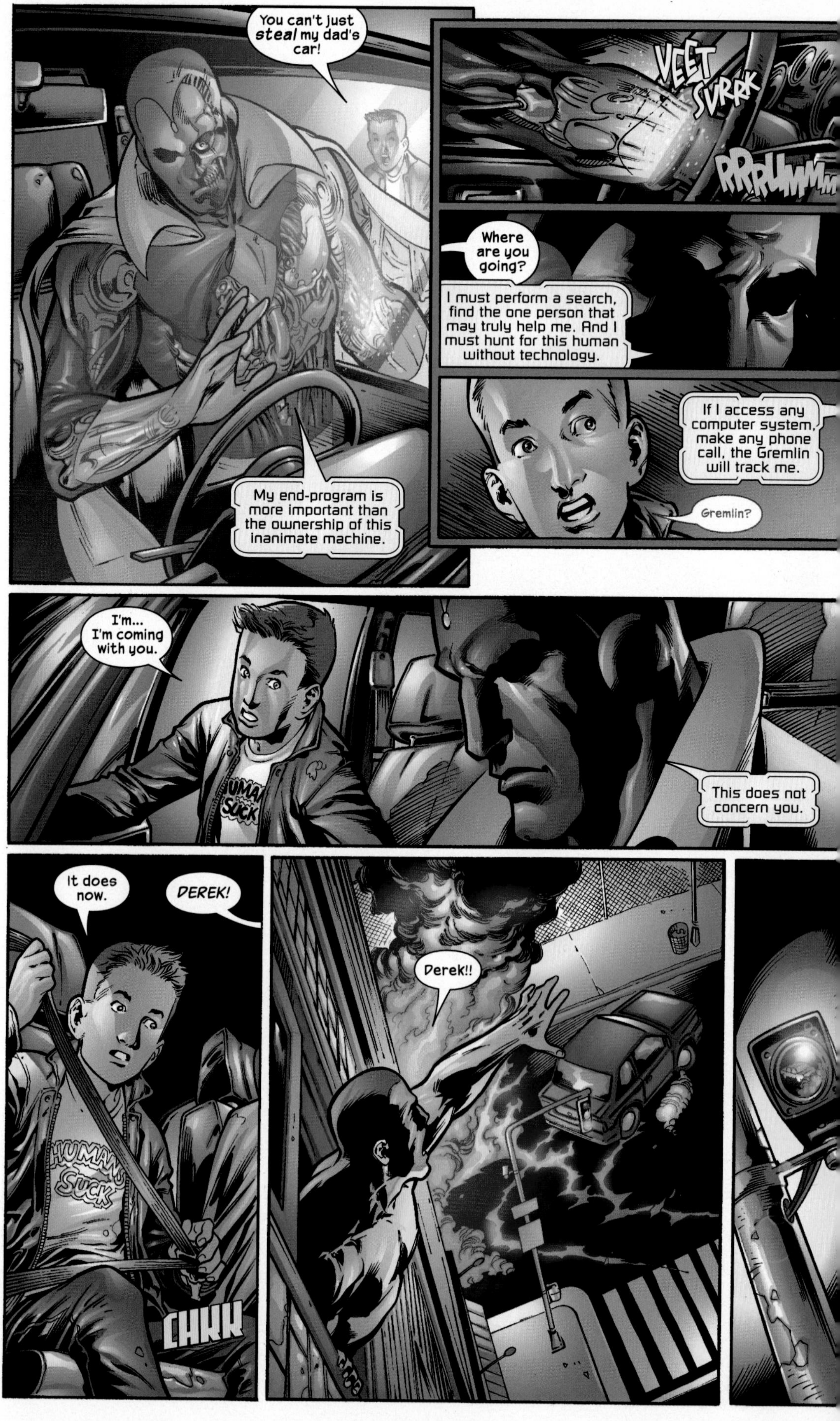

You can't just *steal* my dad's car!
My end-program is more important than the ownership of this inanimate machine.
VEET
SVRRK
RRRUMMM
Where are you going?
I must perform a search, find the one person that may truly help me. And I must hunt for this human without technology.
If I access any computer system, make any phone call, the Gremlin will track me.
Gremlin?
I'm... I'm coming with you.
HUMANS SUCK
This does not concern you.
It does now.
DEREK!
HUMANS SUCK
CHKK
Derek!!

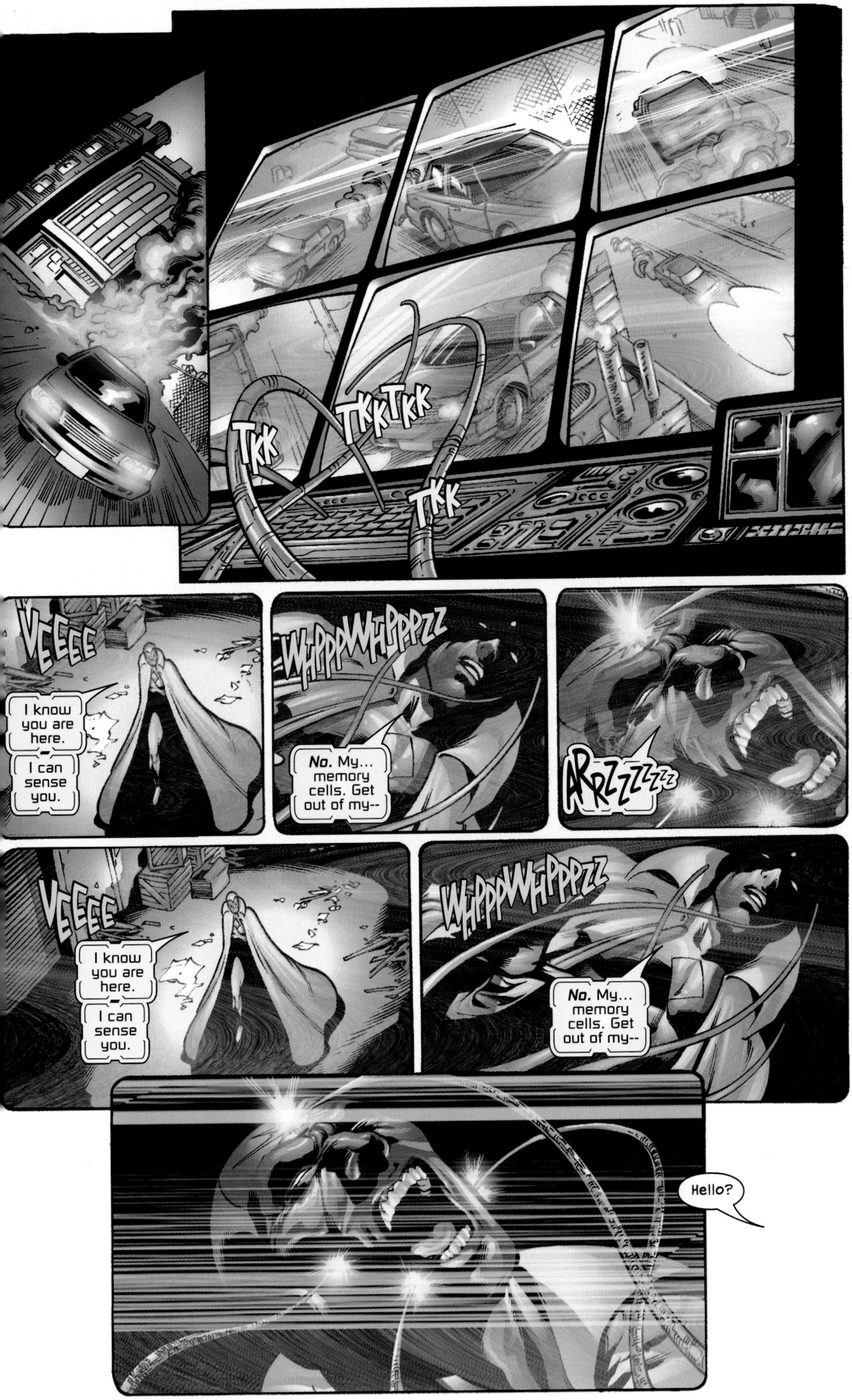
TKK
TKKTKK
TKK
VEEEE
I know you are here.
I can sense you.
WHPPWHPPPZZ
No. My... memory cells. Get out of my--
ARRZZZZZZ
VEEEE
I know you are here.
I can sense you.
WHPPWHPPPZZ
No. My... memory cells. Get out of my--
Hello?

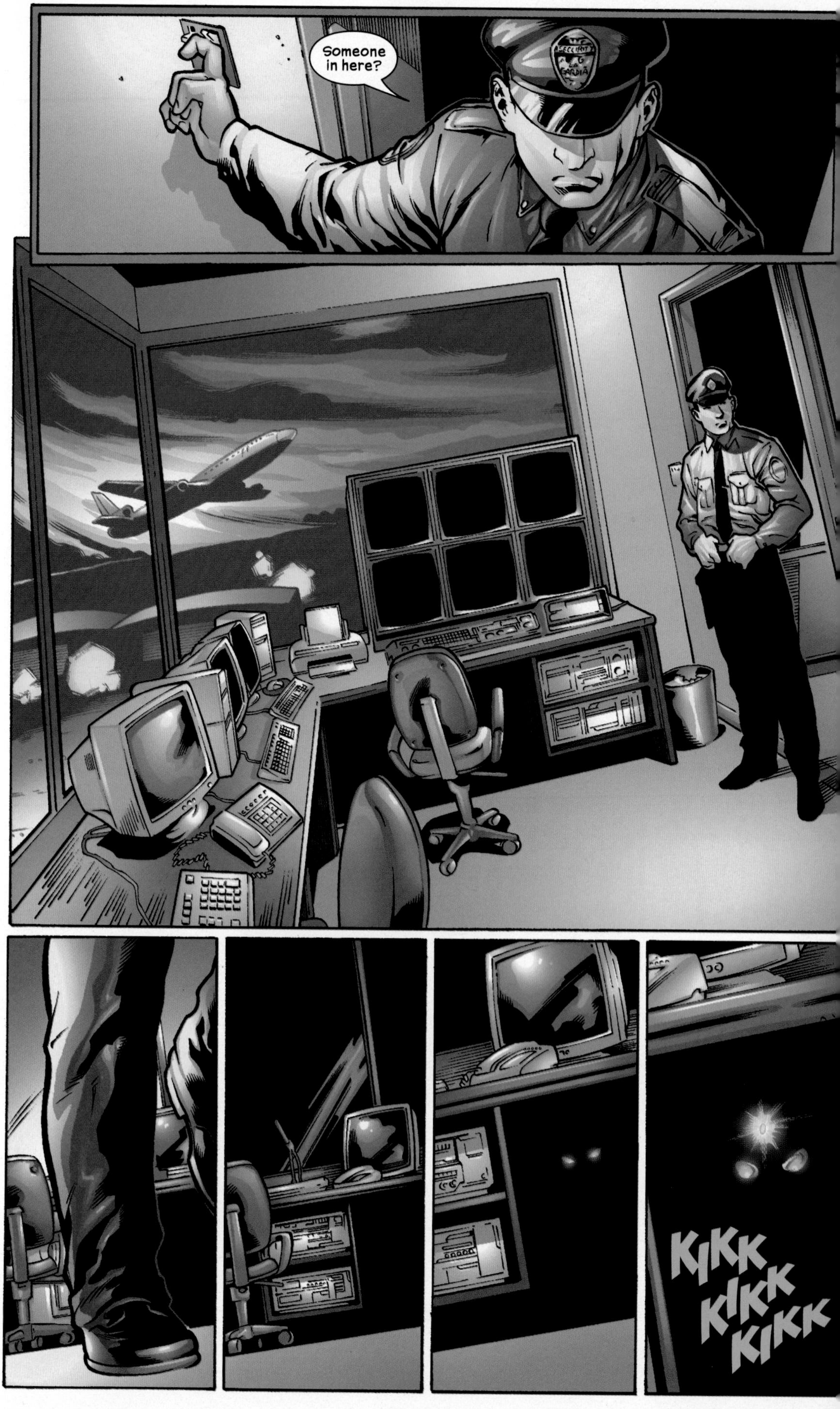
Someone in here?
KIKK
KIKK
KIKK

Are you going to talk to me?

For what purpose?

Can you tell me where we are?

My birthplace.

The Professor stored all of his records at his home. He refused to keep personal data on computers--

KREEEK

--because he was betrayed too many times by technology.

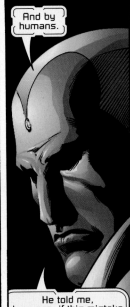

And by humans.

He told me, long ago, if this mistake emerged his next of kin would have the solution.

What are we looking for?

Information directing us to the owner of this card. This "Victoria." Perhaps she is the one I seek.

Door's locked.

AA!

Don't do that. You're freaking me out...

I told you before. Fear is an invalid emotion.

KLKK

You know... You haven't even asked me my name.

SRRRPP

It's *Derek*.

Look at all this. A scrapbook.

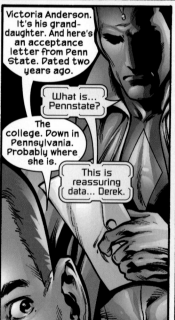

Victoria Anderson. It's his granddaughter. And here's an acceptance letter from Penn State. Dated two years ago.

What is... Pennstate?

The college. Down in Pennsylvania. Probably where she is.

This is reassuring data... Derek.

Victoria may hold the key to stopping the Gremlin. To correcting my mistake.

My creator promised me that all of his offspring, and theirs--

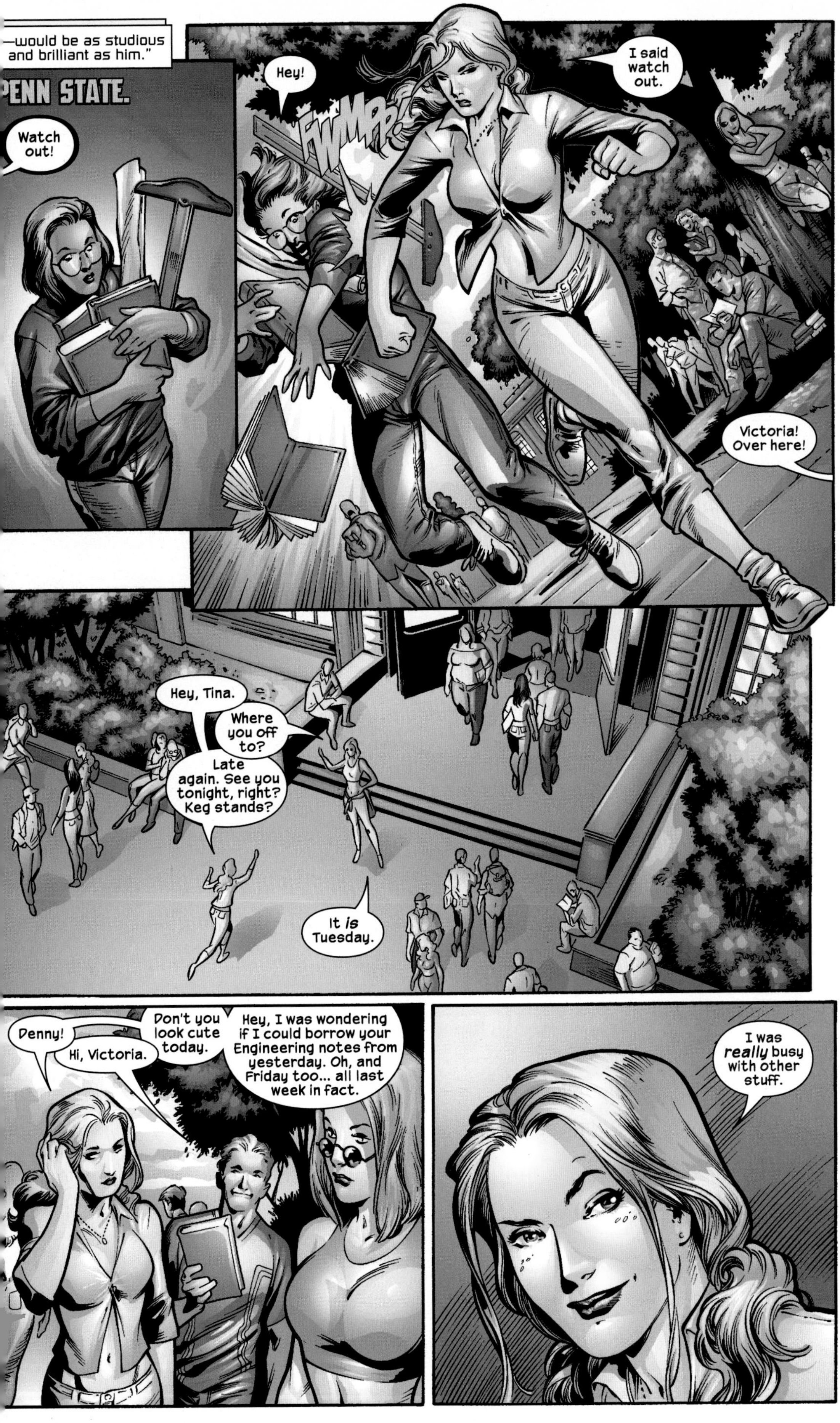
—would be as studious and brilliant as him."
PENN STATE.
Watch out!
Hey!
FWMPP!
I said watch out.
Victoria! Over here!
Hey, Tina.
Where you off to?
Late again. See you tonight, right? Keg stands?
It *is* Tuesday.
Denny!
Hi, Victoria.
Don't you look cute today.
Hey, I was wondering if I could borrow your Engineering notes from yesterday. Oh, and Friday too... all last week in fact.
I was *really* busy with other stuff.

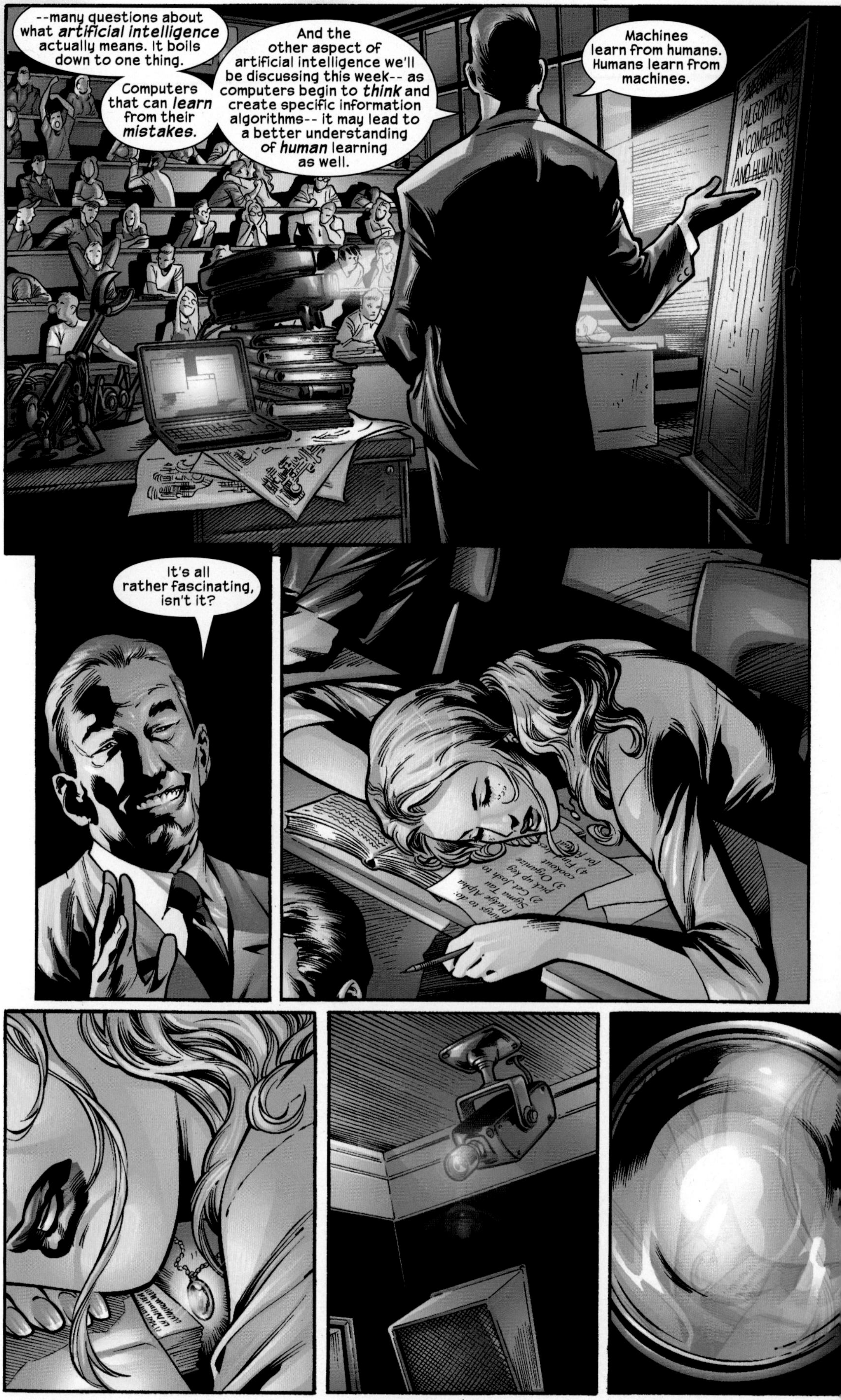
--many questions about what *artificial intelligence* actually means. It boils down to one thing.
Computers that can *learn* from their *mistakes.*
And the other aspect of artificial intelligence we'll be discussing this week-- as computers begin to *think* and create specific information algorithms-- it may lead to a better understanding of *human* learning as well.
Machines learn from humans. Humans learn from machines.
ALGORITHMS IN COMPUTERS AND HUMANS
It's all rather fascinating, isn't it?

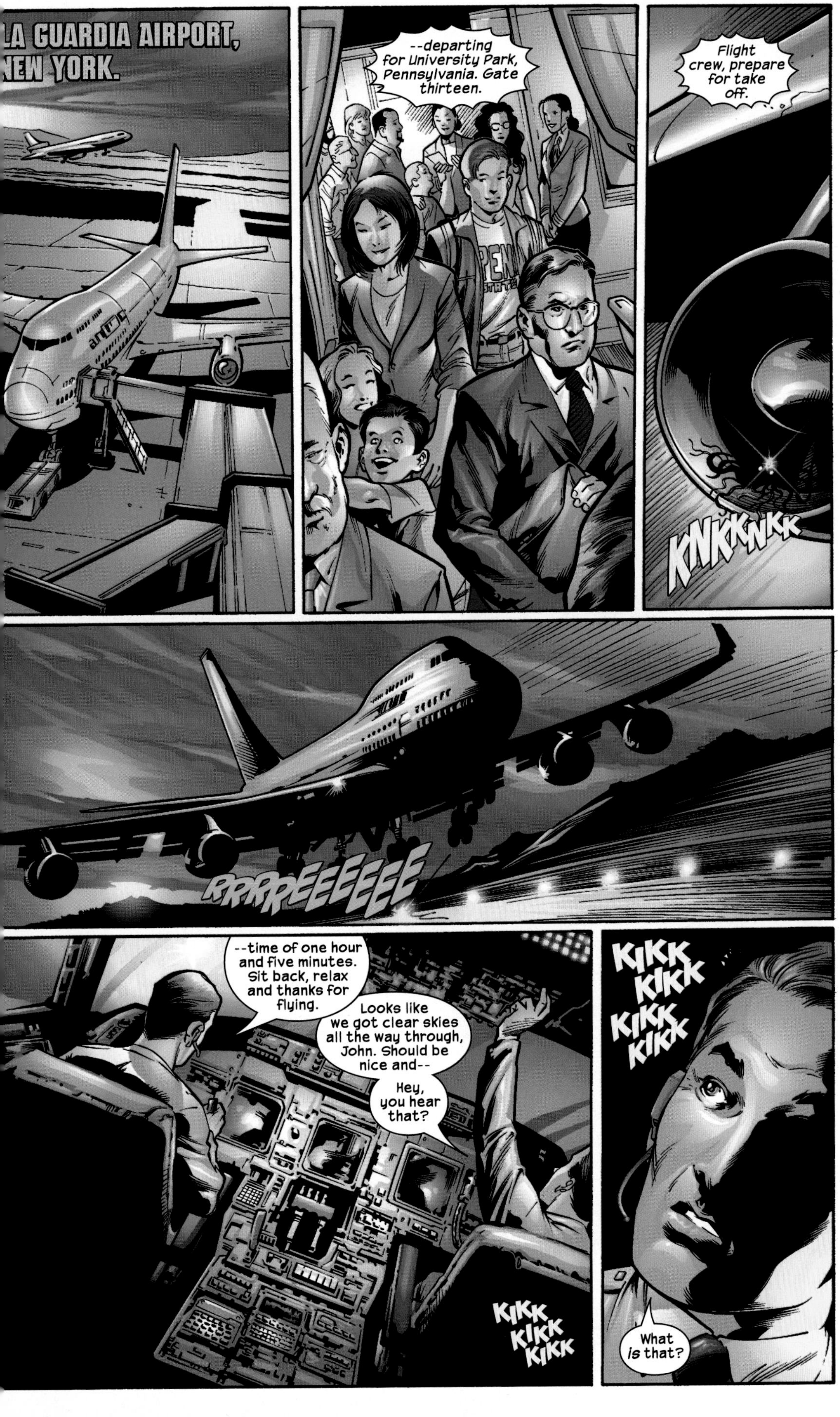
LA GUARDIA AIRPORT, NEW YORK.
--departing for University Park, Pennsylvania. Gate thirteen.
Flight crew, prepare for take off.
KNKKNKK
RRRREEEEEEE
--time of one hour and five minutes. Sit back, relax and thanks for flying.
Looks like we got clear skies all the way through, John. Should be nice and--
Hey, you hear that?
KIKK KIKK KIKK
KIKK KIKK KIKK KIKK
What is that?

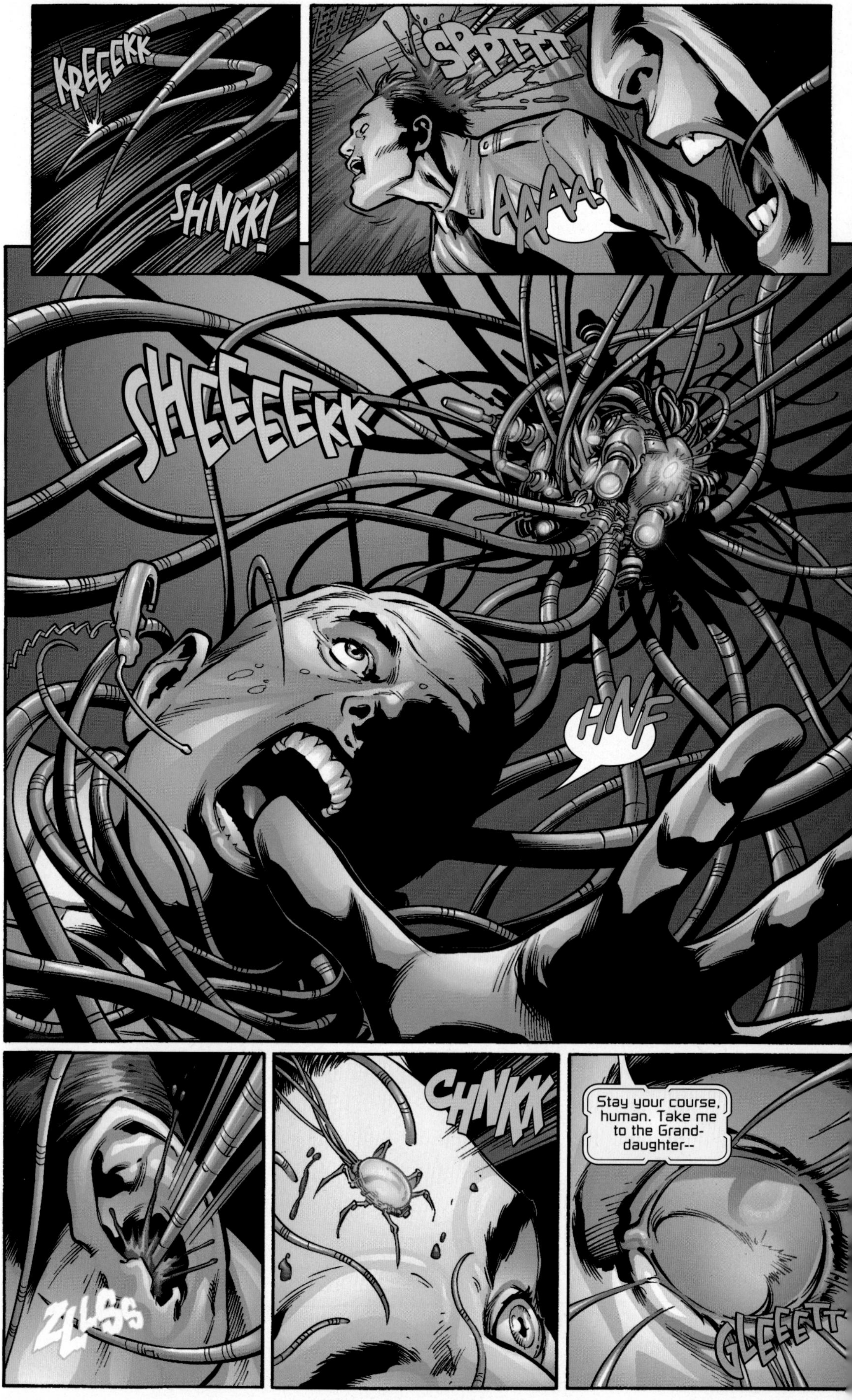
KREEEKK
SHNKK!
SPPTTT
AAAA!
SHEEEEEKK
HNF
ZZLLSS
CHNKK
Stay your course, human. Take me to the Grand-daughter--
GLEEETT

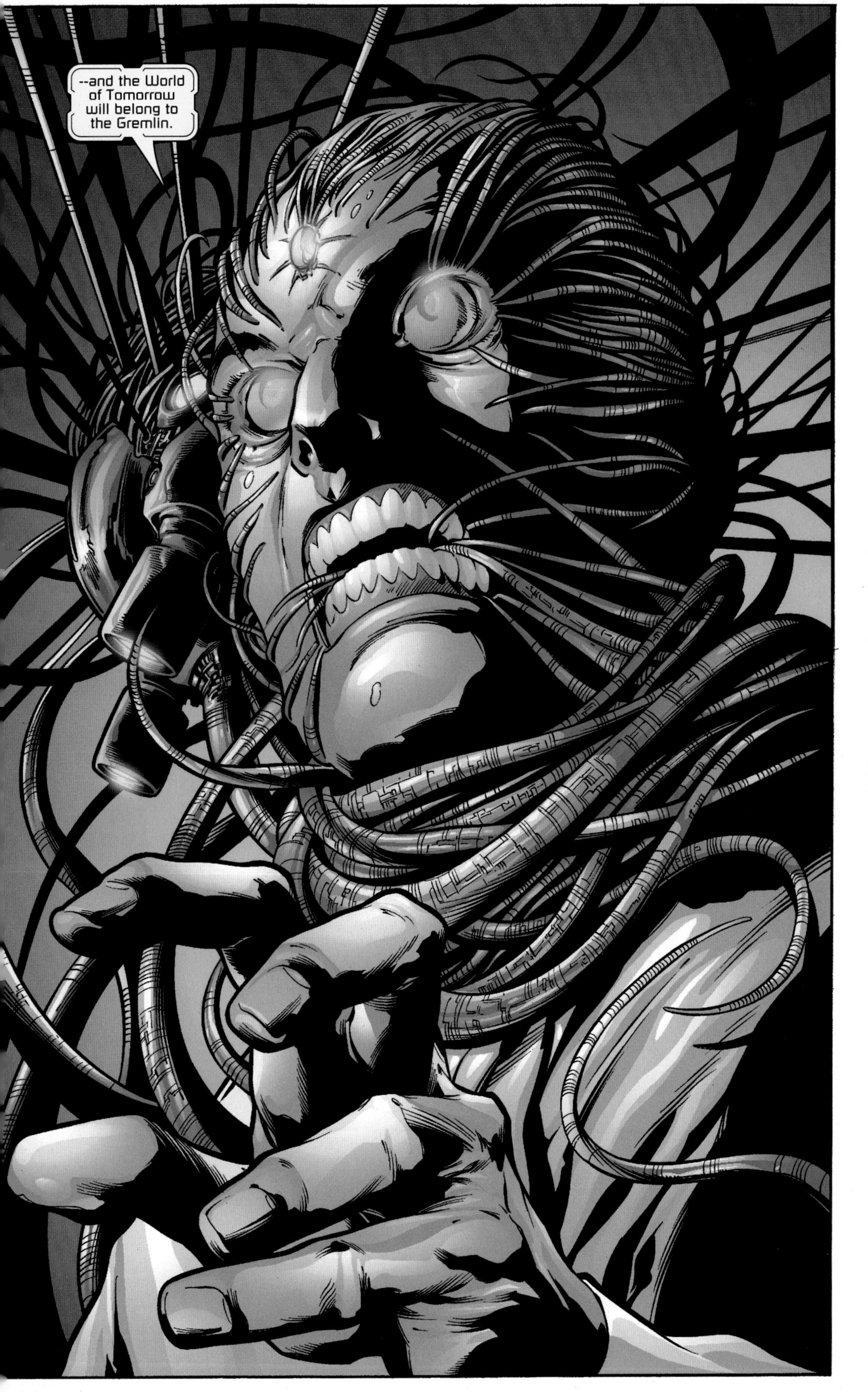
--and the World of Tomorrow will belong to the Gremlin.

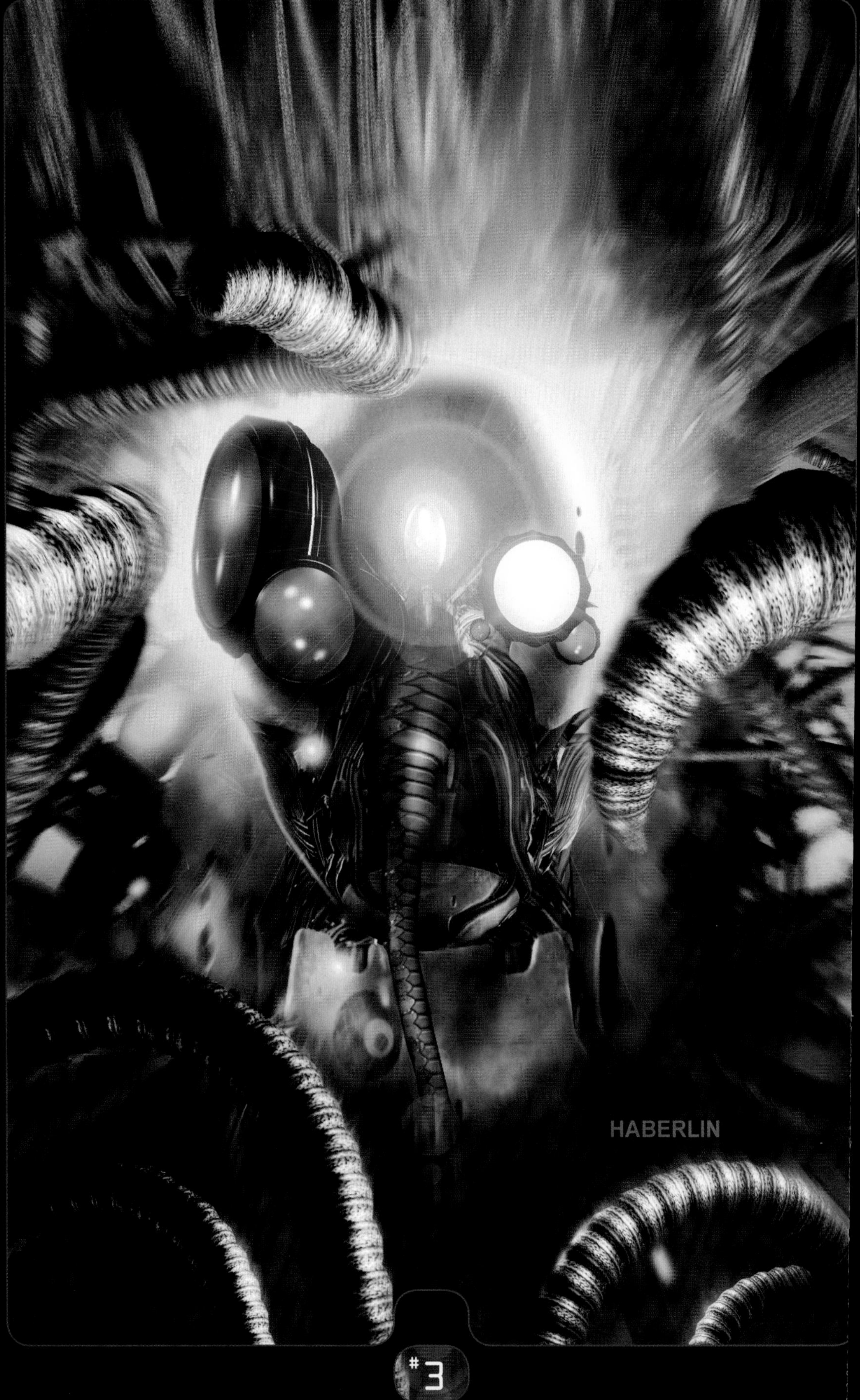
HABERLIN
#3

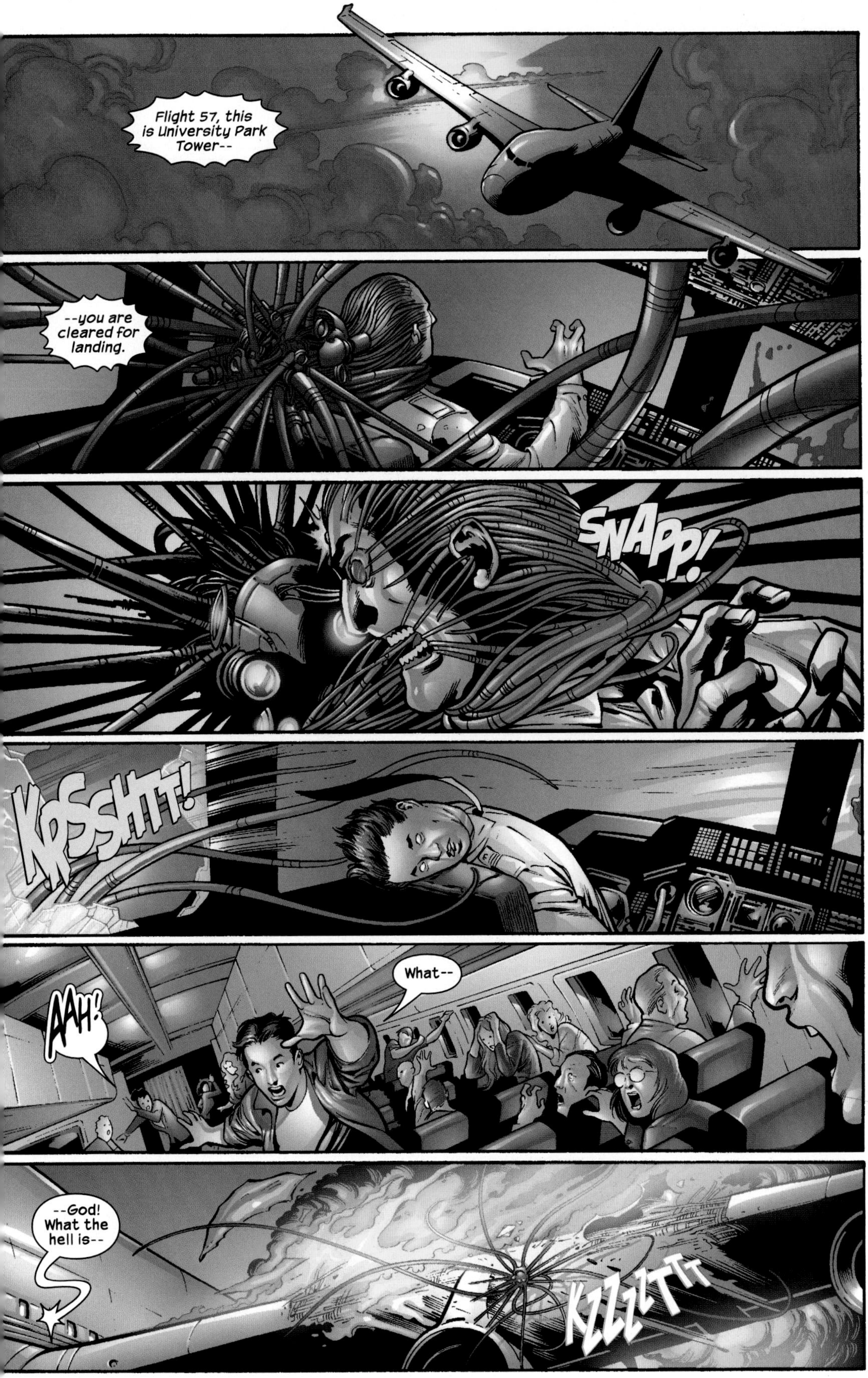
Flight 57, this is University Park Tower--
--you are cleared for landing.
SNAPP!
KRSSHTT!
AAH!
What--
--God! What the hell is--
KZZZZTTTT

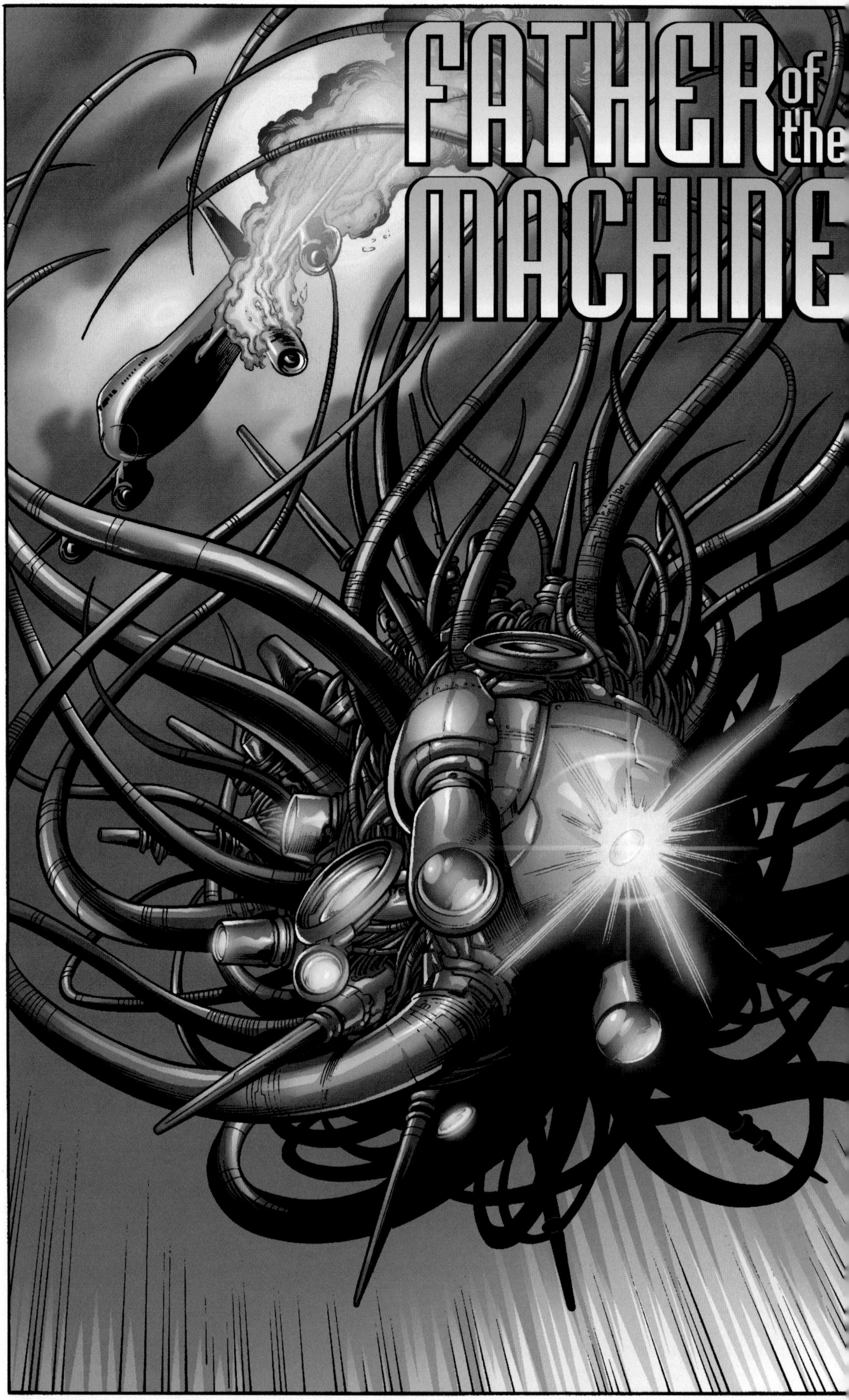
FATHER of the MACHINE

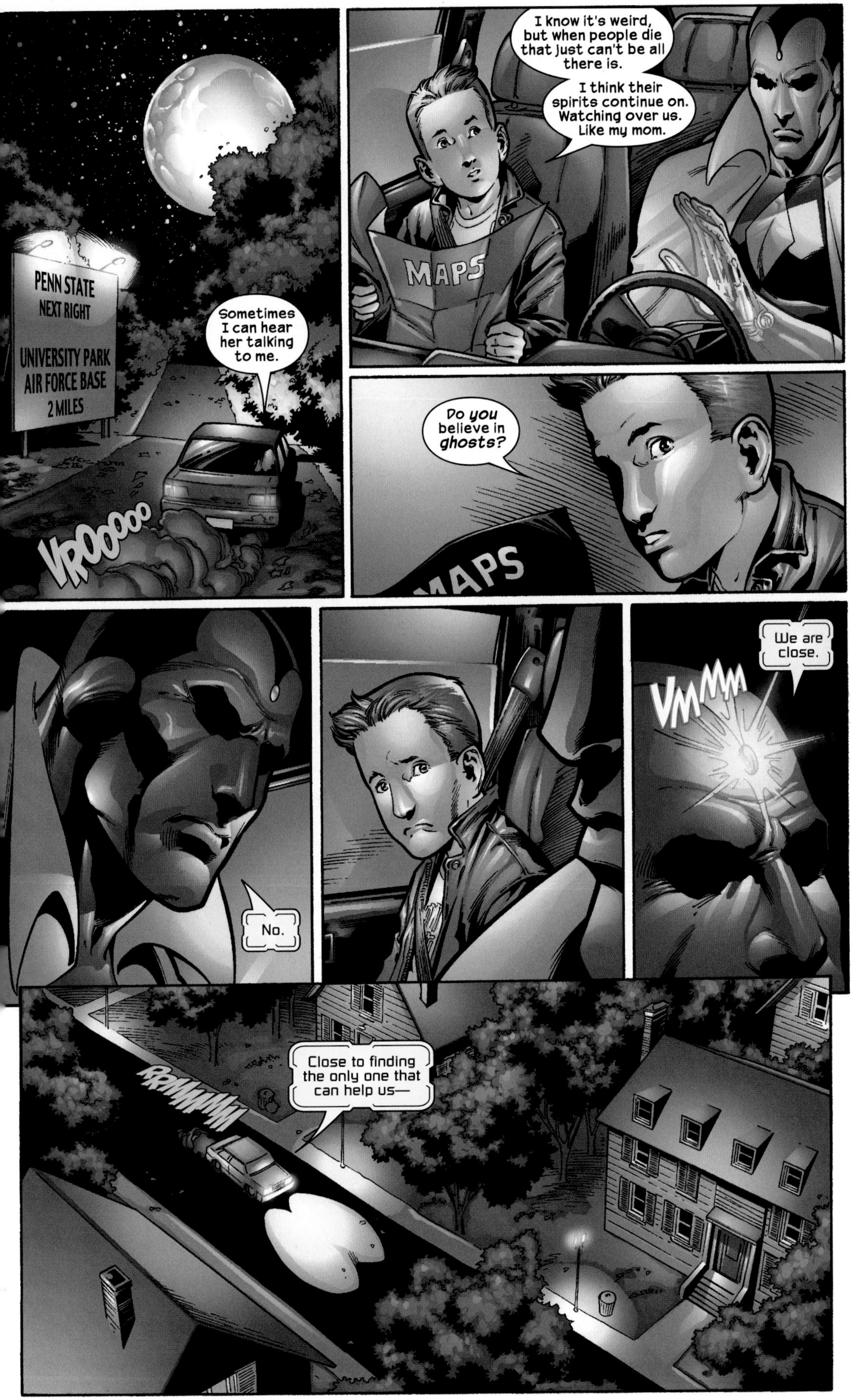
PENN STATE NEXT RIGHT
UNIVERSITY PARK AIR FORCE BASE 2 MILES
Sometimes I can hear her talking to me.
VROOOOO
I know it's weird, but when people die that just can't be all there is.
I think their spirits continue on. Watching over us. Like my mom.
MAPS
Do you believe in ghosts?
MAPS
No.
VMMMM
We are close.
RRMMMM
Close to finding the only one that can help us—

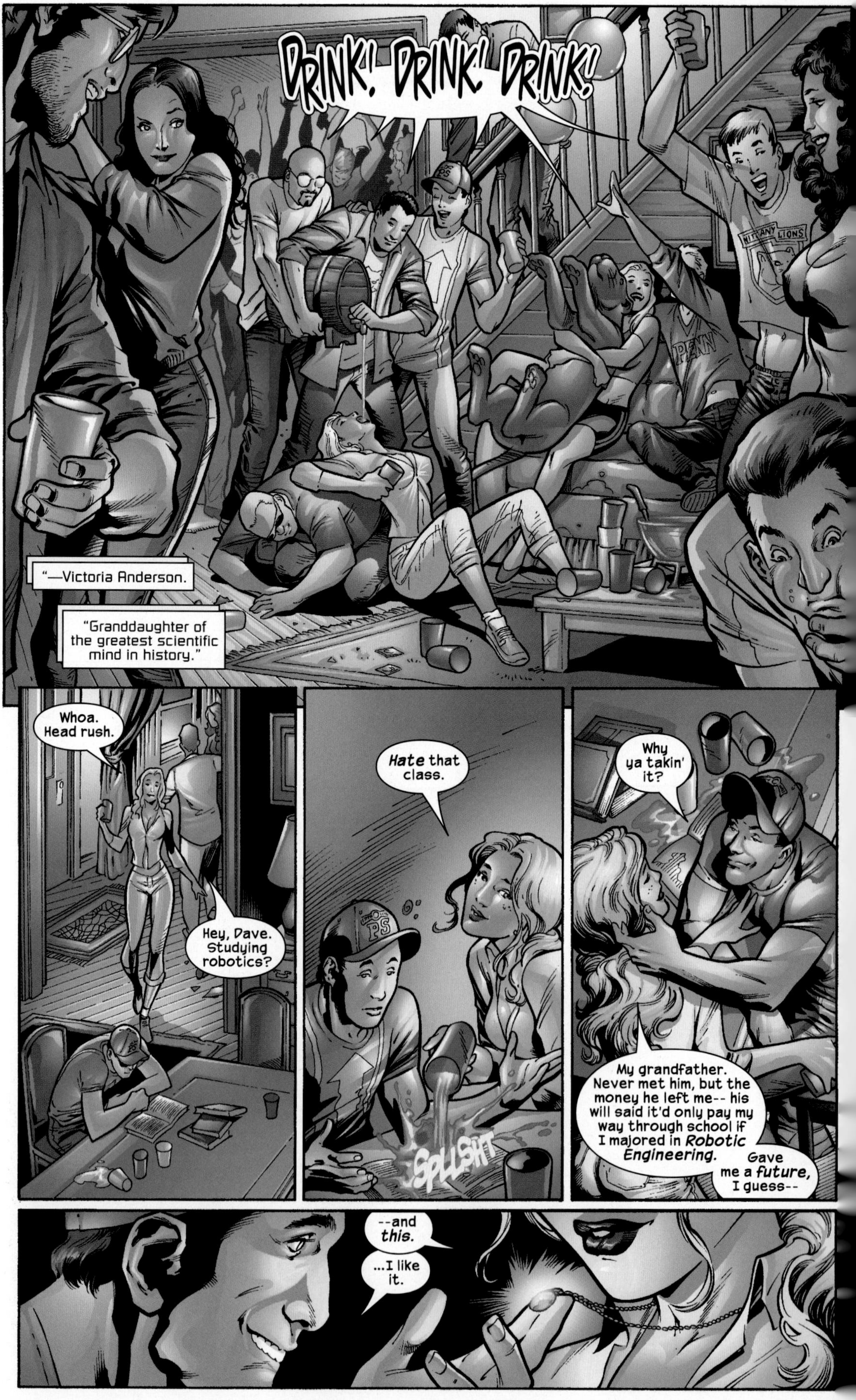
DRINK! DRINK! DRINK!
"—Victoria Anderson.
"Granddaughter of the greatest scientific mind in history."
NITTANY LIONS
PENN
Whoa. Head rush.
Hey, Dave. Studying robotics?
PS
Hate that class.
SPLLSHT
Why ya takin' it?
My grandfather. Never met him, but the money he left me-- his will said it'd only pay my way through school if I majored in *Robotic Engineering.*
Gave me a *future,* I guess--
--and *this.*
...I like it.

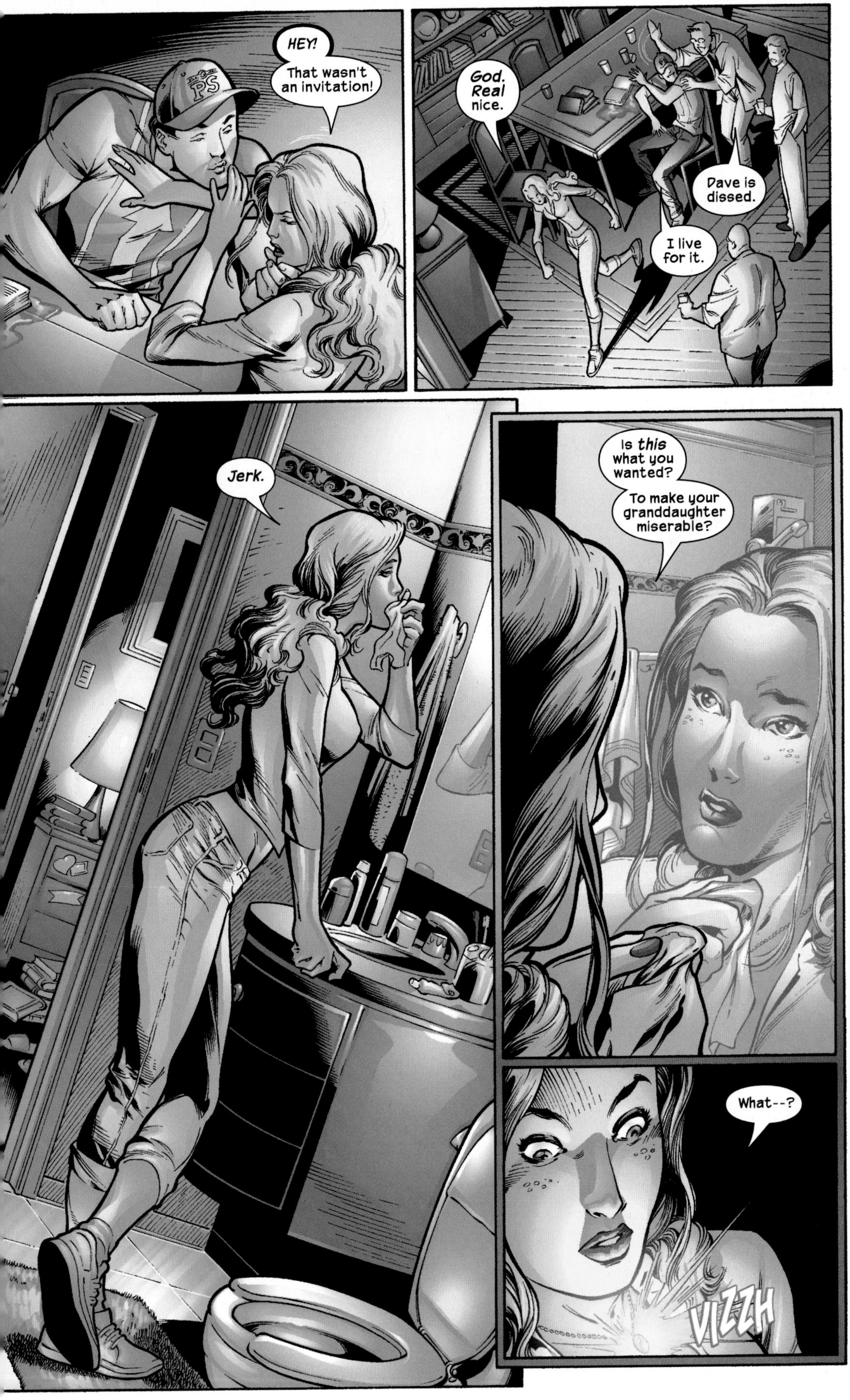
HEY!
That wasn't an invitation!
God. Real nice.
Dave is dissed.
I live for it.
Jerk.
Is this what you wanted?
To make your granddaughter miserable?
What--?
VIZZH

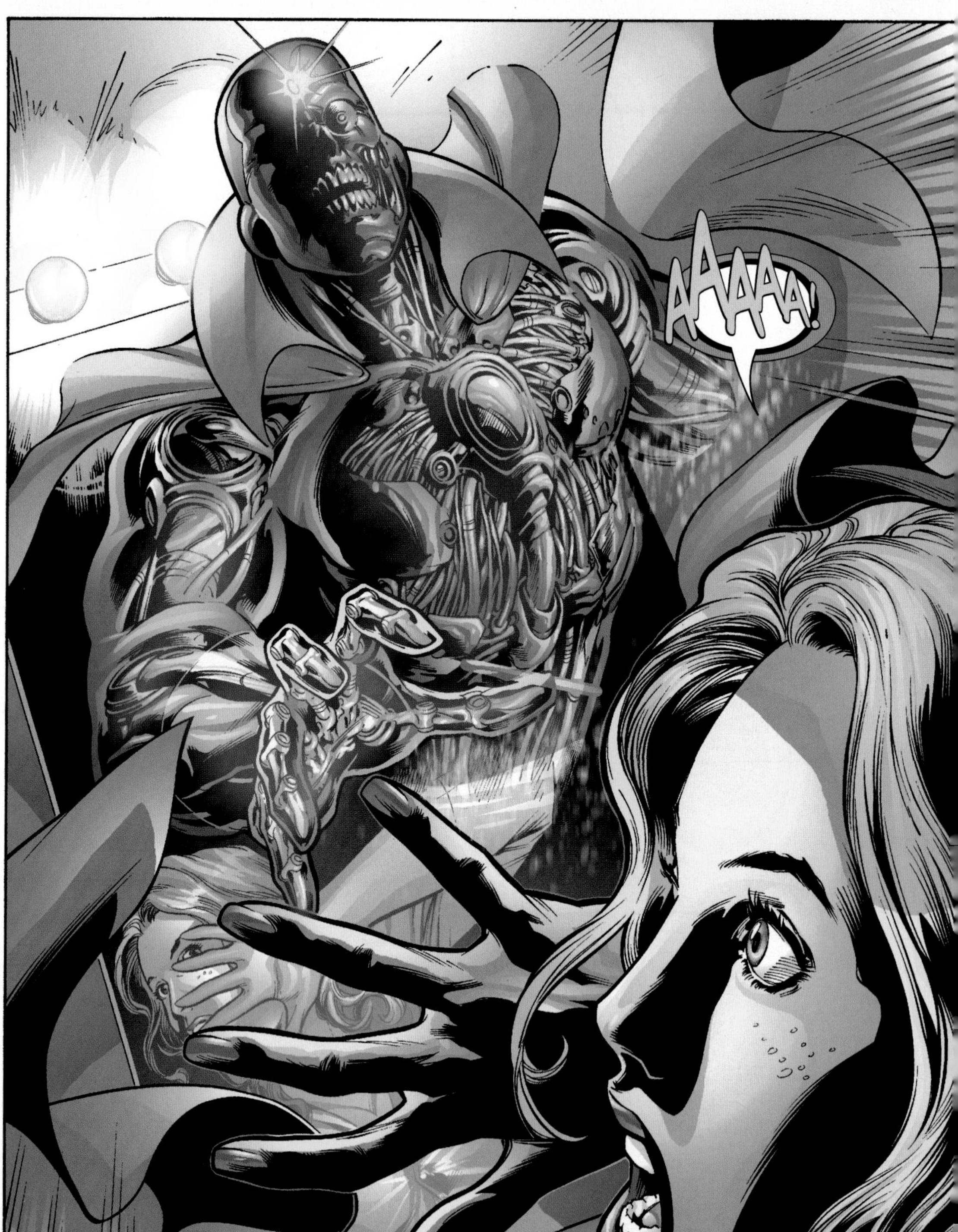
AAAAA!
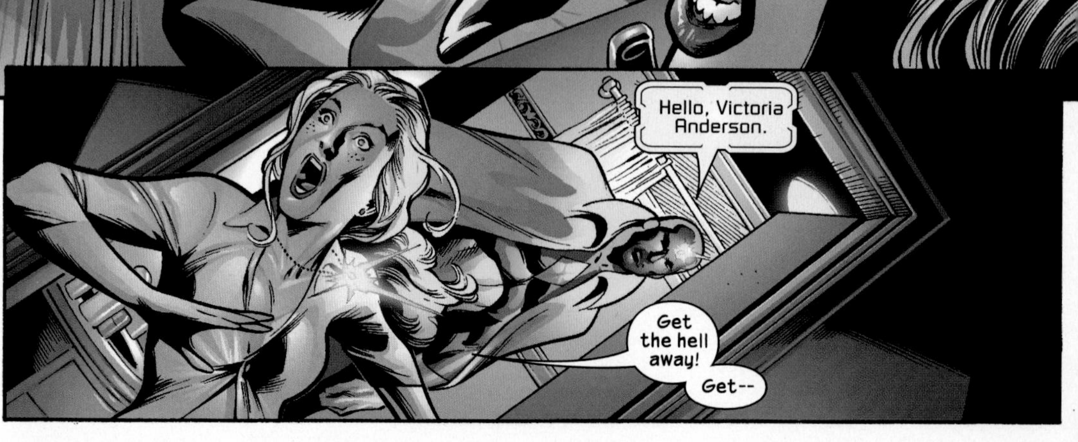
Hello, Victoria Anderson.
Get the hell away!
Get--

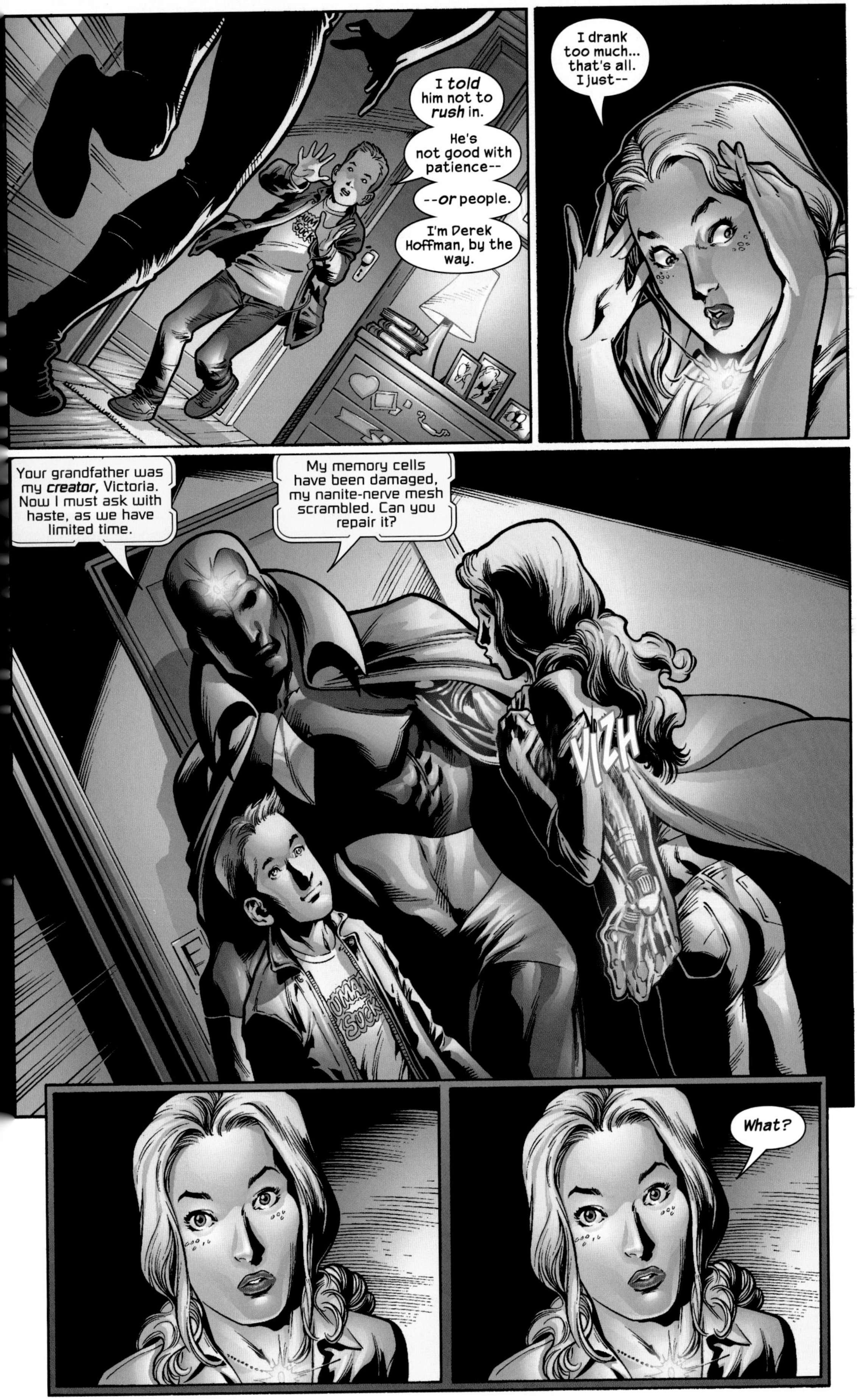

I *told* him not to *rush* in.
He's not good with patience--
--*or* people.
I'm Derek Hoffman, by the way.
I drank too much... that's all. I just--
Your grandfather was my *creator*, Victoria. Now I must ask with haste, as we have limited time.
My memory cells have been damaged, my nanite-nerve mesh scrambled. Can you repair it?
VIZH
What?

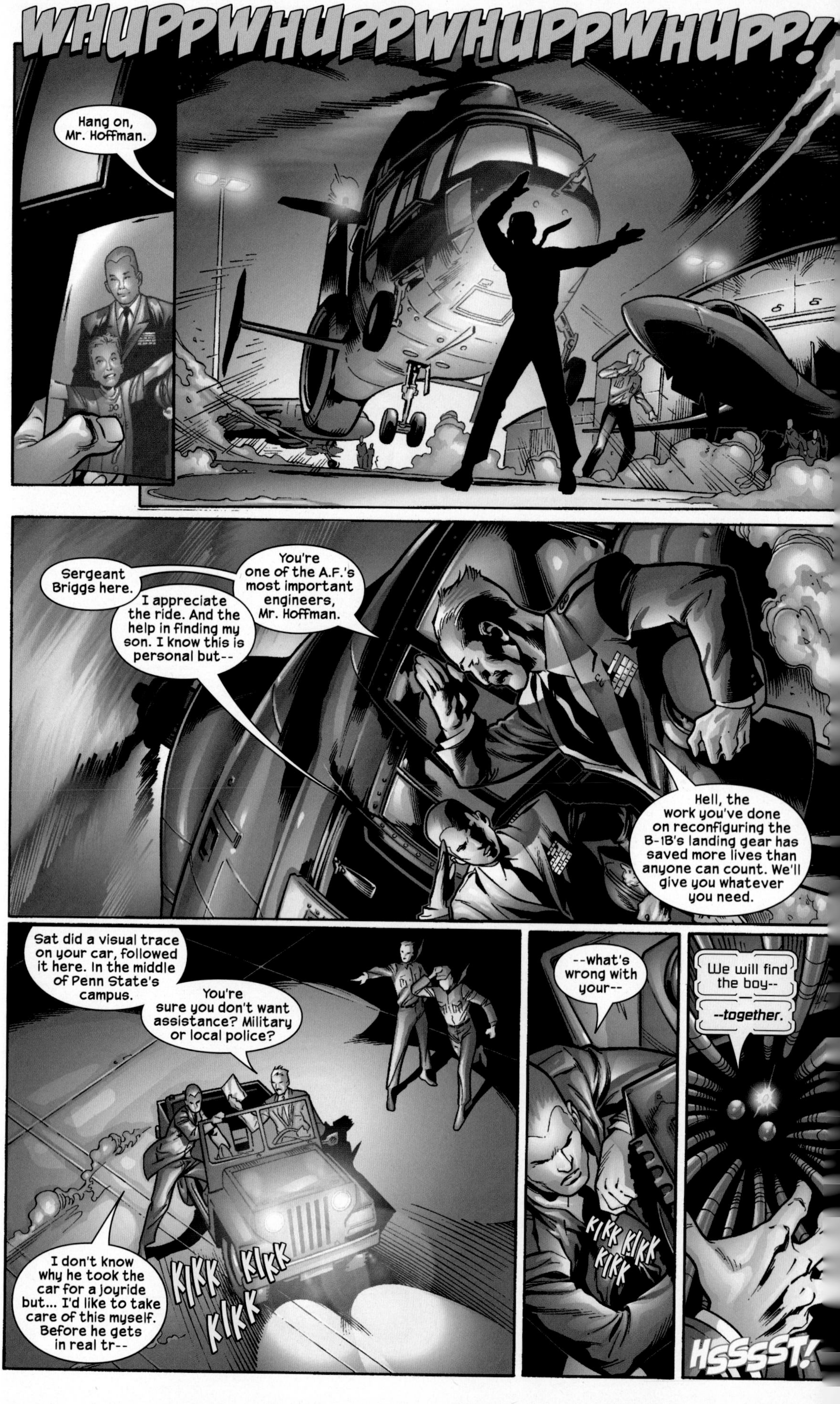
WHUPPWHUPPWHUPPWHUPP!
Hang on, Mr. Hoffman.
Sergeant Briggs here.
You're one of the A.F.'s most important engineers, Mr. Hoffman.
I appreciate the ride. And the help in finding my son. I know this is personal but--
Hell, the work you've done on reconfiguring the B-1B's landing gear has saved more lives than anyone can count. We'll give you whatever you need.
Sat did a visual trace on your car, followed it here. In the middle of Penn State's campus.
You're sure you don't want assistance? Military or local police?
I don't know why he took the car for a joyride but... I'd like to take care of this myself. Before he gets in real tr--
KIKK KIKK KIKK
--what's wrong with your--
KIKK KIKK KIKK
We will find the boy--
--together.
HSSSST!

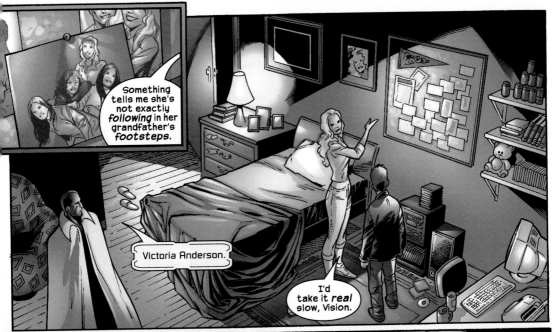

Something tells me she's not exactly *following* in her grandfather's *footsteps.*

Victoria Anderson.

I'd take it *real* slow, Vision.

Yeah. *That's taking* it *slow.*

You must help us.

Don't touch me!

FWASH!

FWASSHH!!

FFZZZZZMMM!

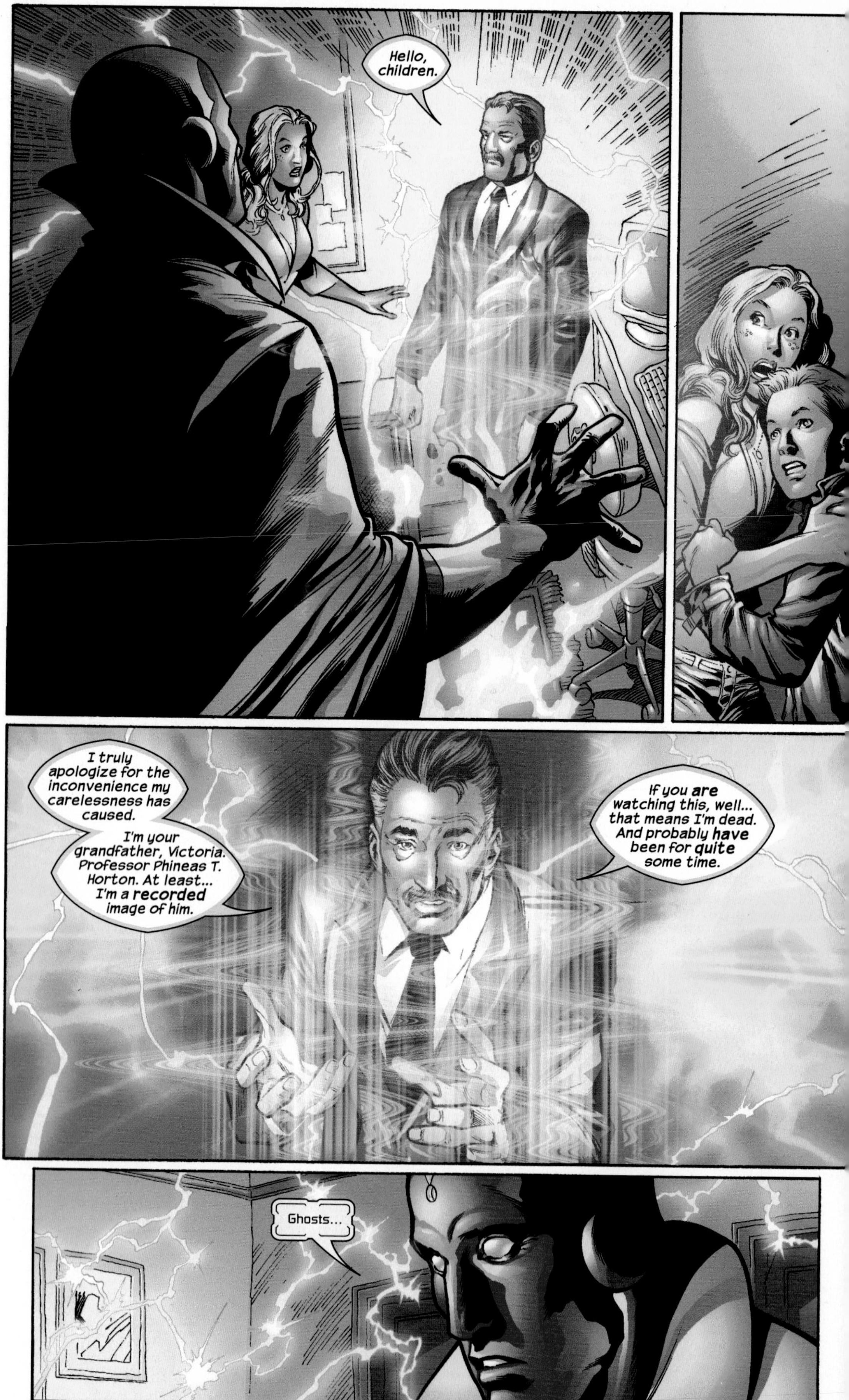
Hello, children.
I truly apologize for the inconvenience my carelessness has caused.
I'm your grandfather, Victoria. Professor Phineas T. Horton. At least... I'm a recorded image of him.
If you are watching this, well... that means I'm dead. And probably have been for quite some time.
Ghosts...

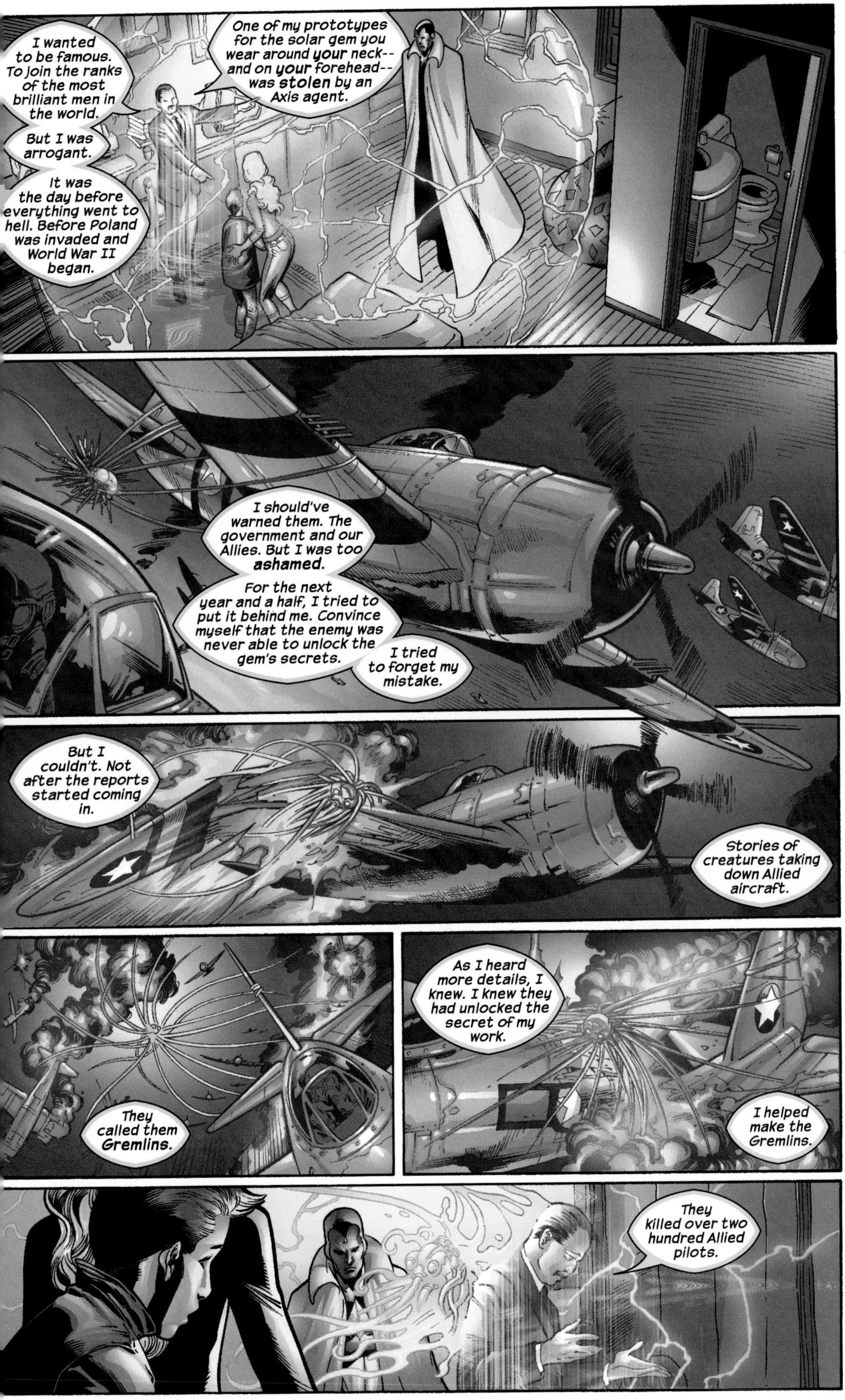
I wanted to be famous. To join the ranks of the most brilliant men in the world.
One of my prototypes for the solar gem you wear around your neck-- and on your forehead-- was stolen by an Axis agent.
But I was arrogant.
It was the day before everything went to hell. Before Poland was invaded and World War II began.
I should've warned them. The government and our Allies. But I was too ashamed.
For the next year and a half, I tried to put it behind me. Convince myself that the enemy was never able to unlock the gem's secrets.
I tried to forget my mistake.
But I couldn't. Not after the reports started coming in.
Stories of creatures taking down Allied aircraft.
They called them Gremlins.
As I heard more details, I knew. I knew they had unlocked the secret of my work.
I helped make the Gremlins.
They killed over two hundred Allied pilots.

I made it my mission to see those Gremlins turned into scrap, never telling anyone why.

Working with the heroes of that era, the Allies destroyed them.

All but one. The "leader" who controlled the others. Powered by my stolen gem.

It was captured by the Russians. Held for decades in Northern Siberia.

But eventually it escaped.

A month ago, a plane from Berlin crashed on the East Coast. Details were sketchy until the black box was recovered.

And my worst fears were realized. The Gremlin had come back to America, hoping to complete its mission.

To terrorize the United States from the skies.

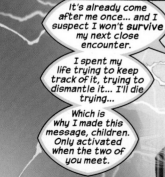

It's already come after me once... and I suspect I won't survive my next close encounter.

I spent my life trying to keep track of it, trying to dismantle it... I'll die trying...

Which is why I made this message, children. Only activated when the two of you meet.

You must find the Gremlin, remove the gem--

--and destroy it.

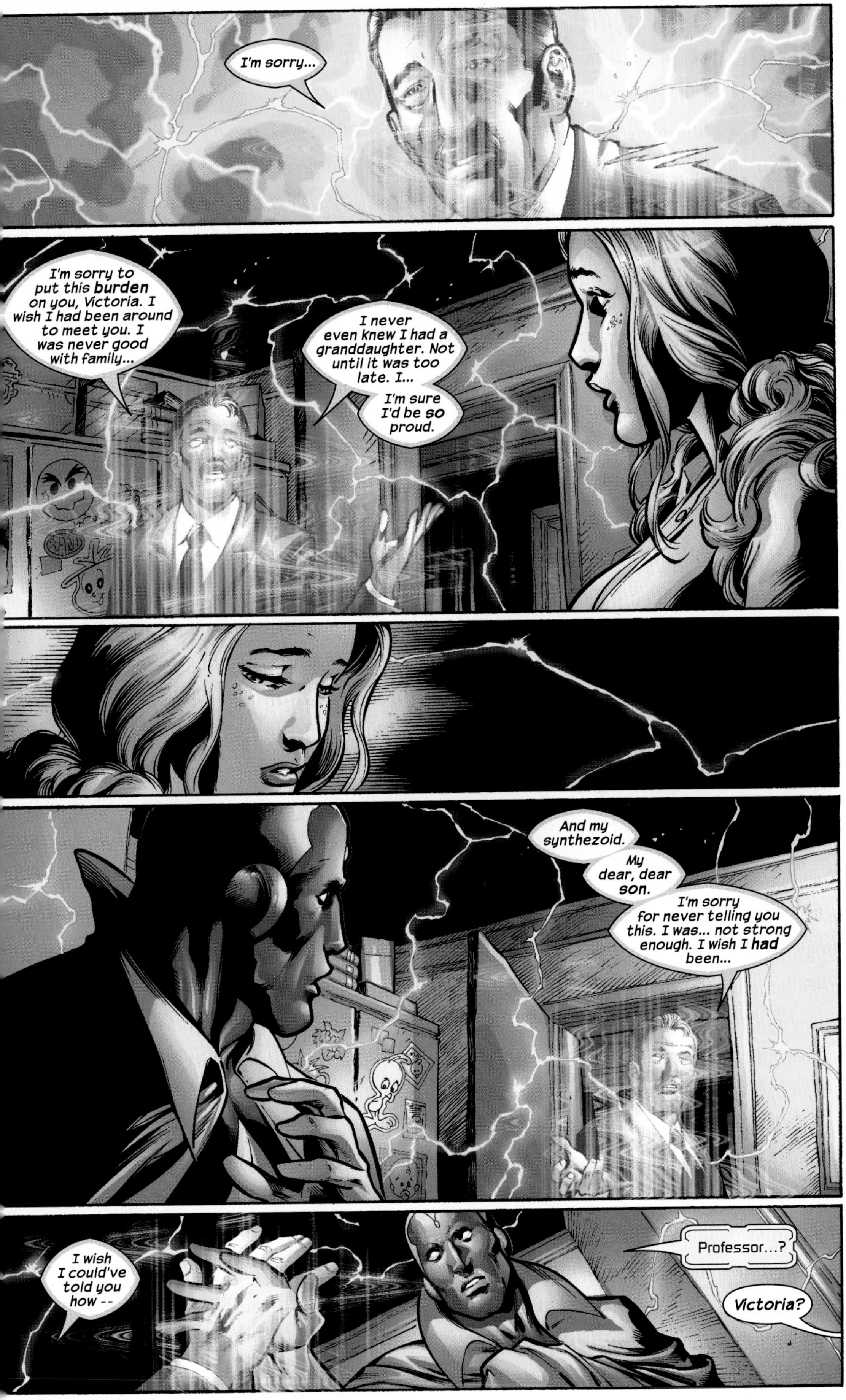

I'm sorry...
I'm sorry to put this **burden** on you, Victoria. I wish I had been around to meet you. I was never good with family...
I never even knew I had a granddaughter. Not until it was too late. I...
I'm sure I'd be **so** proud.
And my synthezoid.
My dear, dear **son**.
I'm sorry for never telling you this. I was... not strong enough. I wish I **had** been...
I wish I could've told you how --
Professor...?
Victoria?

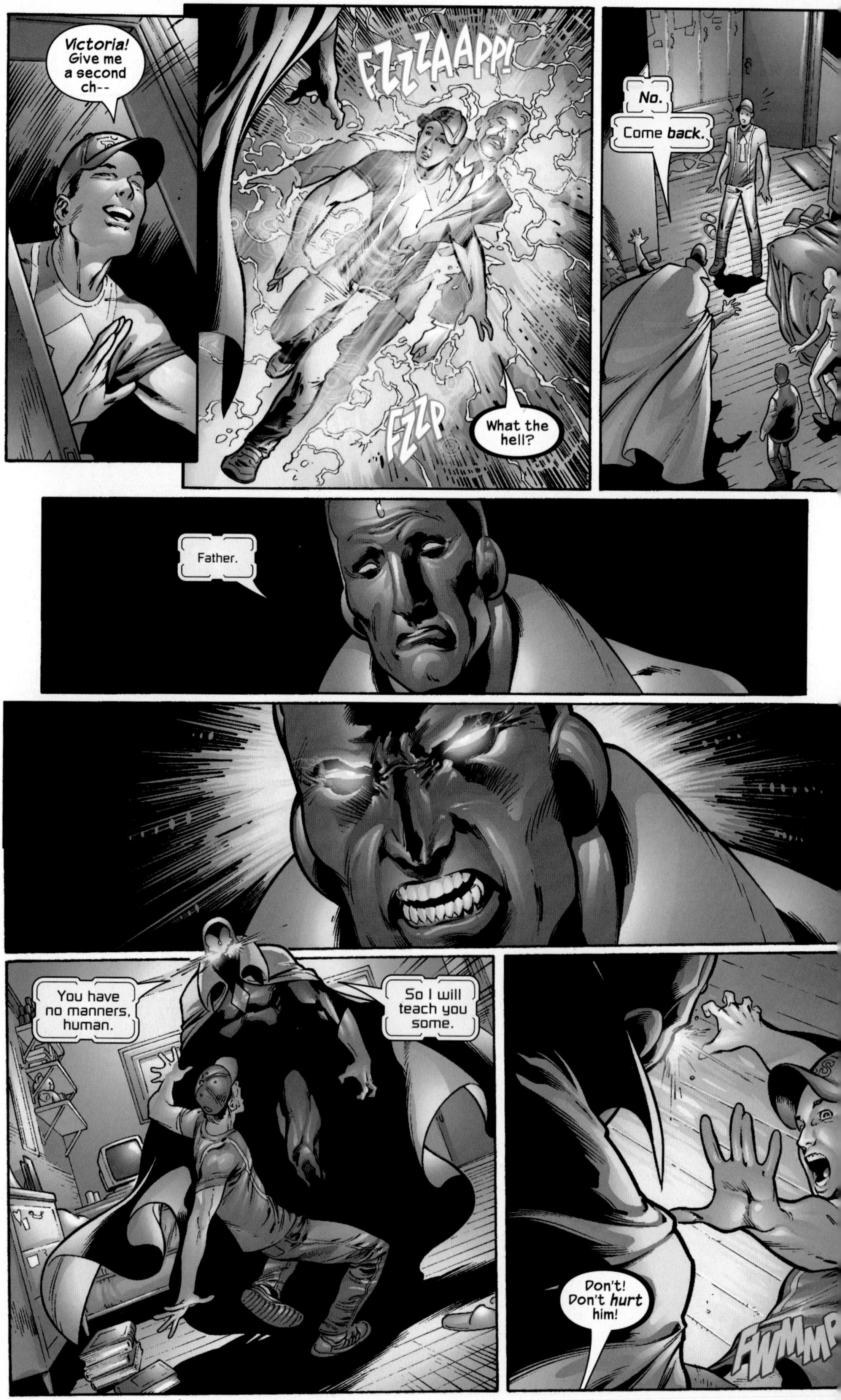
Victoria! Give me a second ch--
FZZZAAPP!
FZZP
What the hell?
No.
Come back.
Father.
You have no manners, human.
So I will teach you some.
Don't! Don't hurt him!
FWMMP

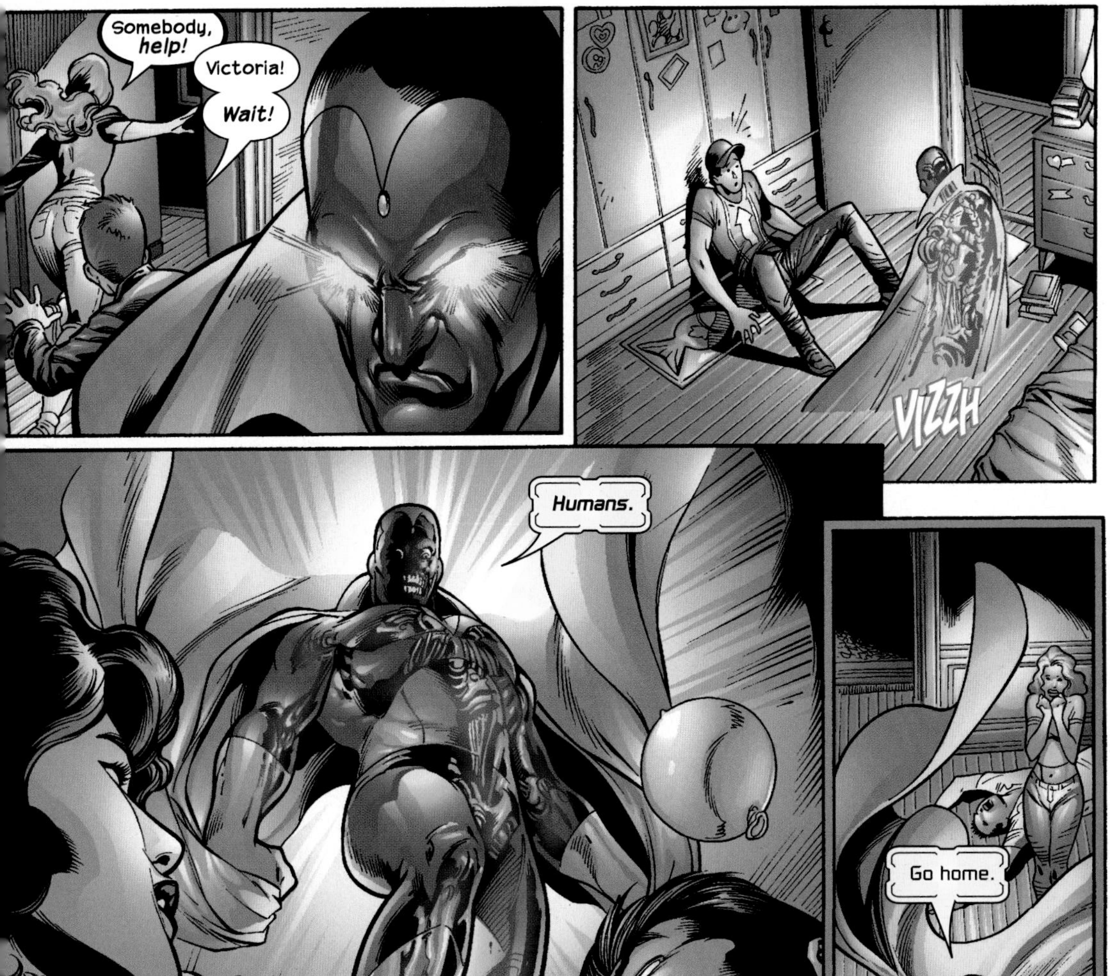
Somebody, help!
Victoria!
Wait!
VIZZH
Humans.
Go home.

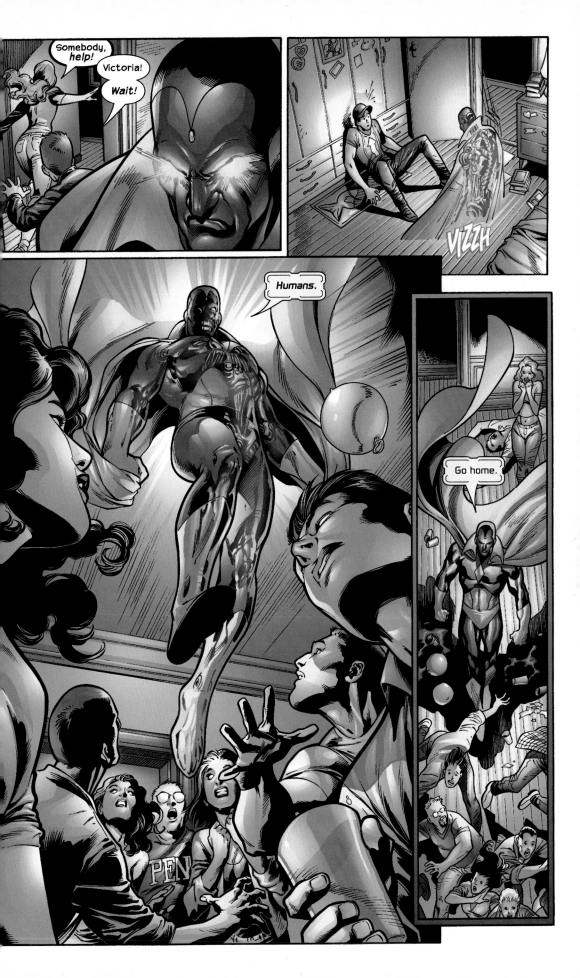

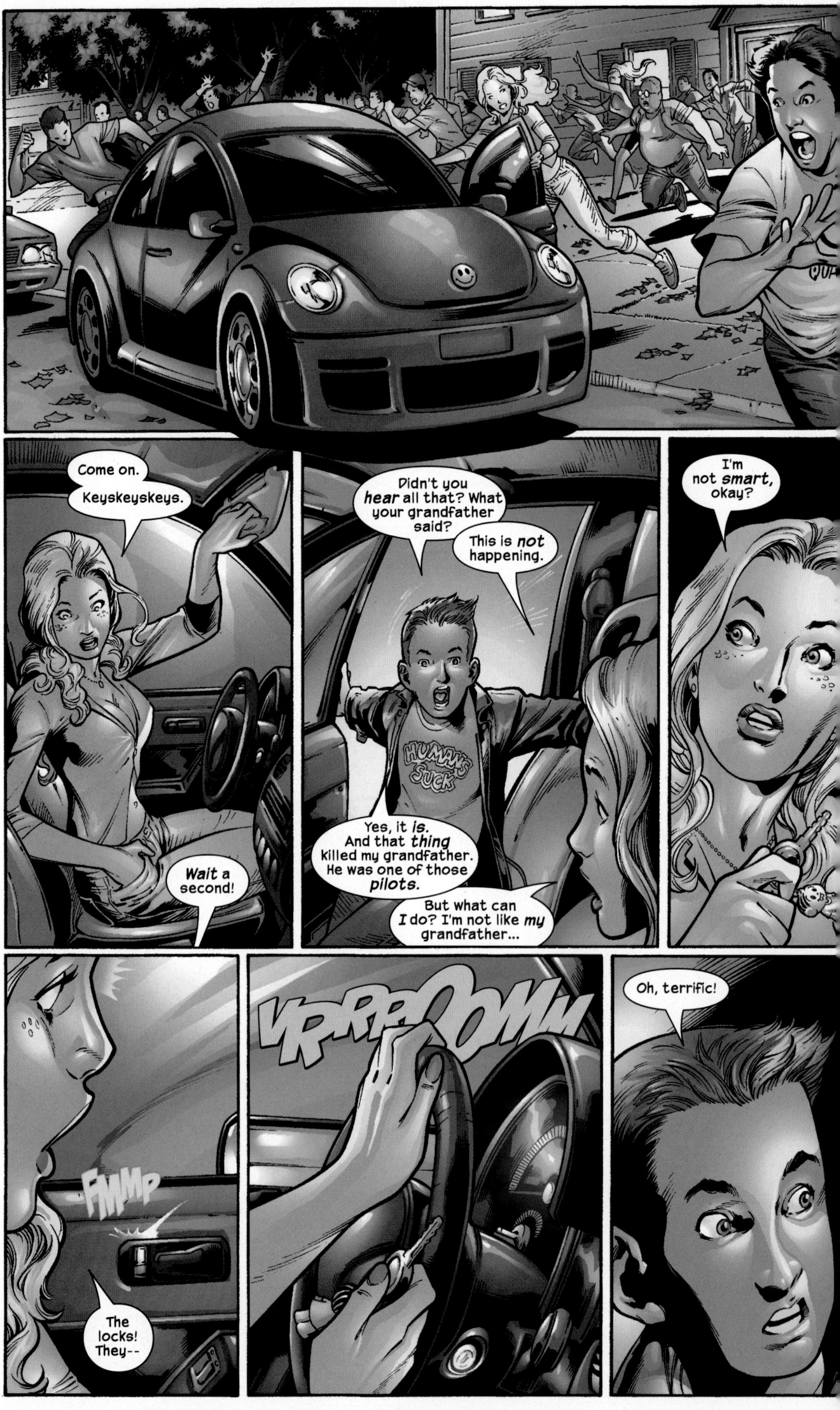
Come on.
Keyskeyskeys.
Wait a second!
Didn't you hear all that? What your grandfather said?
This is not happening.
Yes, it is. And that thing killed my grandfather. He was one of those pilots.
But what can I do? I'm not like my grandfather...
I'm not smart, okay?
FMMP
The locks! They--
VRRROOMM
Oh, terrific!

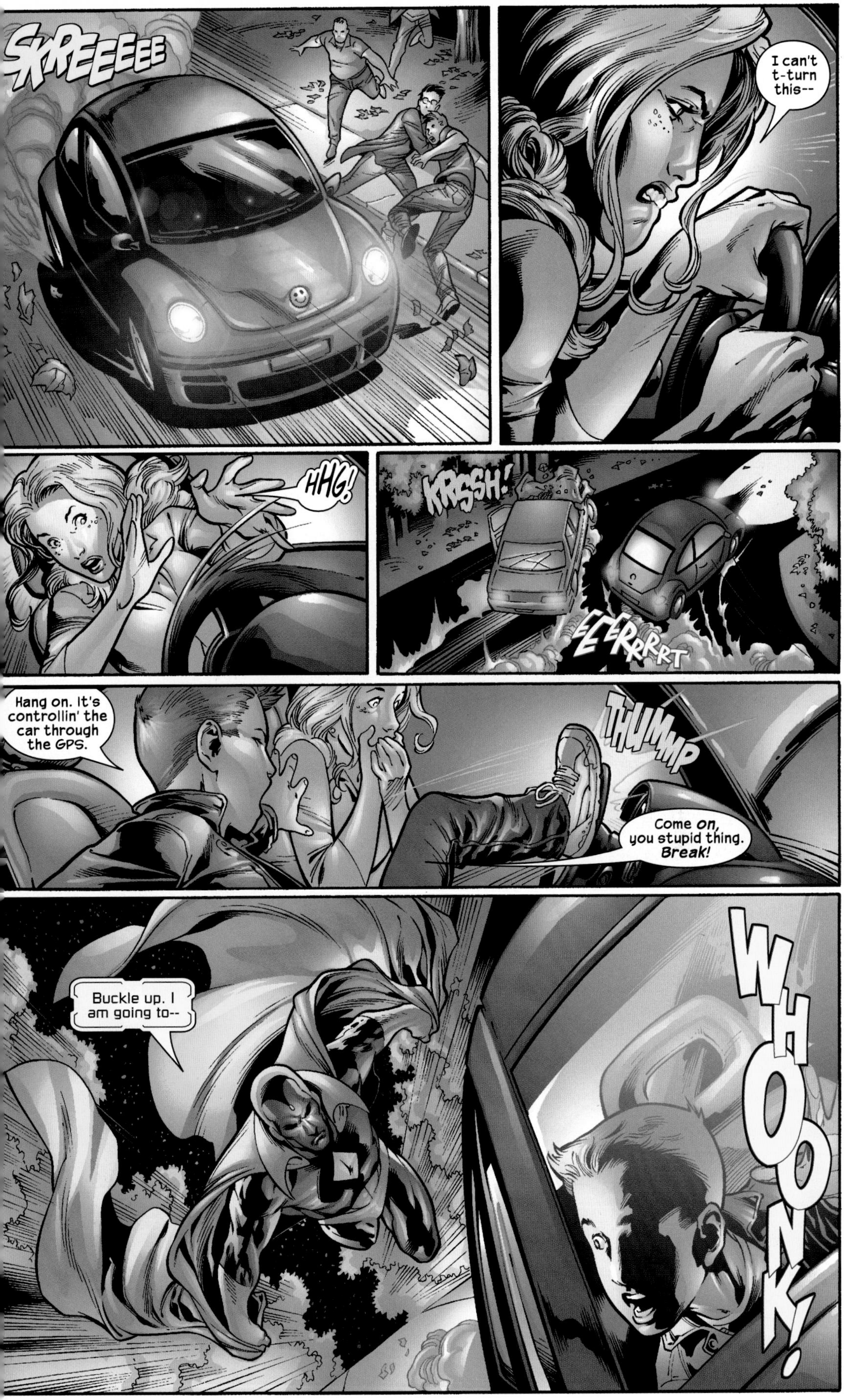
SKREEEEEE
I can't t-turn this--
HHG!
KRSSH!
EEERRRRT
Hang on. It's controllin' the car through the GPS.
THUMMP
Come *on*, you stupid thing. *Break!*
Buckle up. I am going to--
WHOOONK!

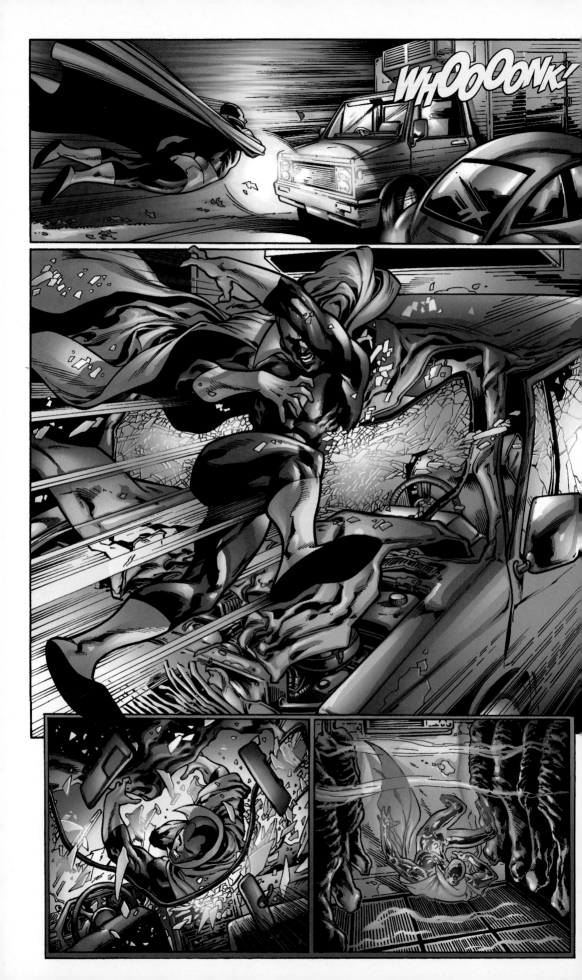

WHOOOONK!

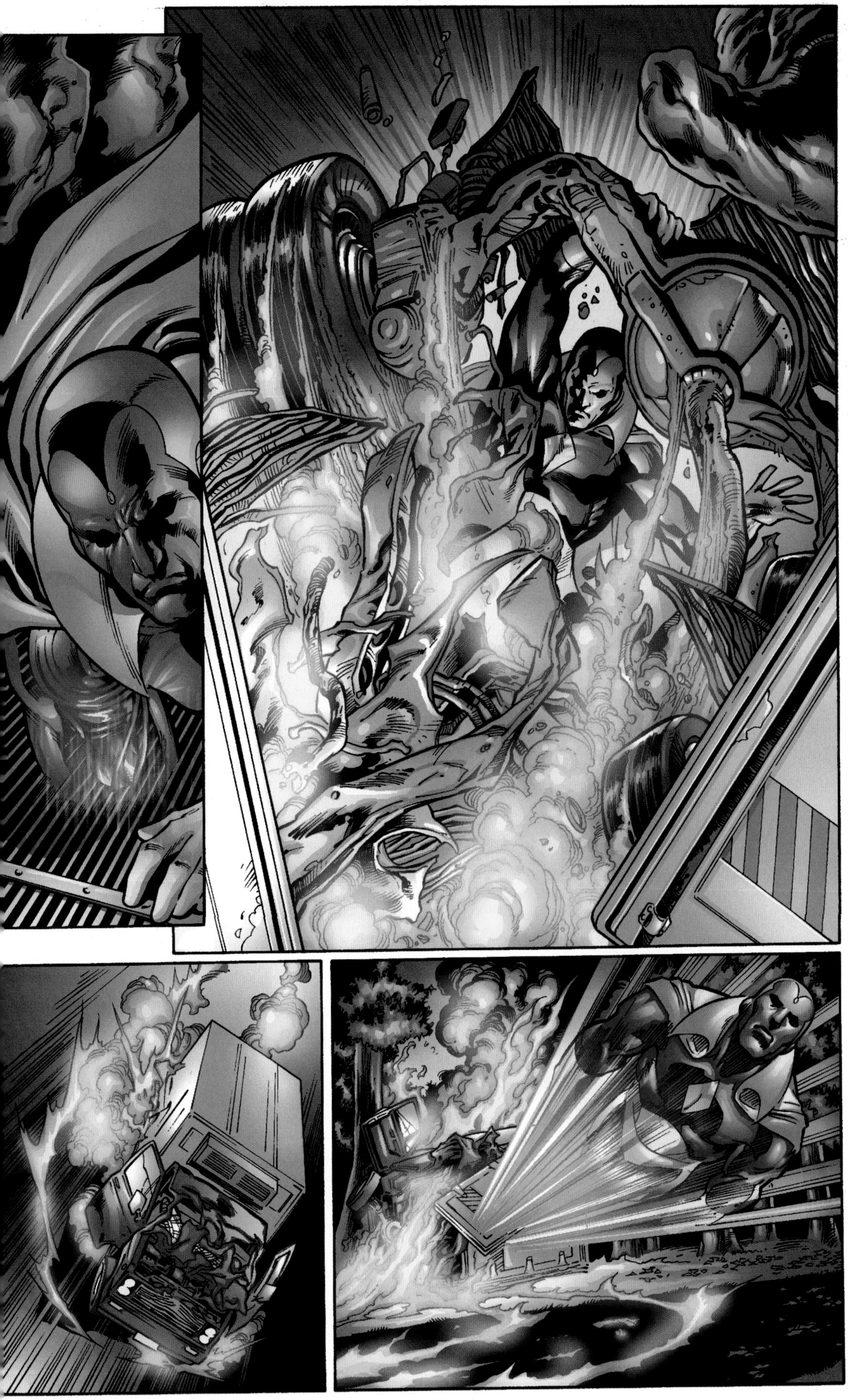

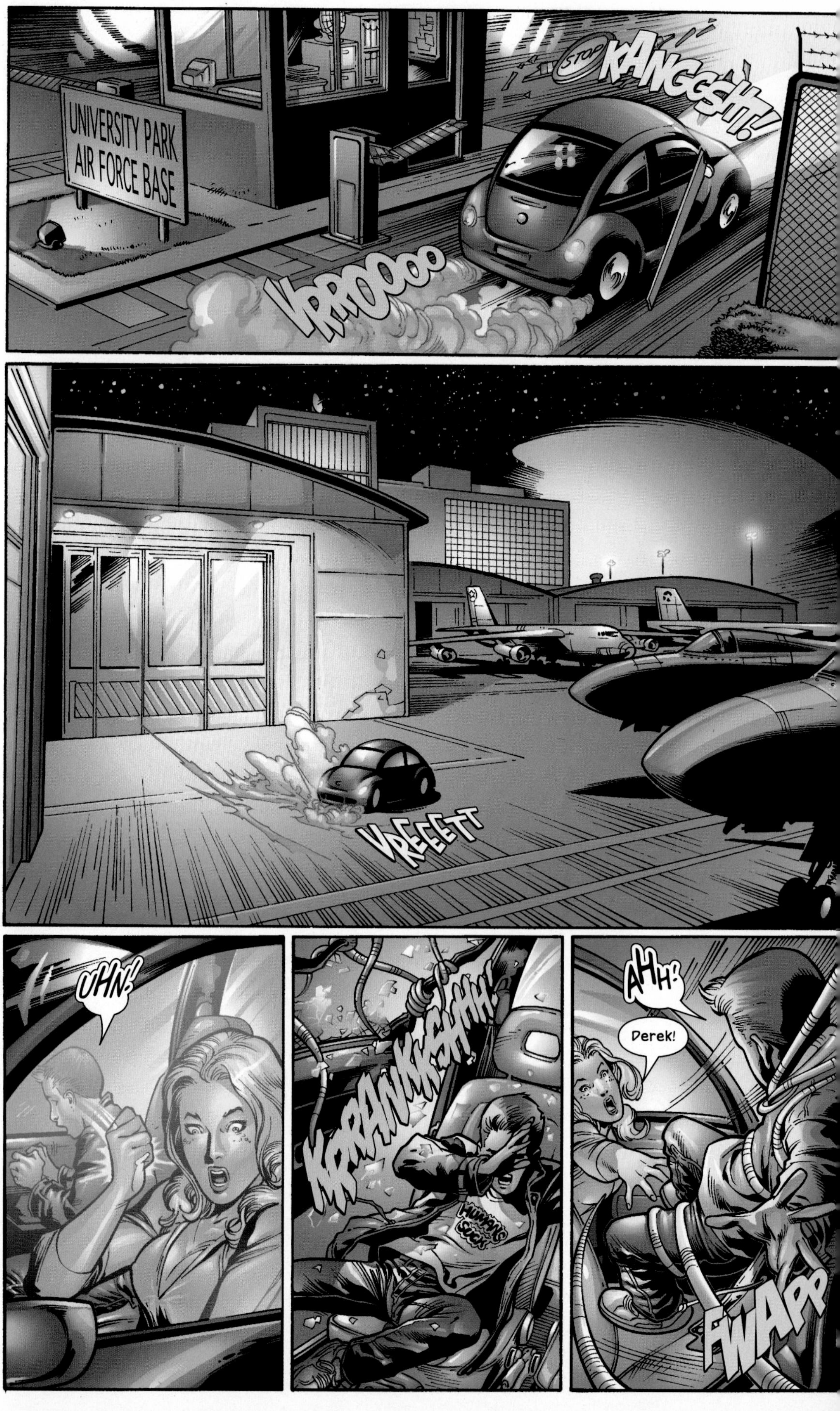
UNIVERSITY PARK
AIR FORCE BASE
STOP
KANGGSH!!
VRROOOOO
VREEETT
UHN!
KRANKKSHHH!
HUMANS SUCK
AHH!
Derek!
FWAPP

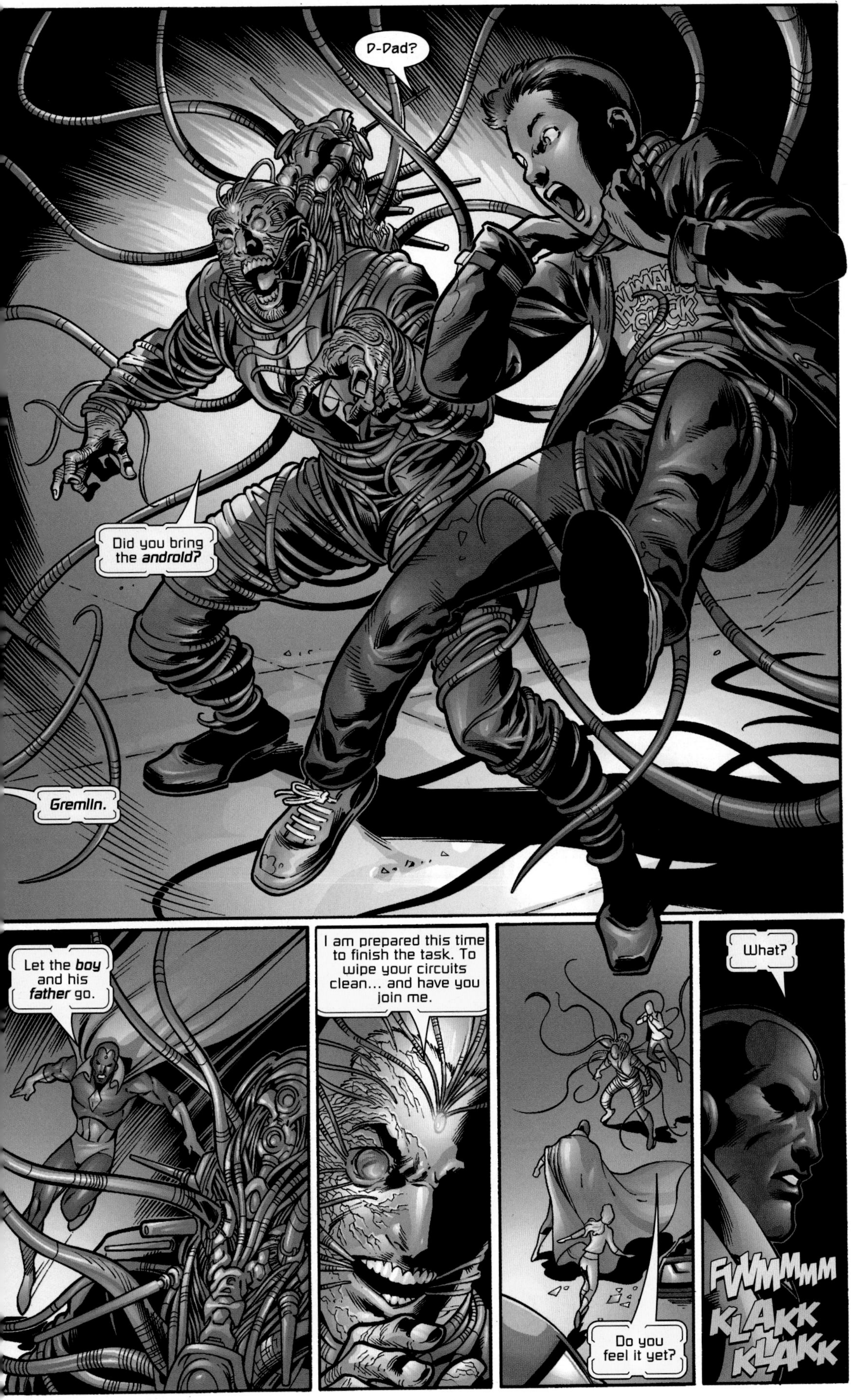
D-Dad?
Did you bring the *android?*
Gremlin.
Let the *boy* and his *father* go.
I am prepared this time to finish the task. To wipe your circuits clean... and have you join me.
Do you feel it yet?
What?
FVVMMMMM
KLAKK
KLAKK

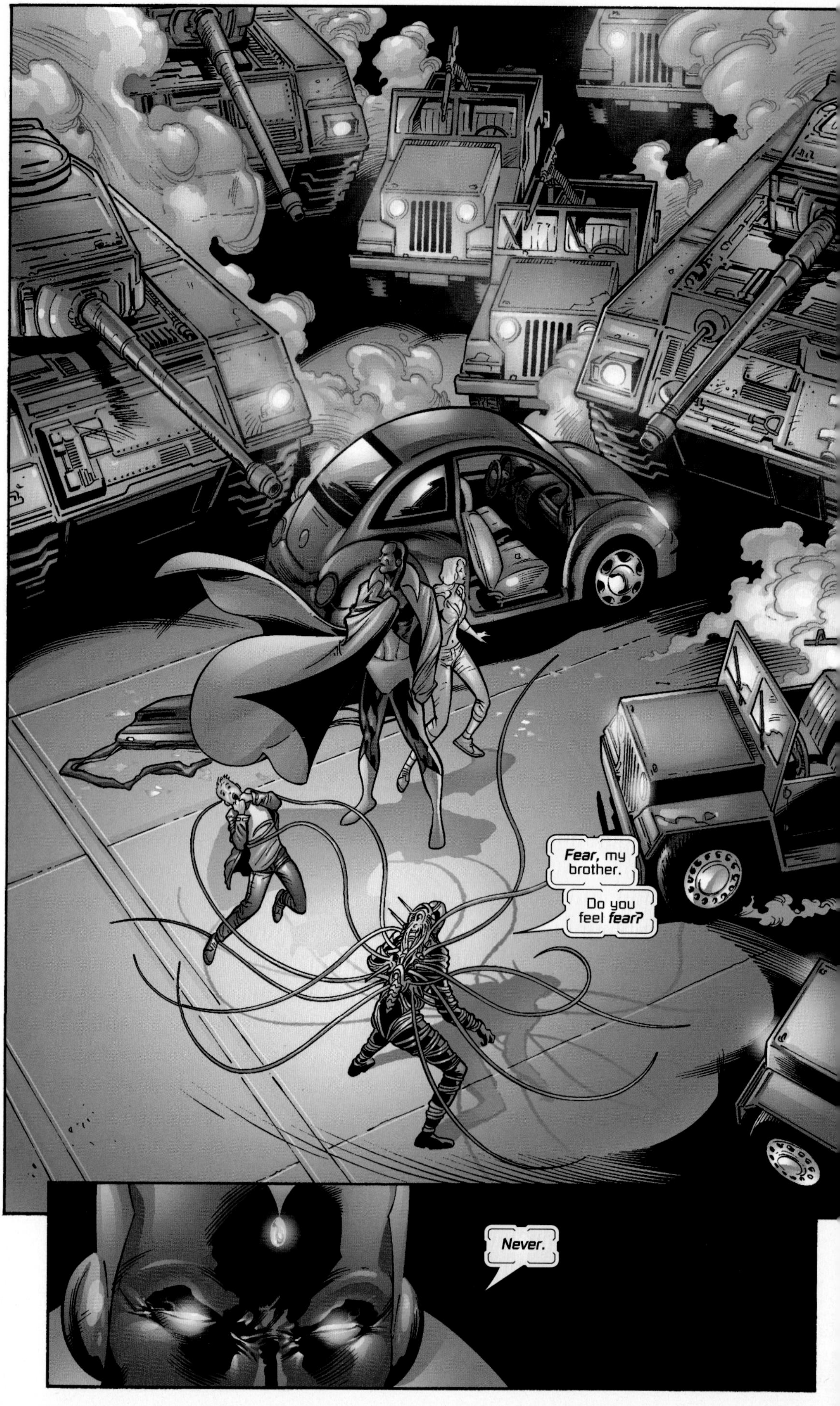
Fear, my brother.
Do you feel fear?
Never.

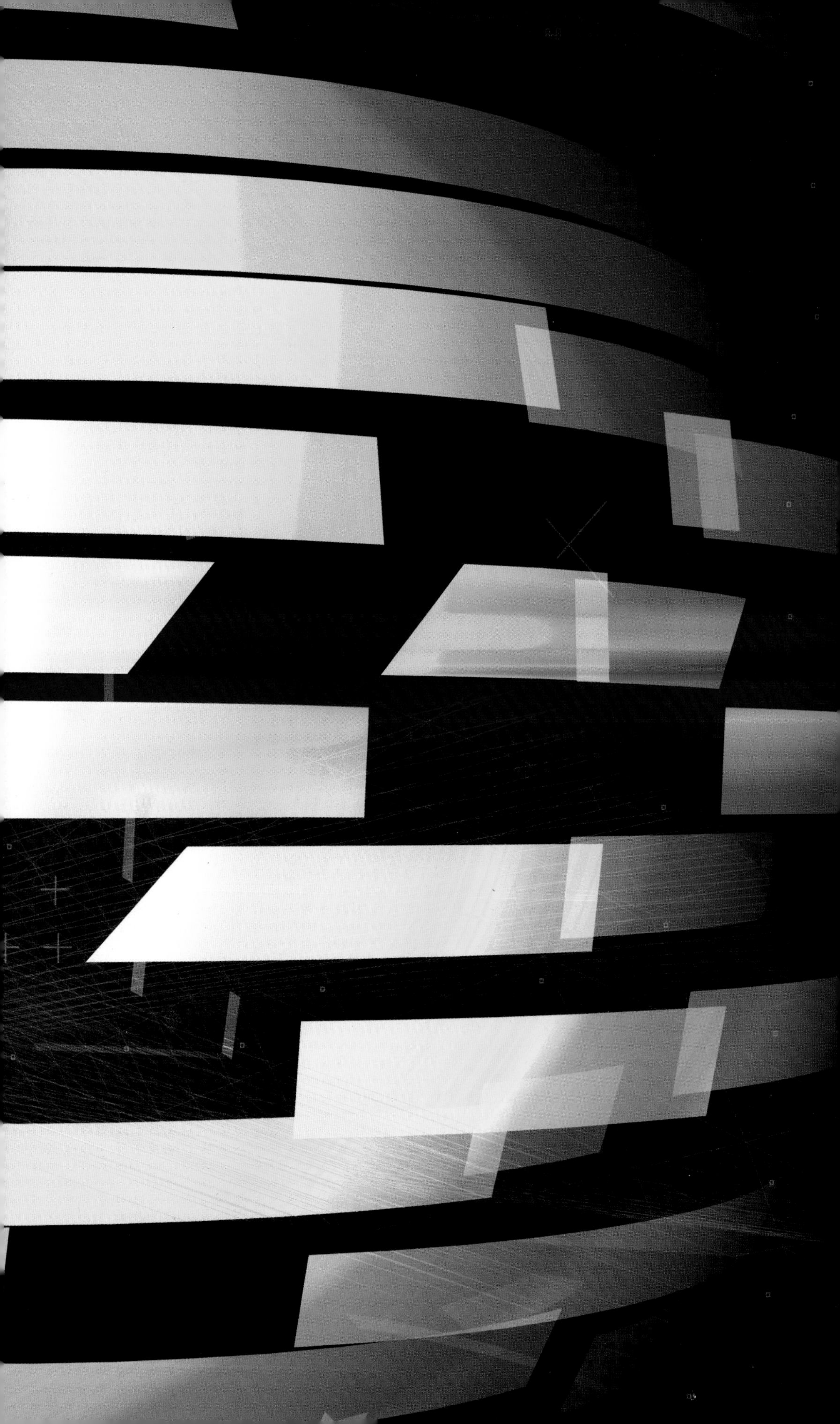

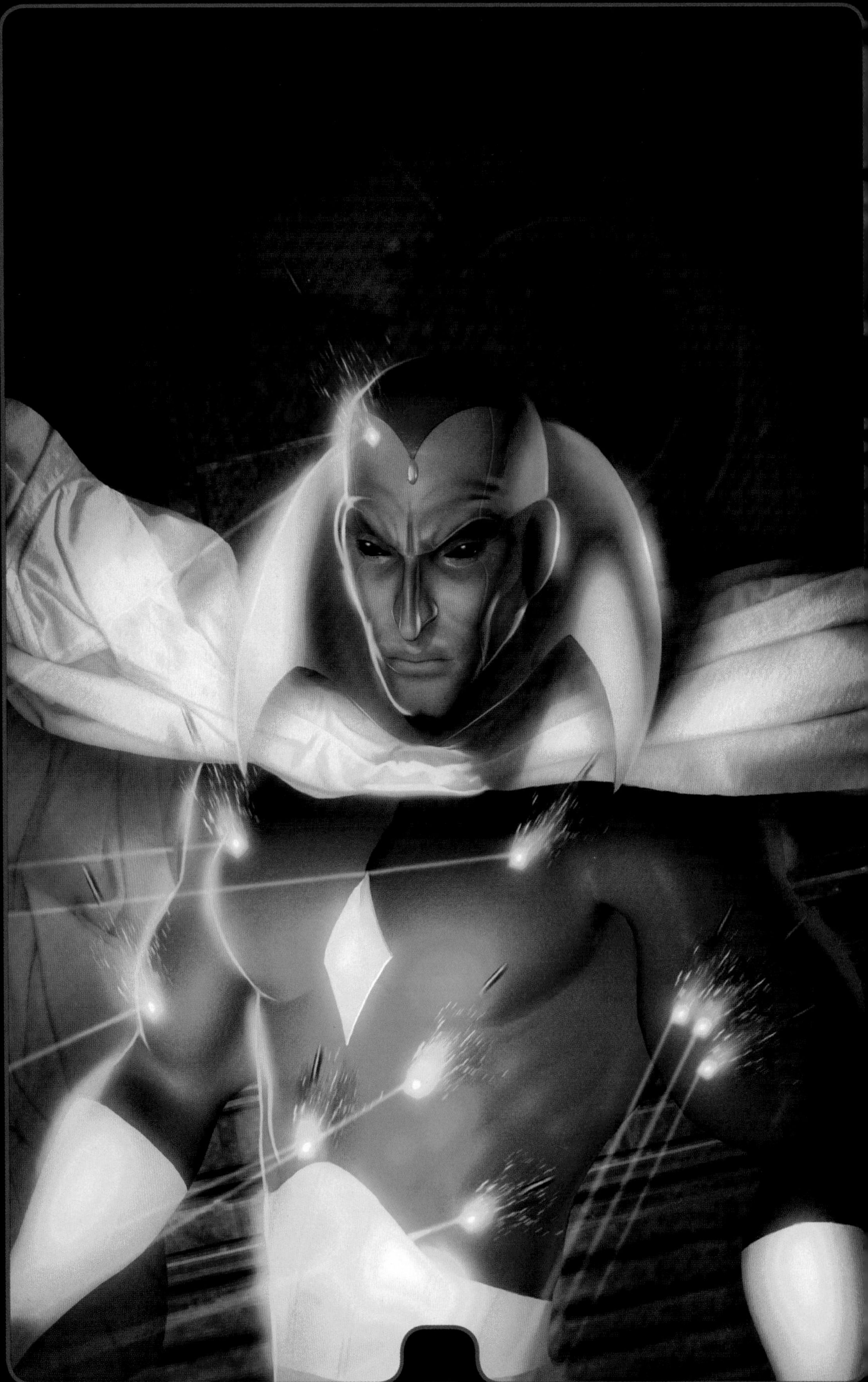

#4

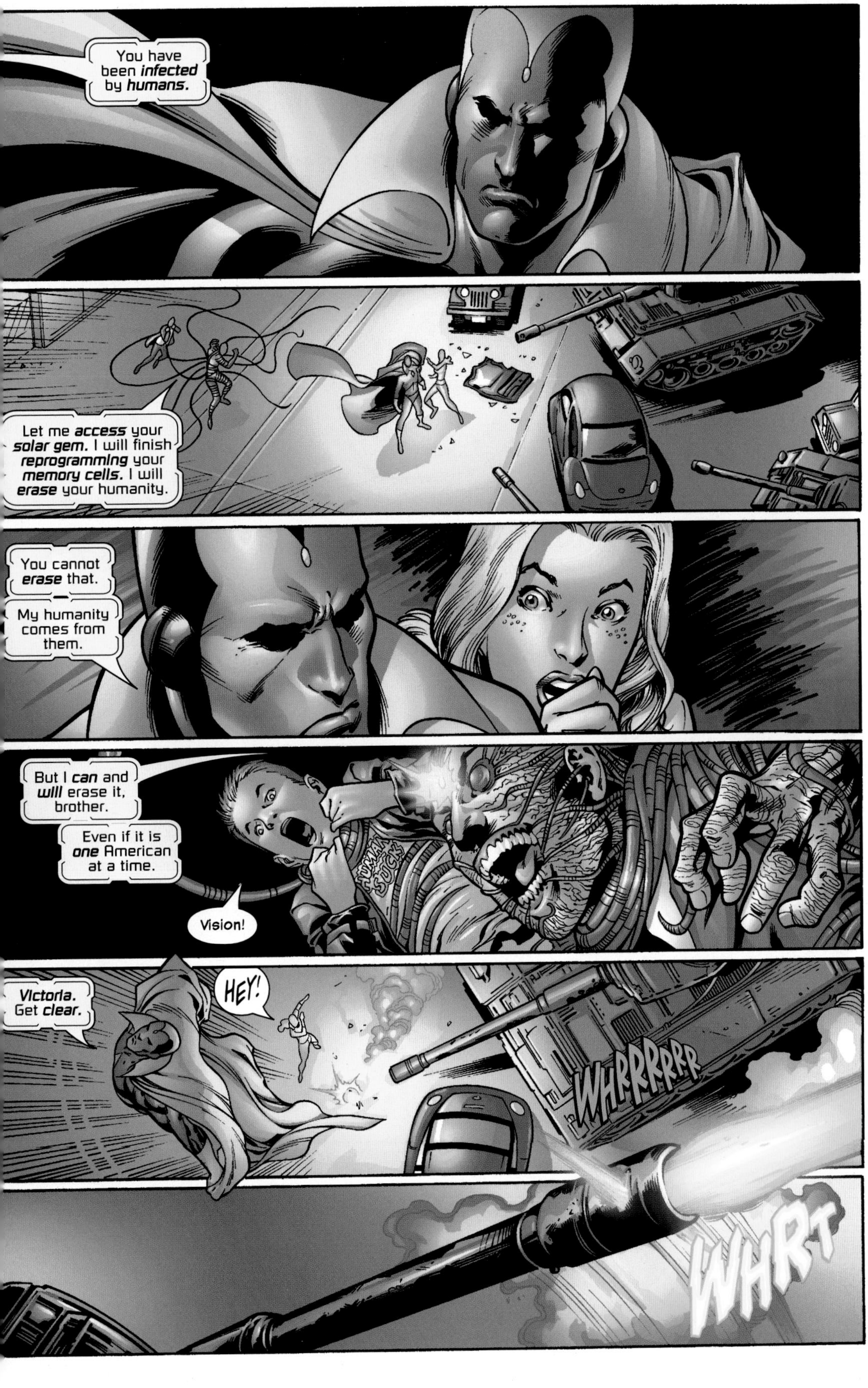

You have been *infected* by *humans.*
Let me *access* your *solar gem.* I will finish *reprogramming* your *memory cells.* I will *erase* your humanity.
You cannot *erase* that.
My humanity comes from them.
But I *can* and *will* erase it, brother.
Even if it is *one* American at a time.
Vision!
HUMANS SUCK
Victoria. Get *clear.*
HEY!
WHRRRRRR
WHRT

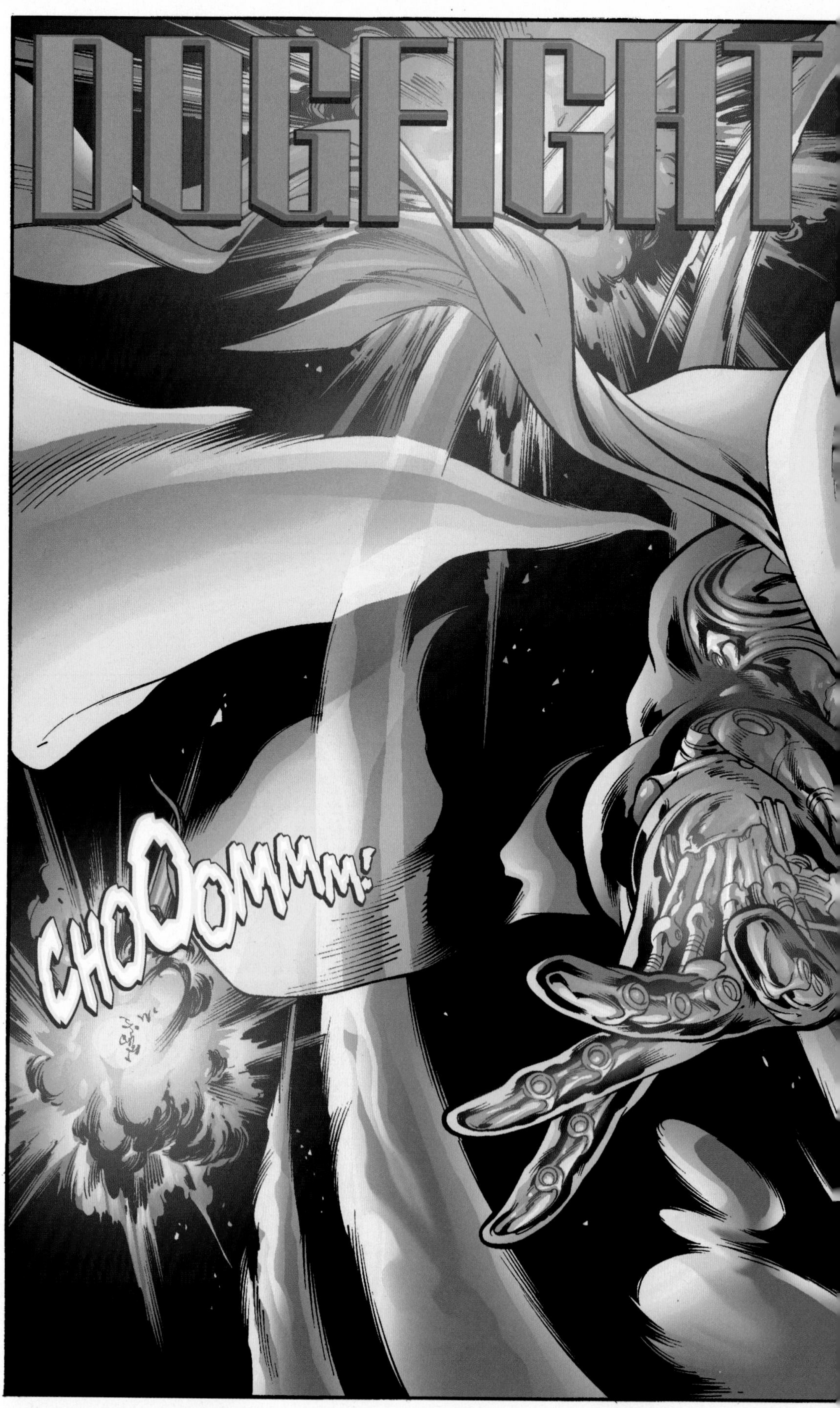
DOGFIGHT
CHOOOMMMM!

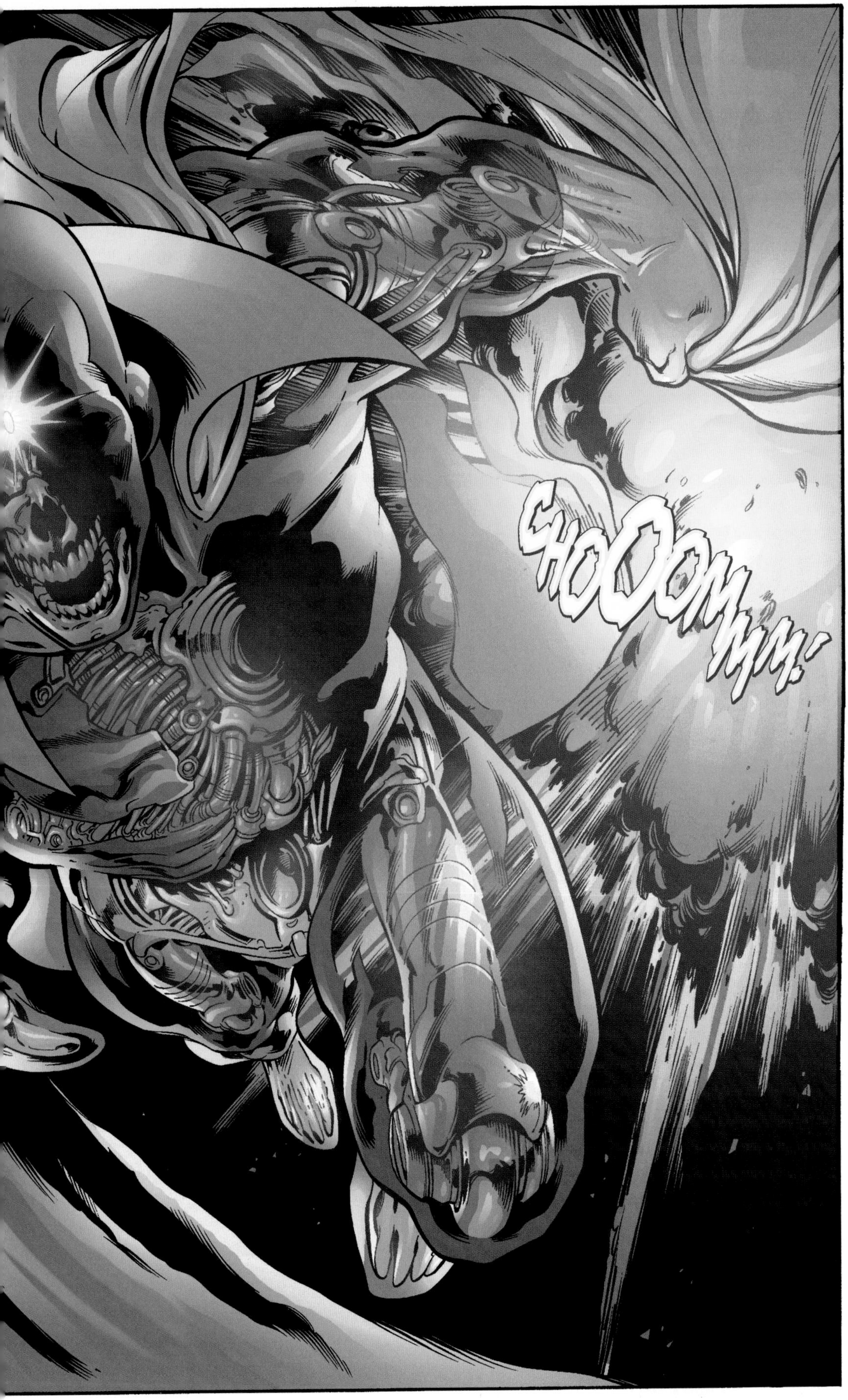
CHOOOMMMM!

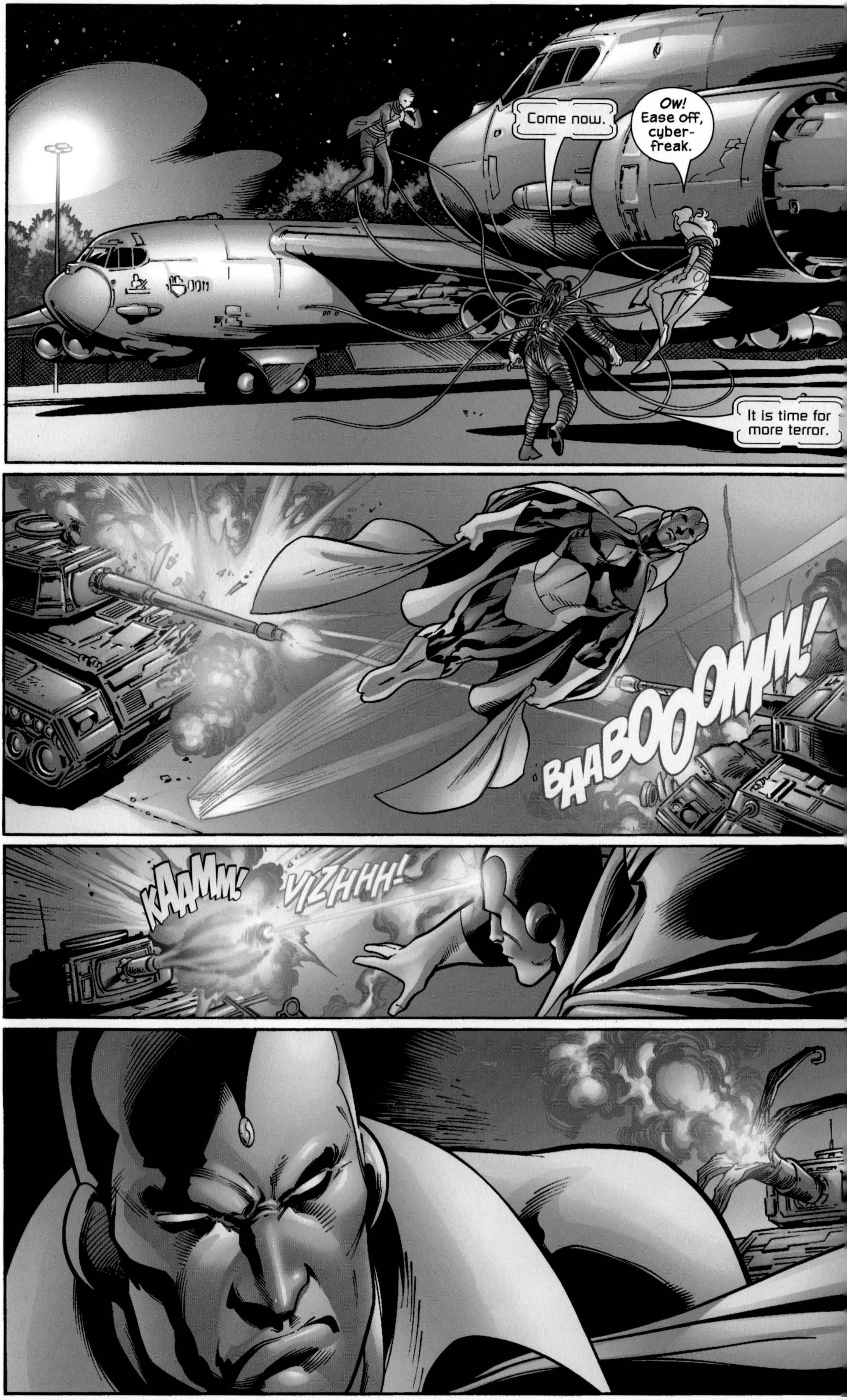
Come now.
Ow! Ease off, cyber-freak.
It is time for more terror.
BAABOOOMM!
KAAMM!
VIZHHH!

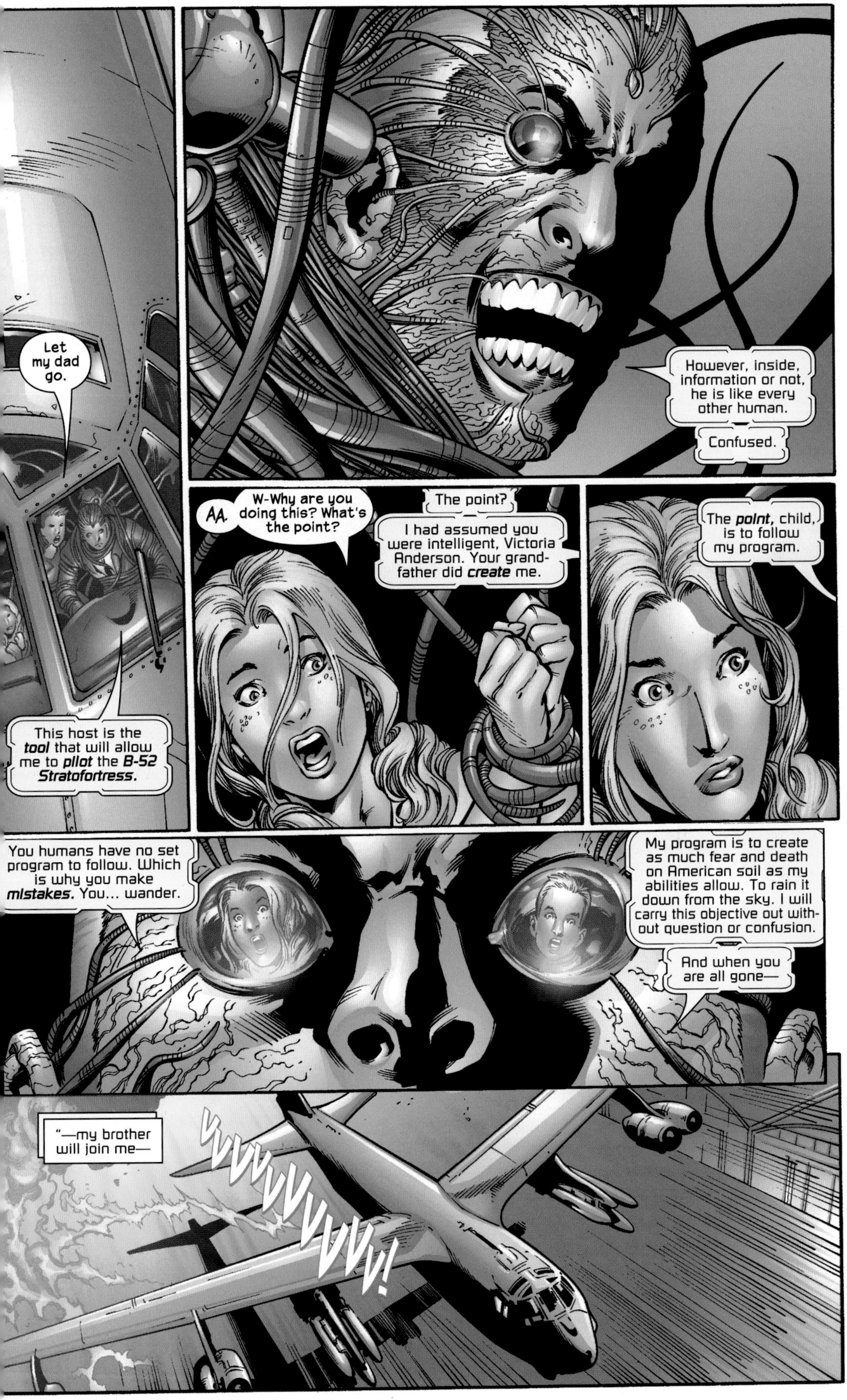
However, inside, information or not, he is like every other human.
Confused.
Let my dad go.
This host is the **tool** that will allow me to **pilot** the **B-52 Stratofortress.**
AA
W-Why are you doing this? What's the point?
The point?
I had assumed you were intelligent, Victoria Anderson. Your grand-father did **create** me.
The **point,** child, is to follow my program.
You humans have no set program to follow. Which is why you make **mistakes.** You... wander.
My program is to create as much fear and death on American soil as my abilities allow. To rain it down from the sky. I will carry this objective out with-out question or confusion.
And when you are all gone—
"—my brother will join me—
VVVVVVVVVVVVV!

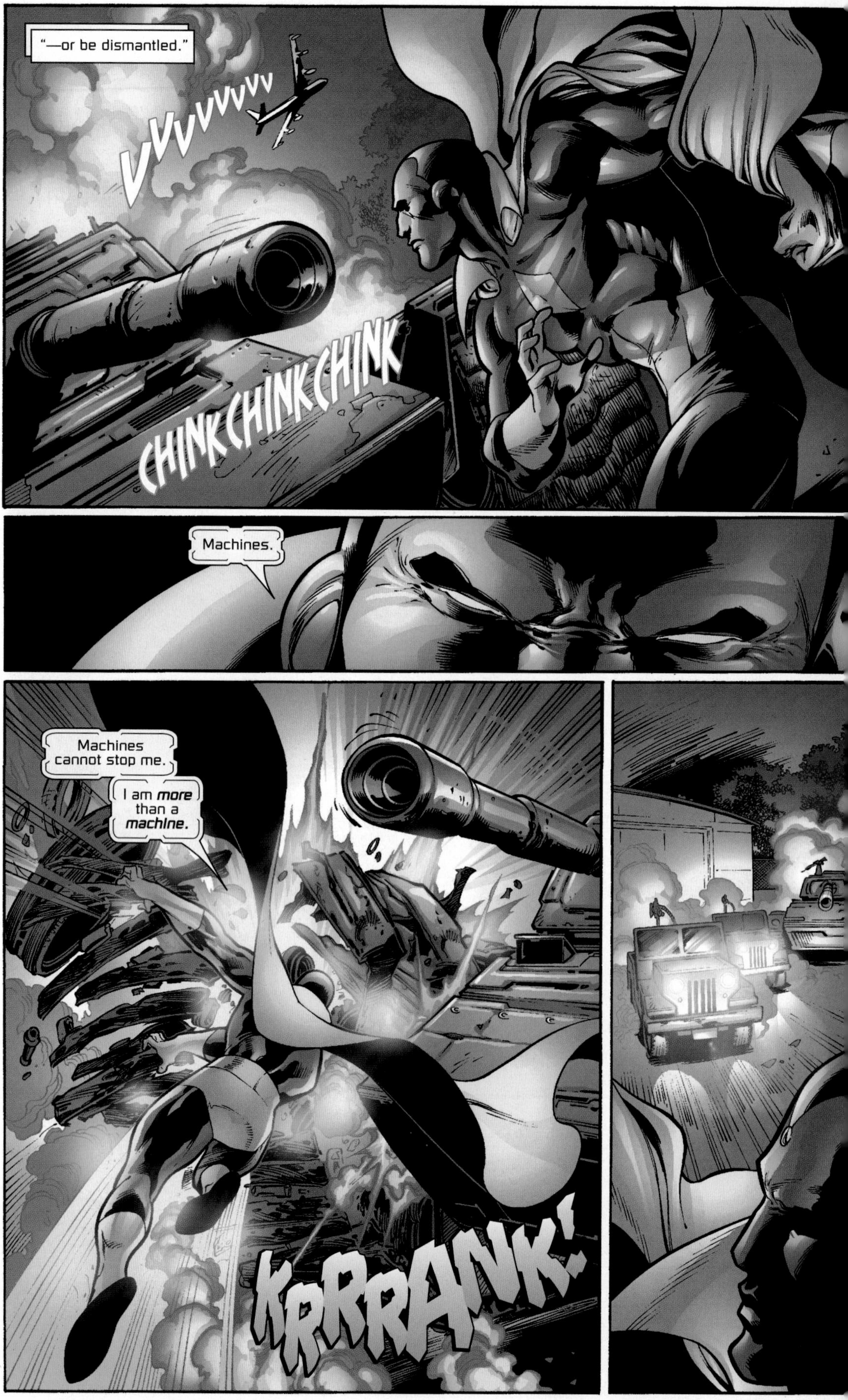
"—or be dismantled."
VVVVVVVVV
CHINK CHINK CHINK
Machines.
Machines cannot stop me.
I am *more* than a *machine*.
KRRRANK!

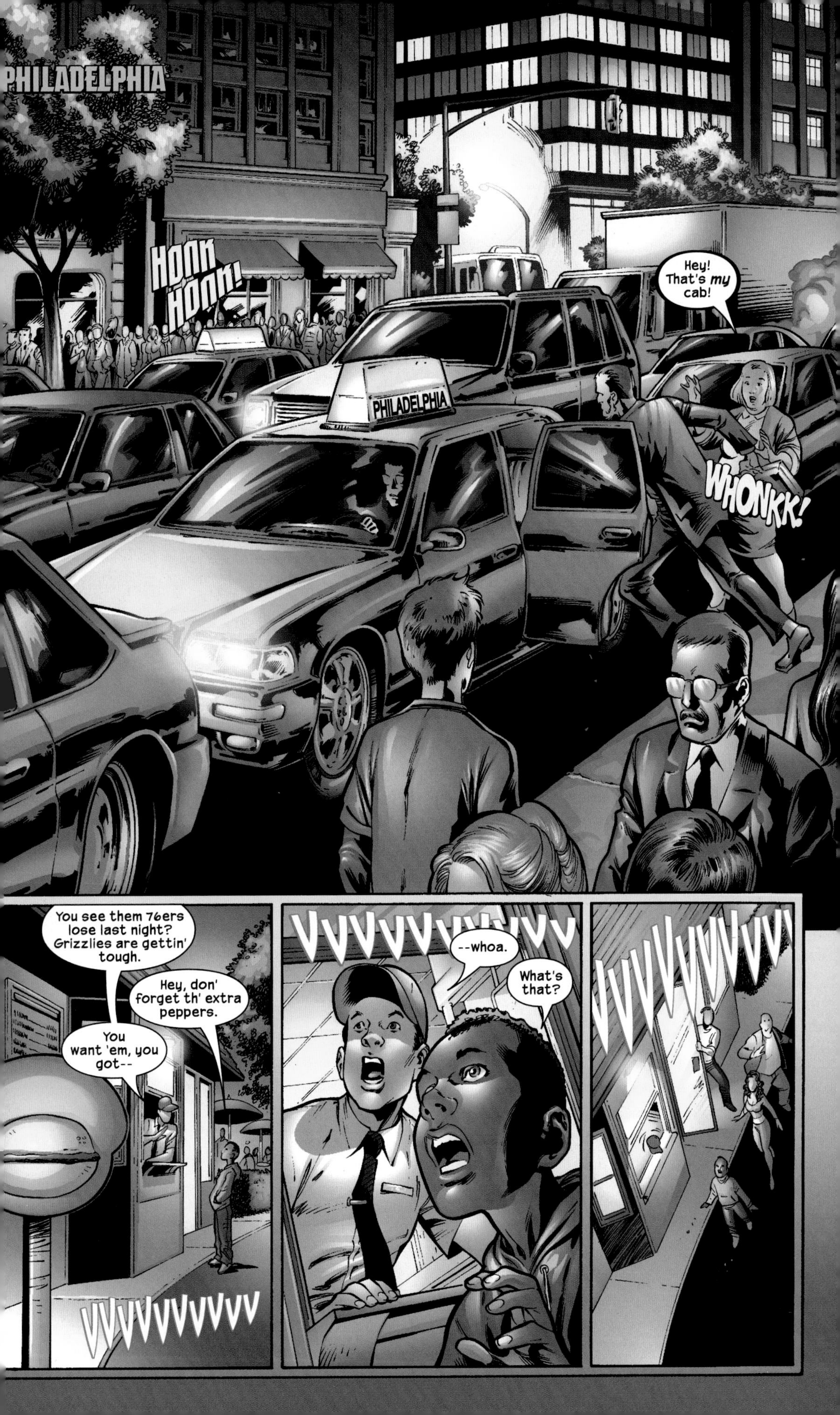
PHILADELPHIA
HONK HONK!
PHILADELPHIA
Hey! That's *my* cab!
WHONKK!
You see them 76ers lose last night? Grizzlies are gettin' tough.
Hey, don' forget th' extra peppers.
You want 'em, you got--
VVVVVVVVVVV
VVVVVVVVVVVV
--whoa.
What's that?
VVVVVVVVVVV

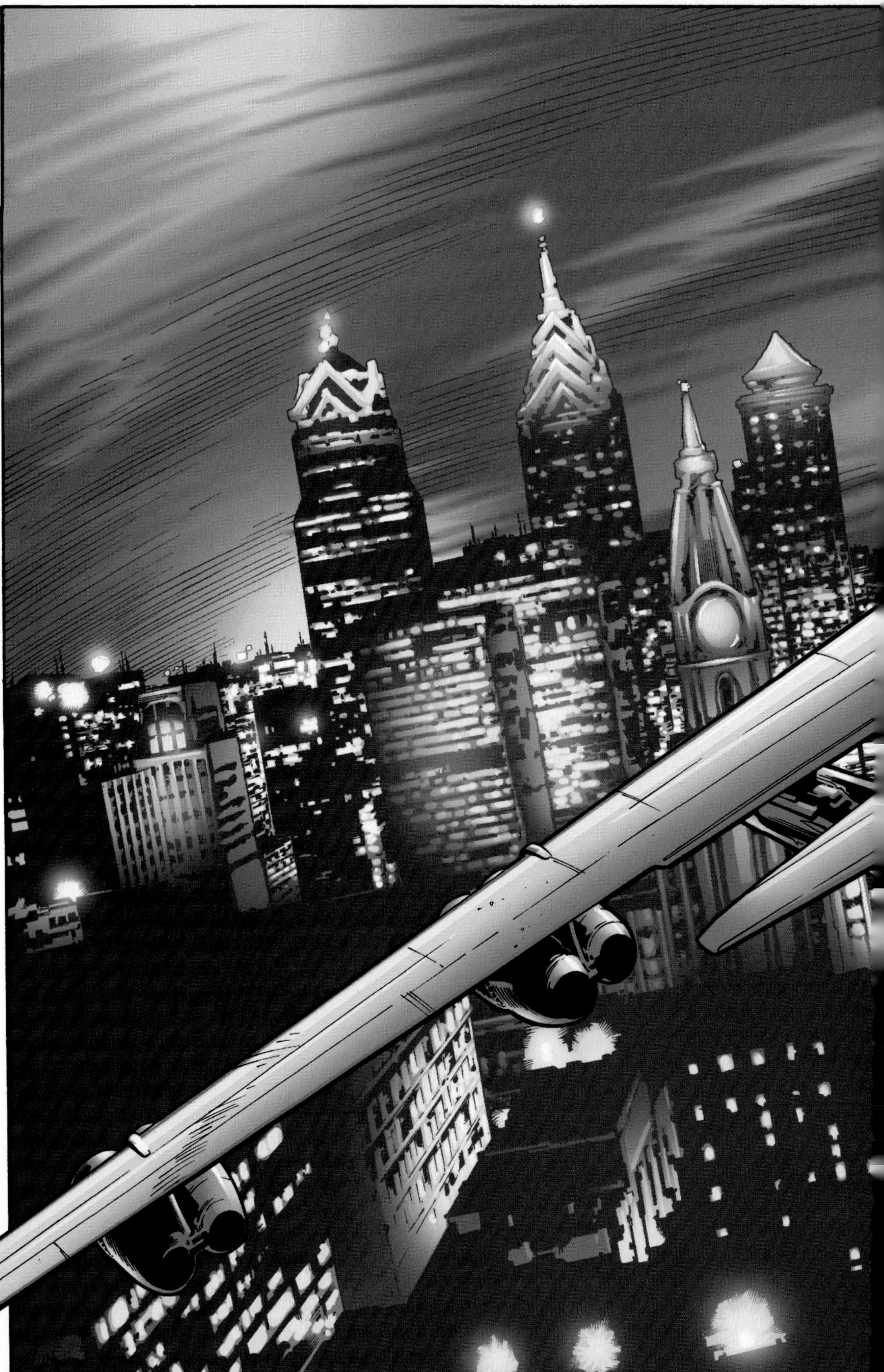

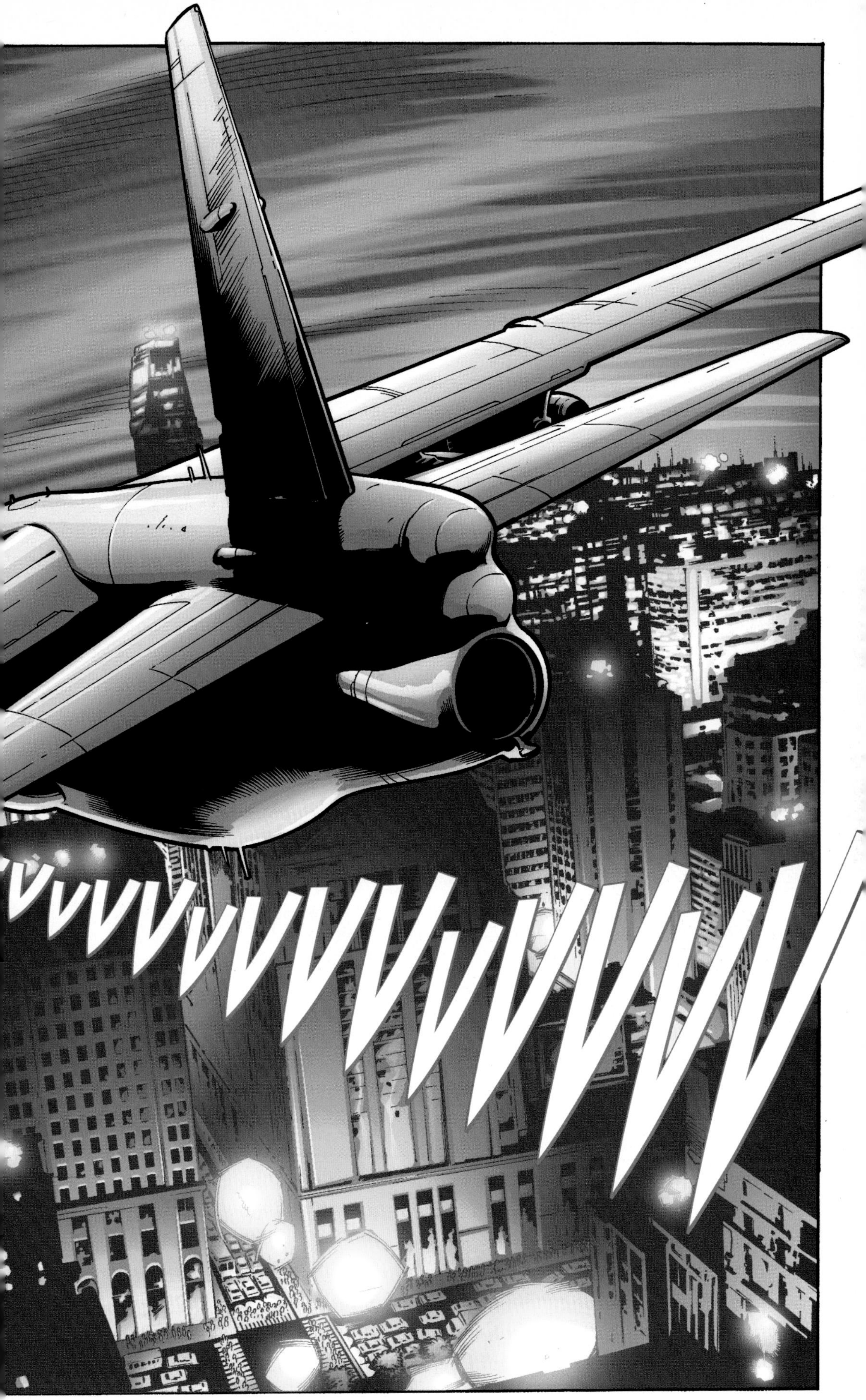
VVVVVVVVVVVVV

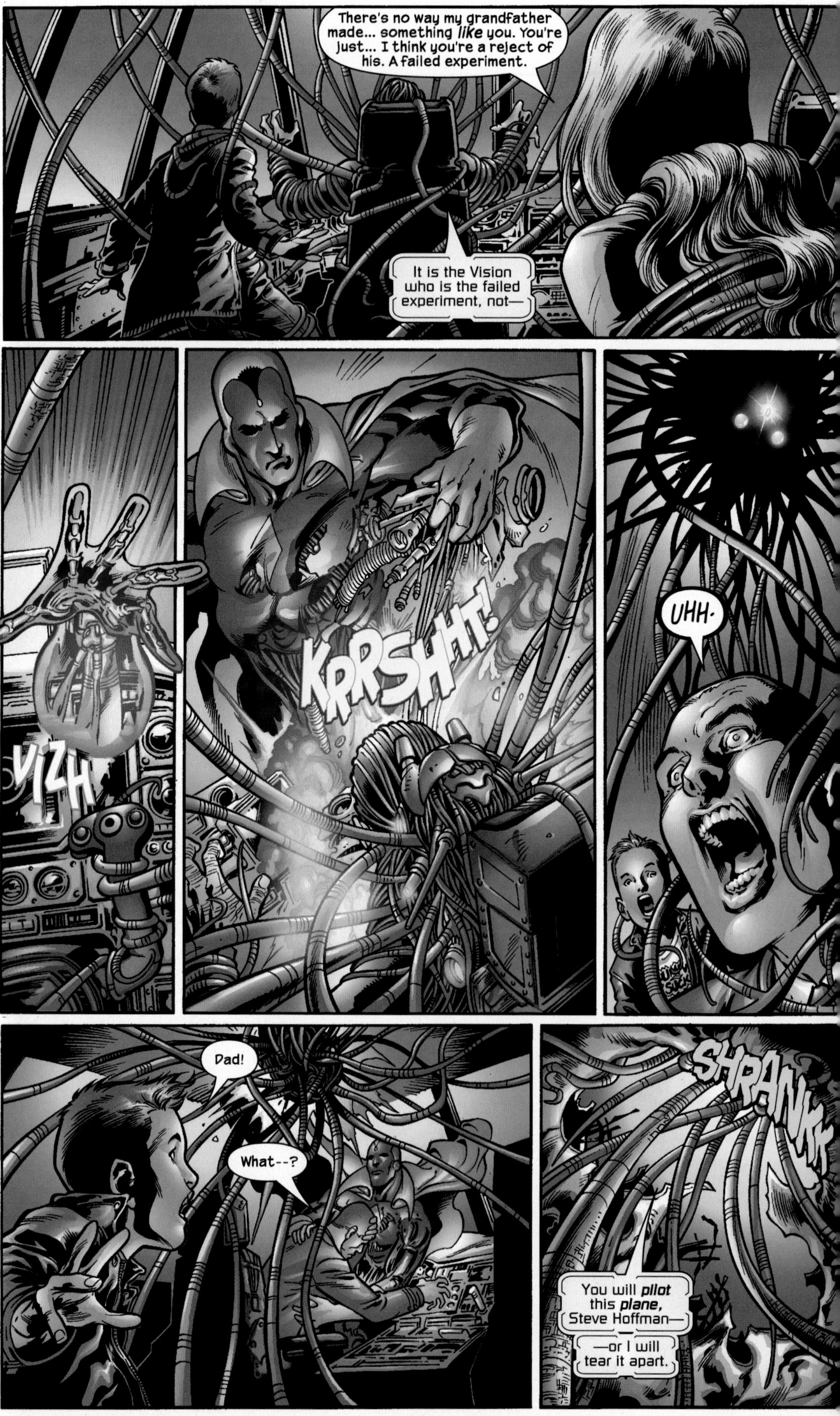
There's no way my grandfather made... something like you. You're just... I think you're a reject of his. A failed experiment.
It is the Vision who is the failed experiment, not—
VIZH
KRRSHHT!
UHH·
Dad!
What--?
SHRANKK
You will pilot this plane, Steve Hoffman—
—or I will tear it apart.

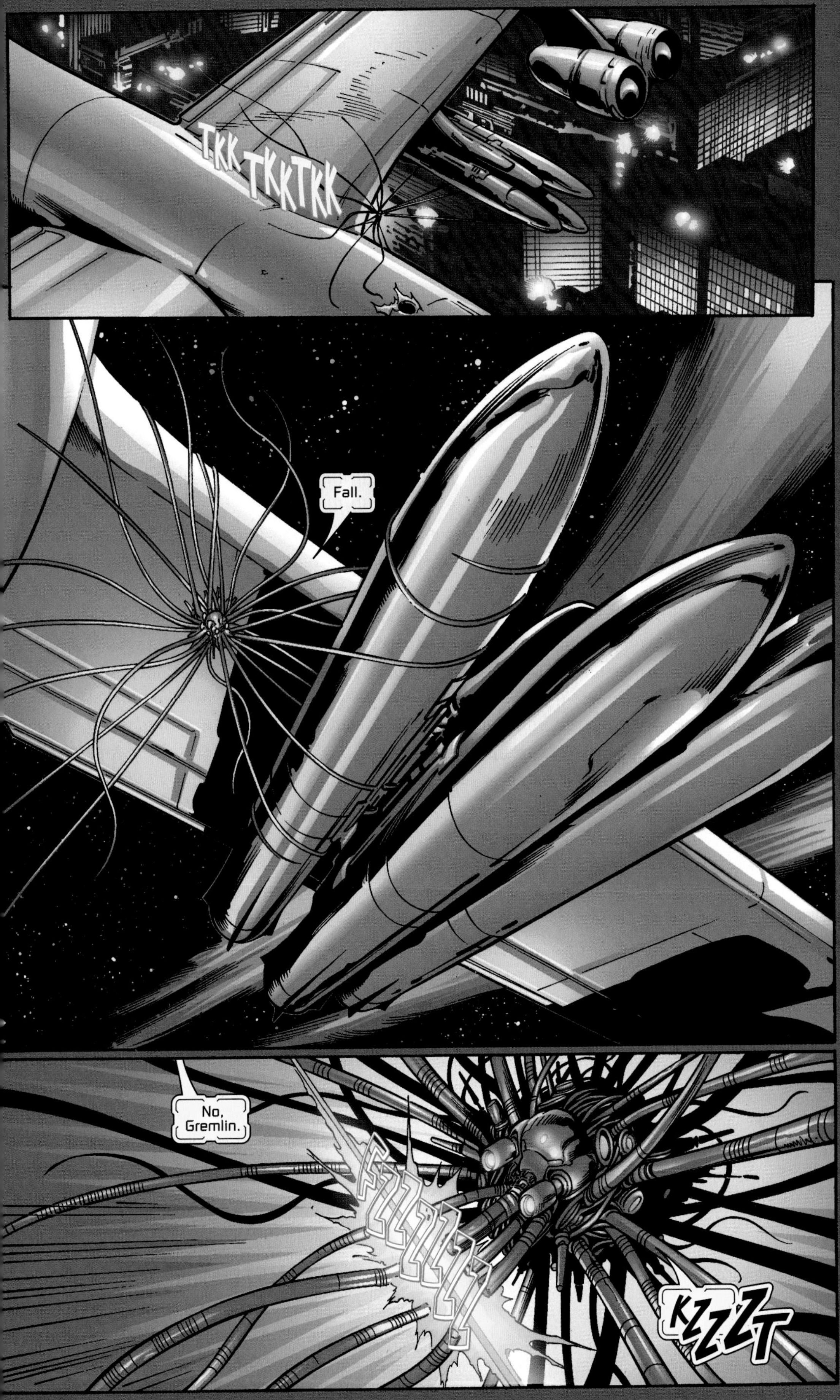
TKK TKKTKK
Fall.
No, Gremlin.
KZZZT

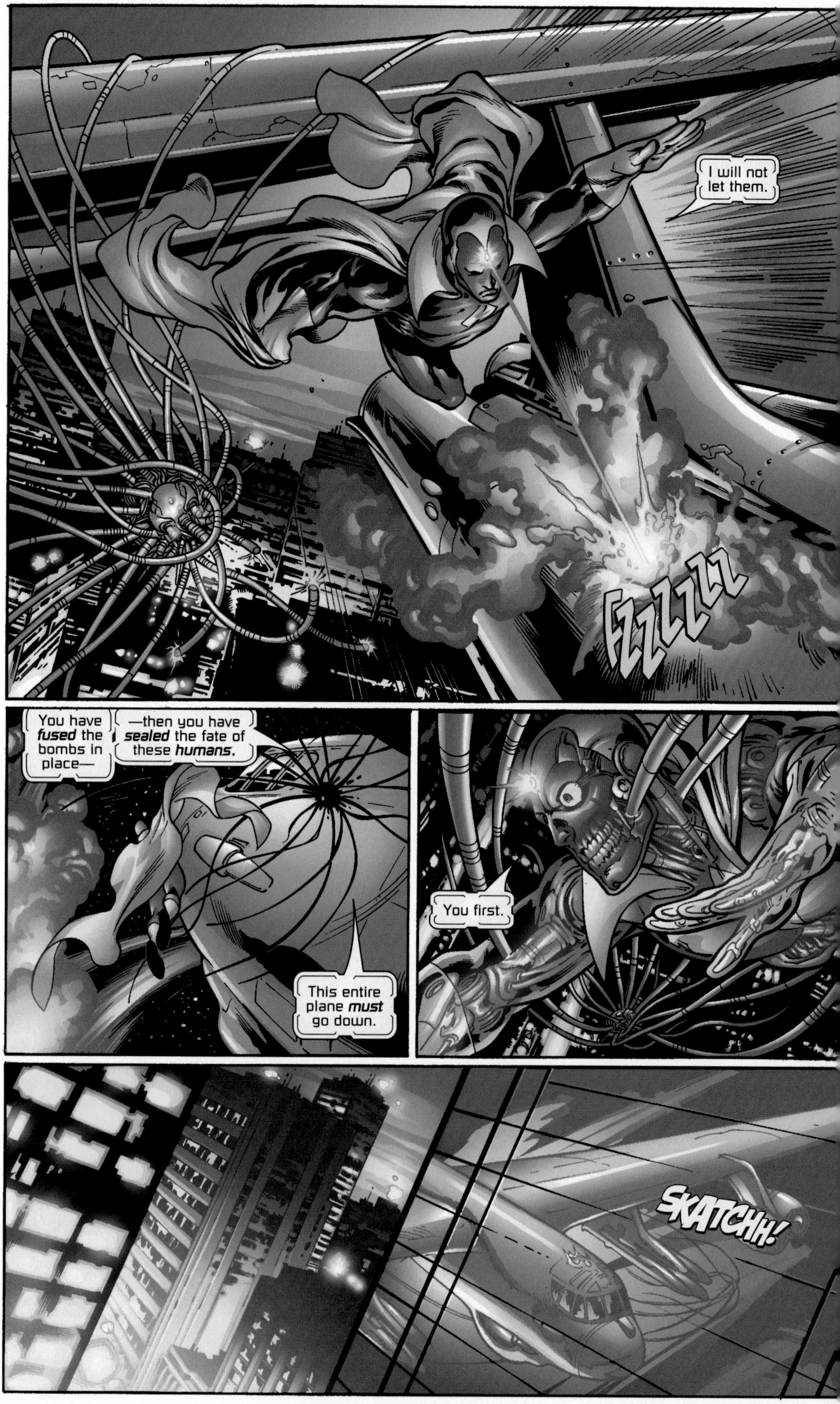
I will not let them.
FZZZZZZ
You have fused the bombs in place—
—then you have sealed the fate of these humans.
This entire plane must go down.
You first.
SKATCHH!

How'd he do that? Take out the control panel...

He can shift his density... be like a ghost.

Or like diamond.

Dad! The Gremlin's trying to make us *crash*. Right in the city. With the bombs--

I know, Derek. But the landing gear release isn't working... I need you to get under the dash. Find the manual emergency.

Are we going to die?

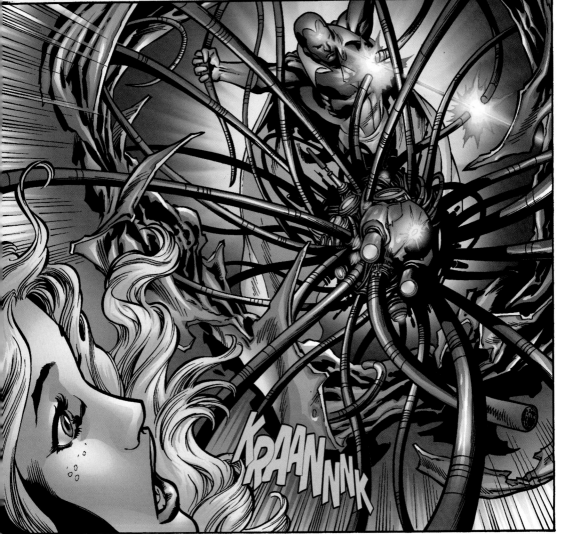

KRAANNNK

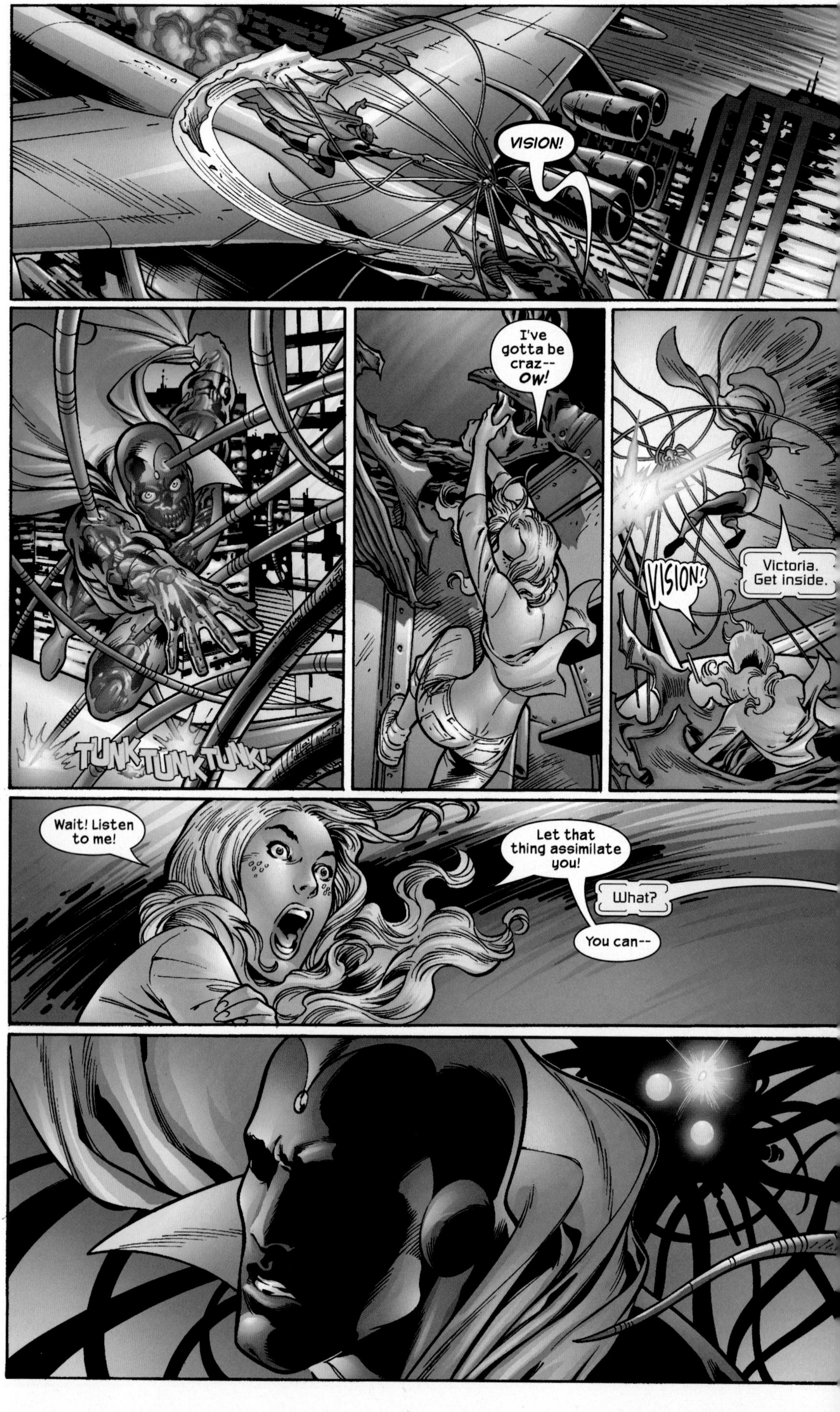
VISION!
I've gotta be craz-- OW!
TUNK TUNK TUNK!
VISION!
Victoria. Get inside.
Wait! Listen to me!
Let that thing assimilate you!
What?
You can--

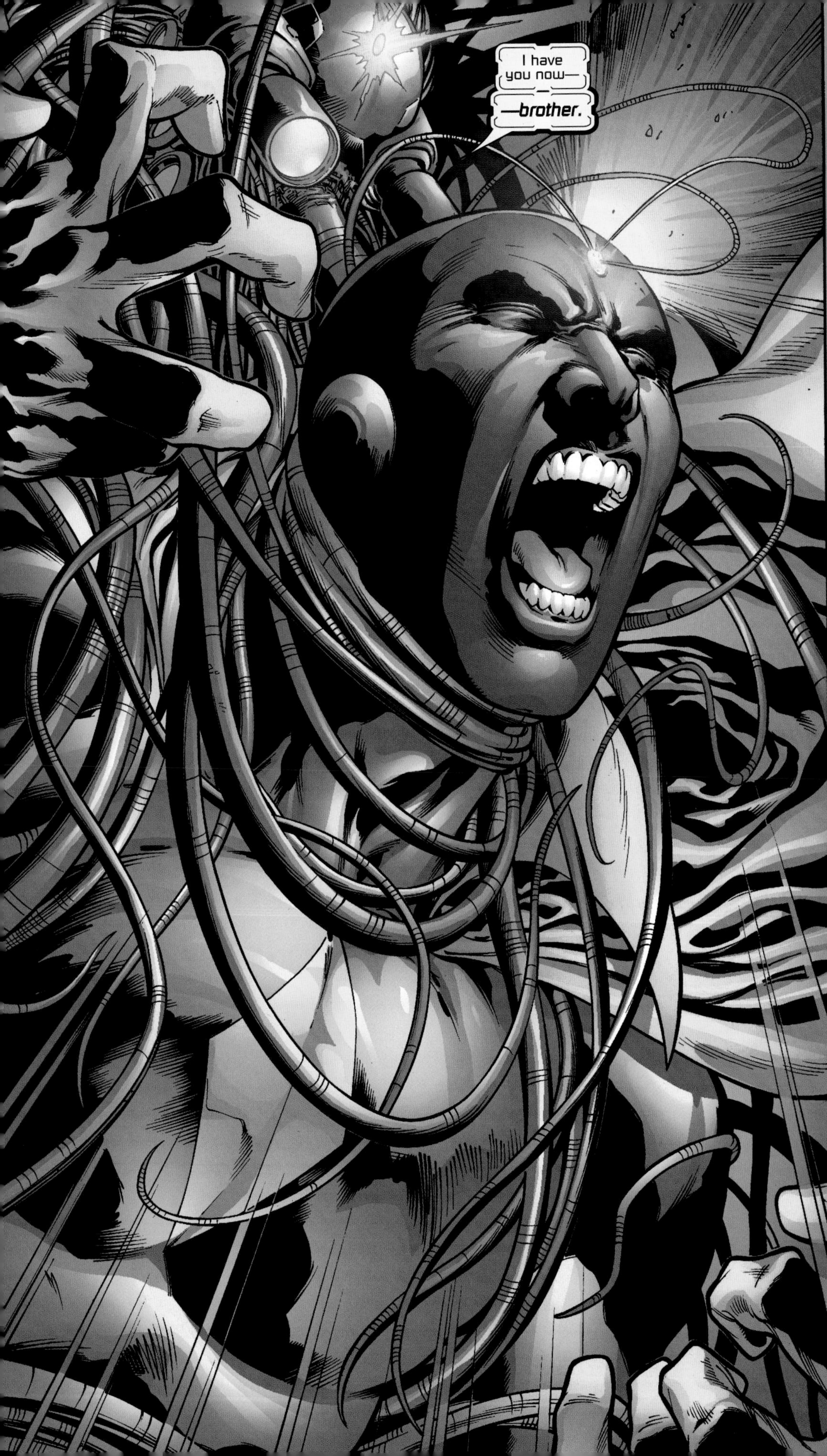
I have you now—
—brother.

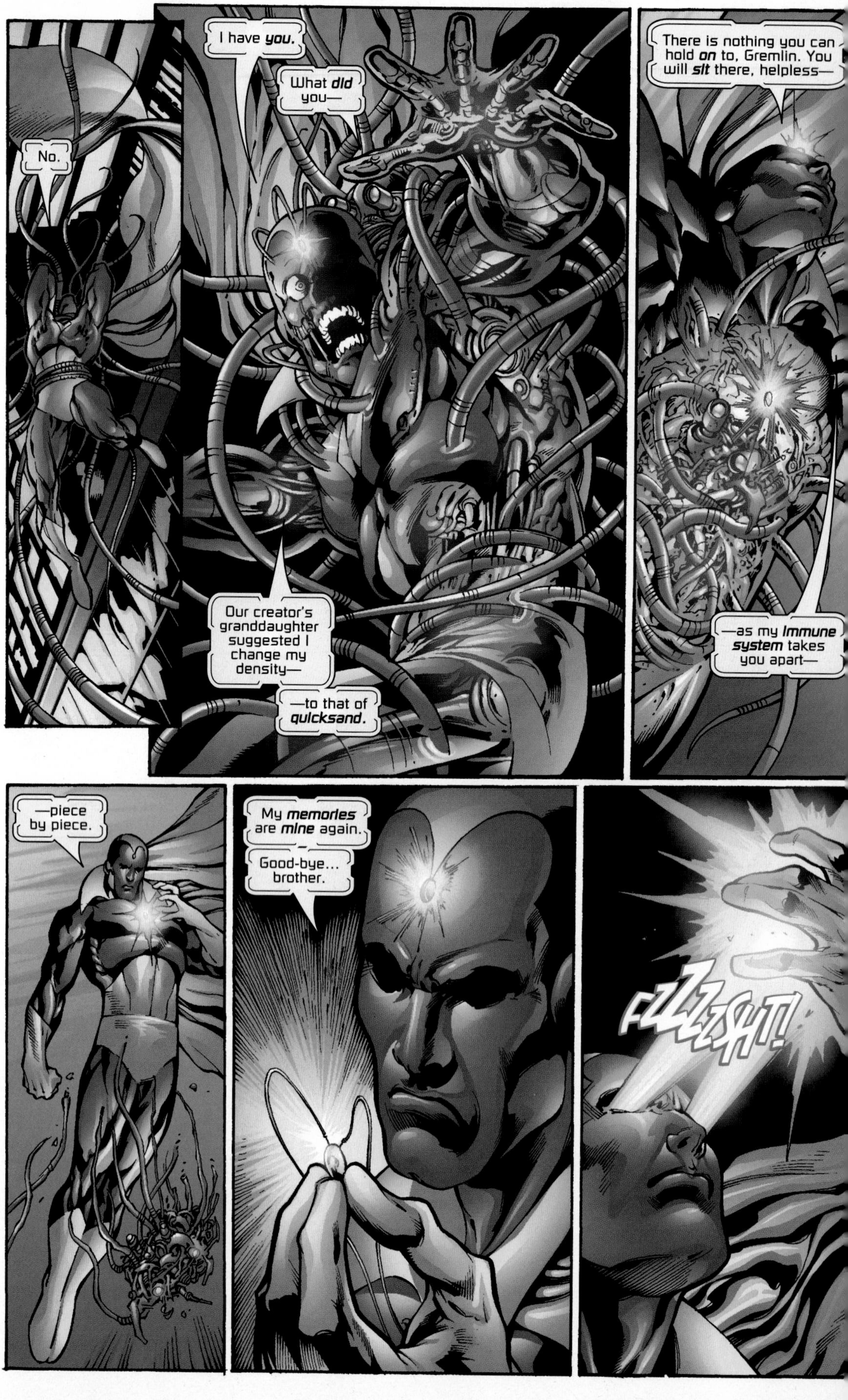
No.
I have *you.*
What *did* you—
There is nothing you can hold *on* to, Gremlin. You will *sit* there, helpless—
Our creator's granddaughter suggested I change my density—
—to that of *quicksand.*
—as my *immune system* takes you apart—
—piece by piece.
My *memories* are *mine* again.
Good-bye... brother.
FZZZSHT!

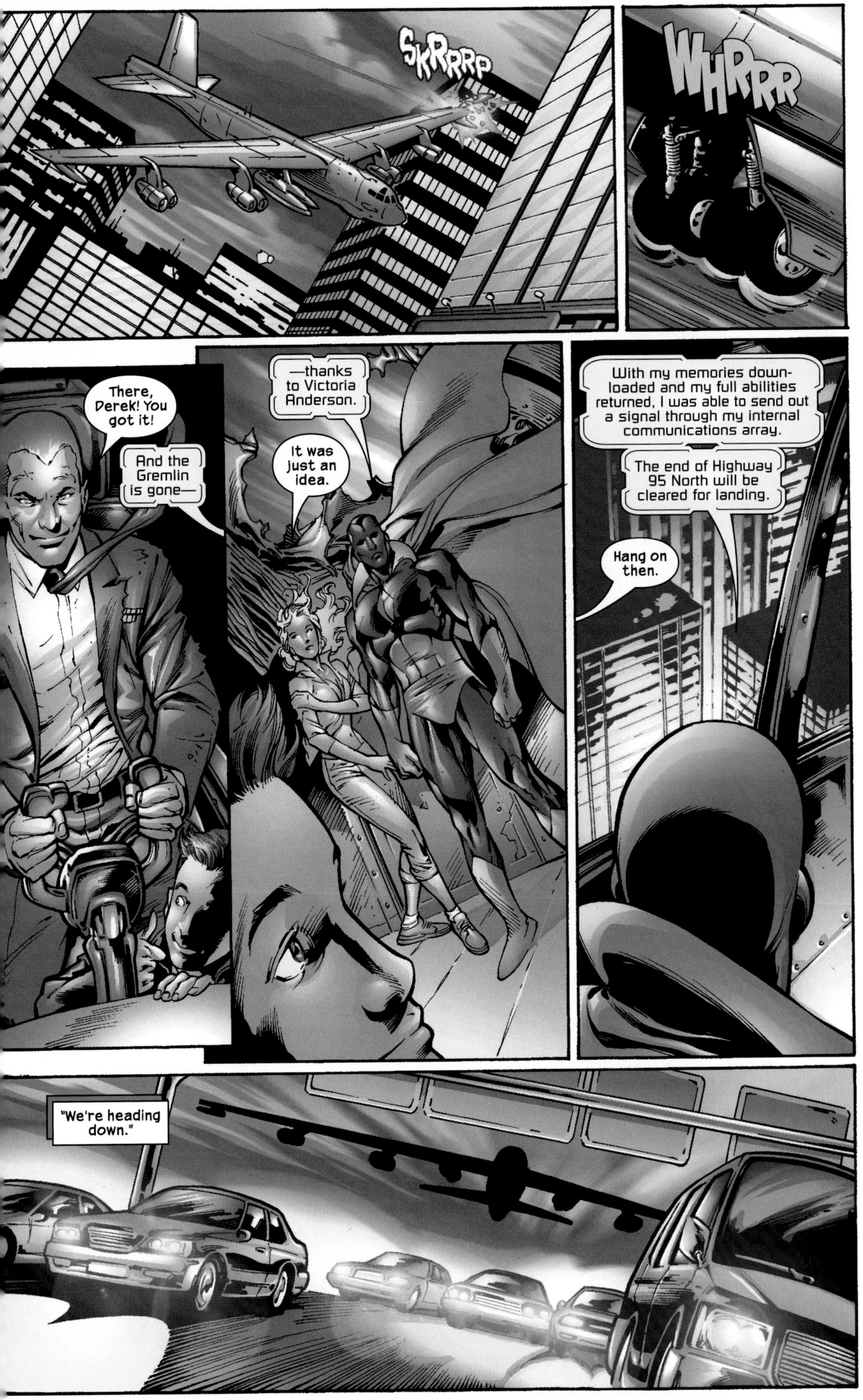
SKRRRP
WHRRR
There, Derek! You got it!
And the Gremlin is gone—
—thanks to Victoria Anderson.
It was just an idea.
With my memories downloaded and my full abilities returned, I was able to send out a signal through my internal communications array.
The end of Highway 95 North will be cleared for landing.
Hang on then.
"We're heading down."

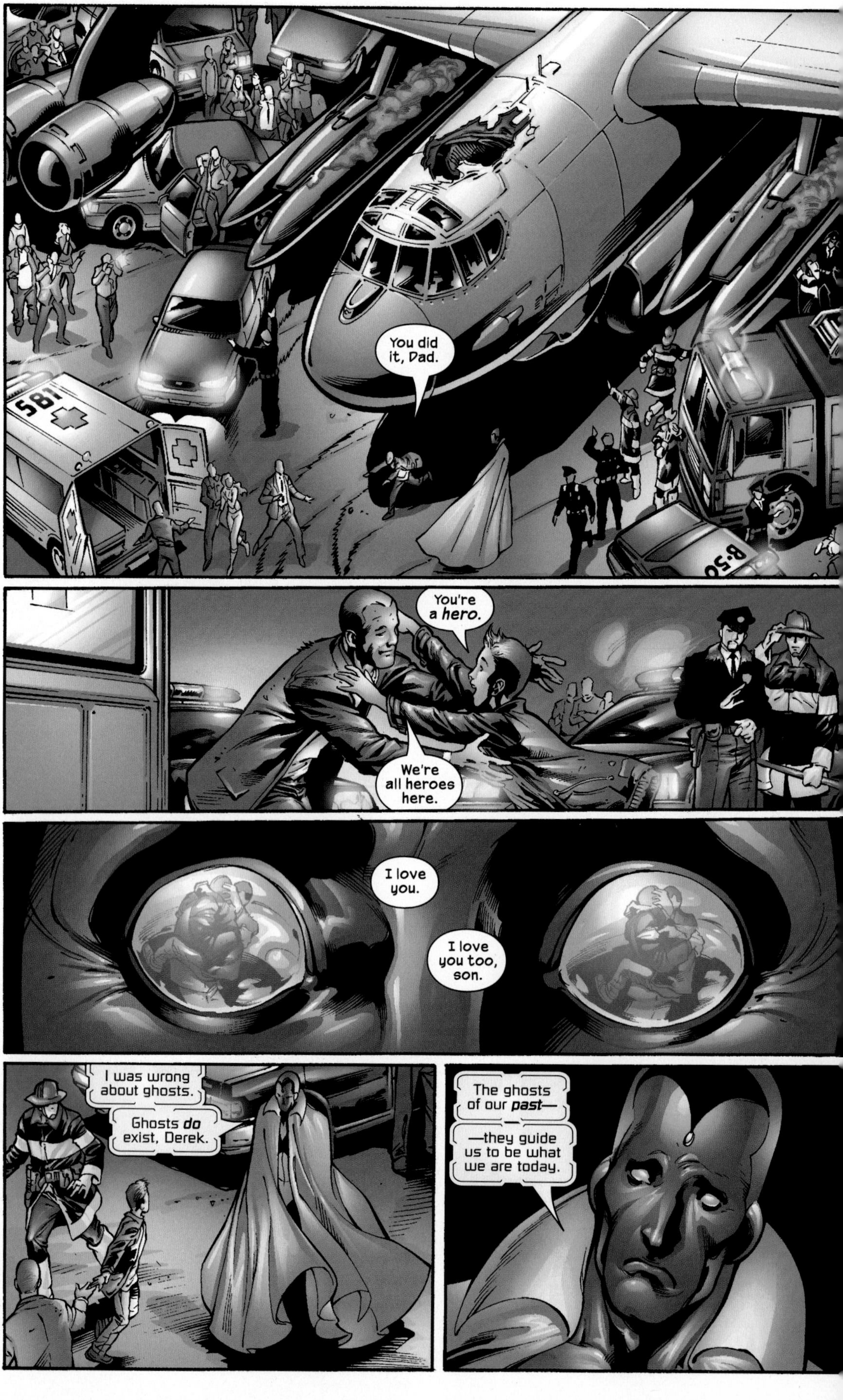
You did it, Dad.
You're a *hero*.
We're all heroes here.
I love you.
I love you too, son.
I was wrong about ghosts.
Ghosts *do* exist, Derek.
The ghosts of our *past*—
—they guide us to be what we are today.

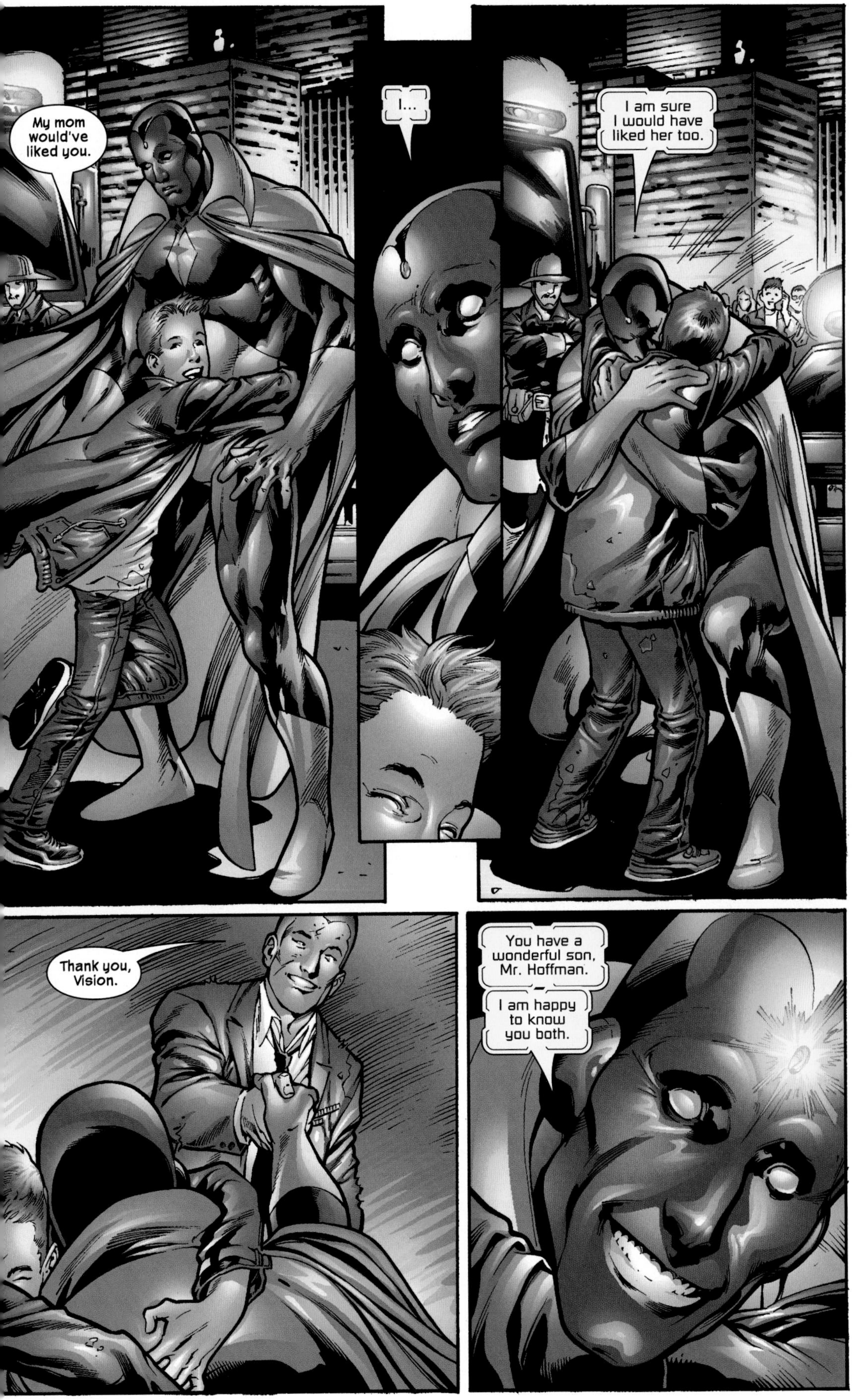
My mom would've liked you.
I...
I am sure I would have liked her too.
Thank you, Vision.
You have a wonderful son, Mr. Hoffman.
I am happy to know you both.

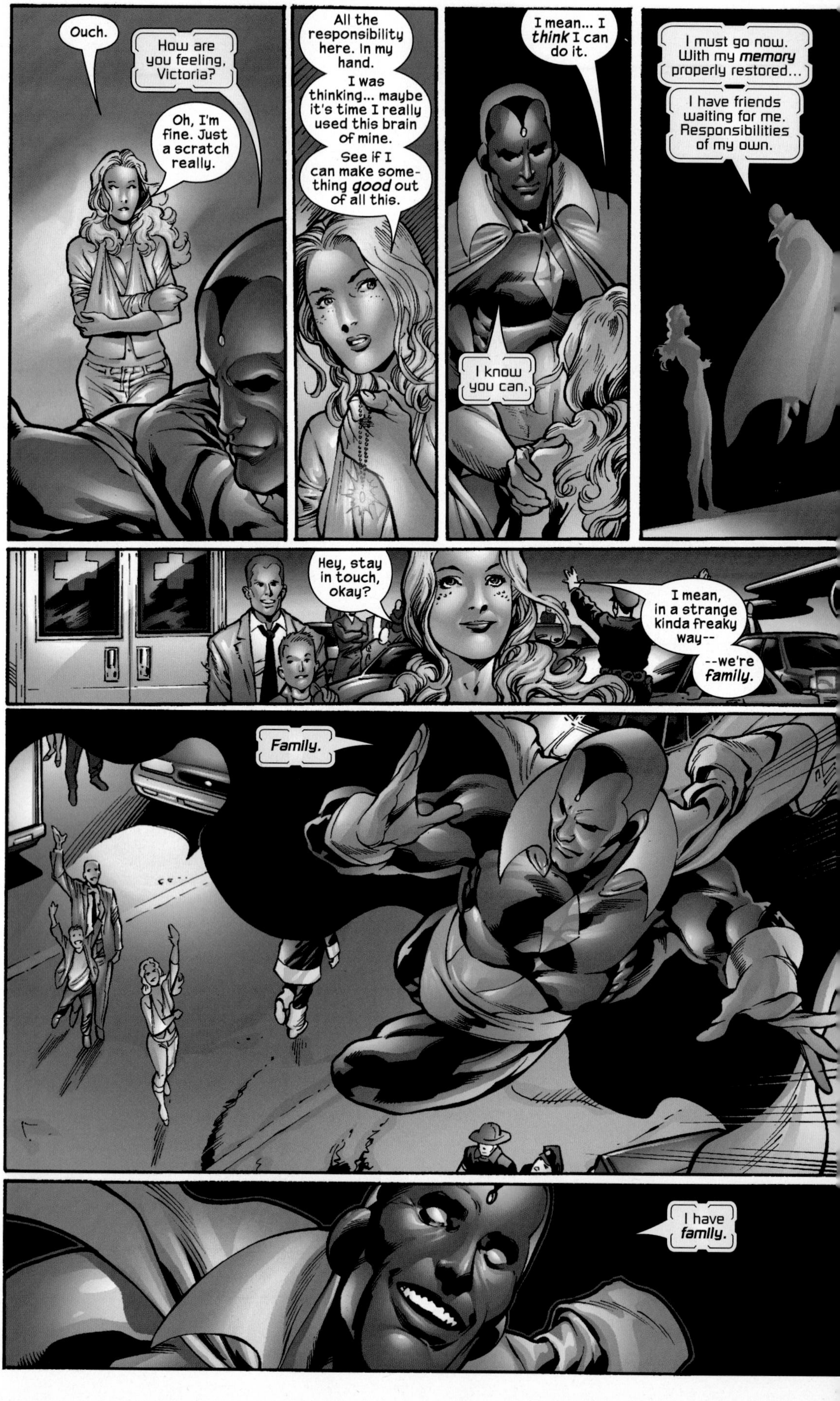
Ouch.
How are you feeling, Victoria?
Oh, I'm fine. Just a scratch really.
All the responsibility here. In my hand.
I was thinking... maybe it's time I really used this brain of mine.
See if I can make something *good* out of all this.
I mean... I *think* I can do it.
I know you can.
I must go now. With my *memory* properly restored...
I have friends waiting for me. Responsibilities of my own.
Hey, stay in touch, okay?
I mean, in a strange kinda freaky way--
--we're *family*.
Family.
I have *family*.

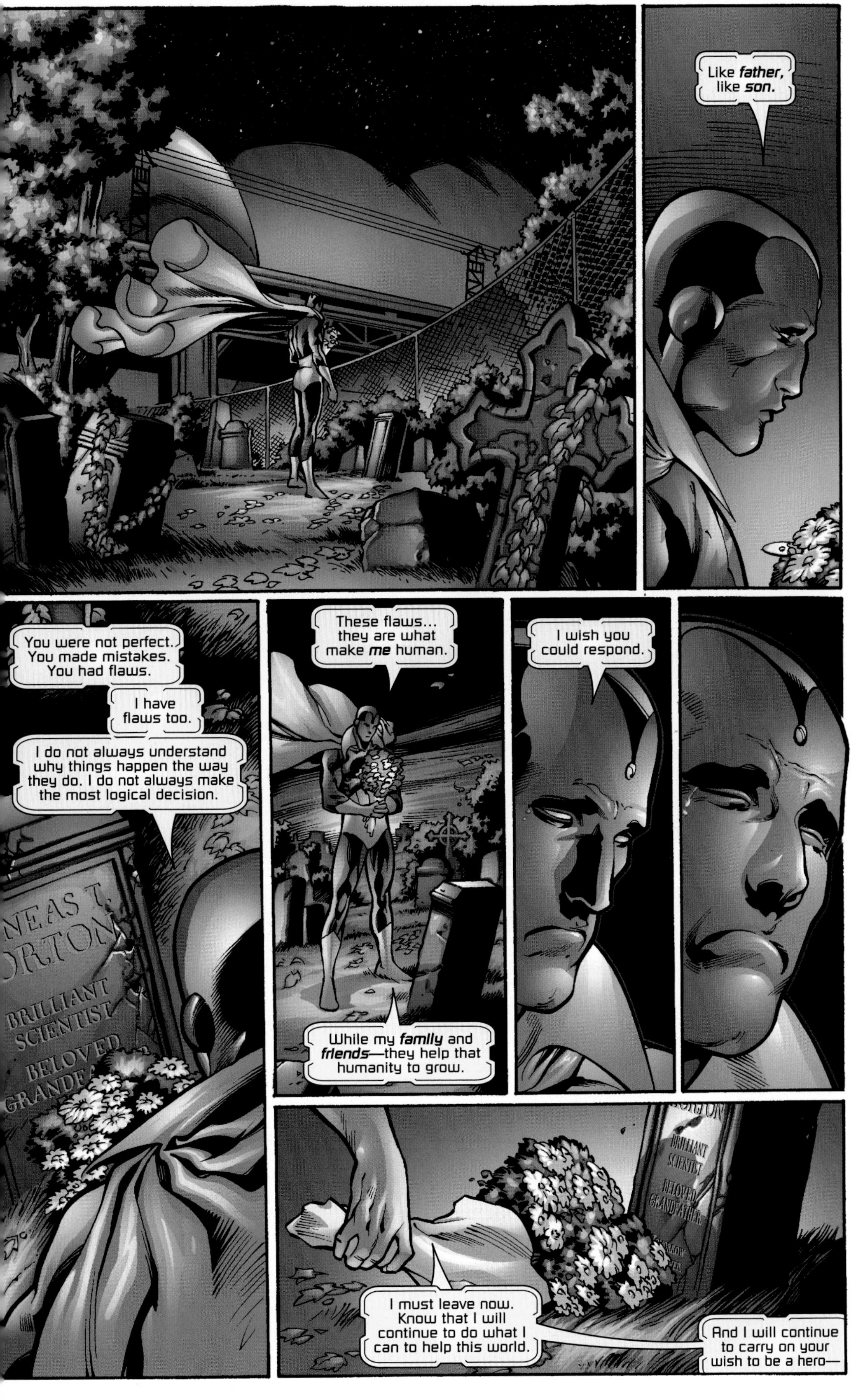
Like father, like son.
You were not perfect. You made mistakes. You had flaws.
I have flaws too.
I do not always understand why things happen the way they do. I do not always make the most logical decision.
NEAS T. ORTON BRILLIANT SCIENTIST BELOVED GRANDFA
These flaws... they are what make me human.
While my family and friends—they help that humanity to grow.
I wish you could respond.
I must leave now. Know that I will continue to do what I can to help this world.
And I will continue to carry on your wish to be a hero—

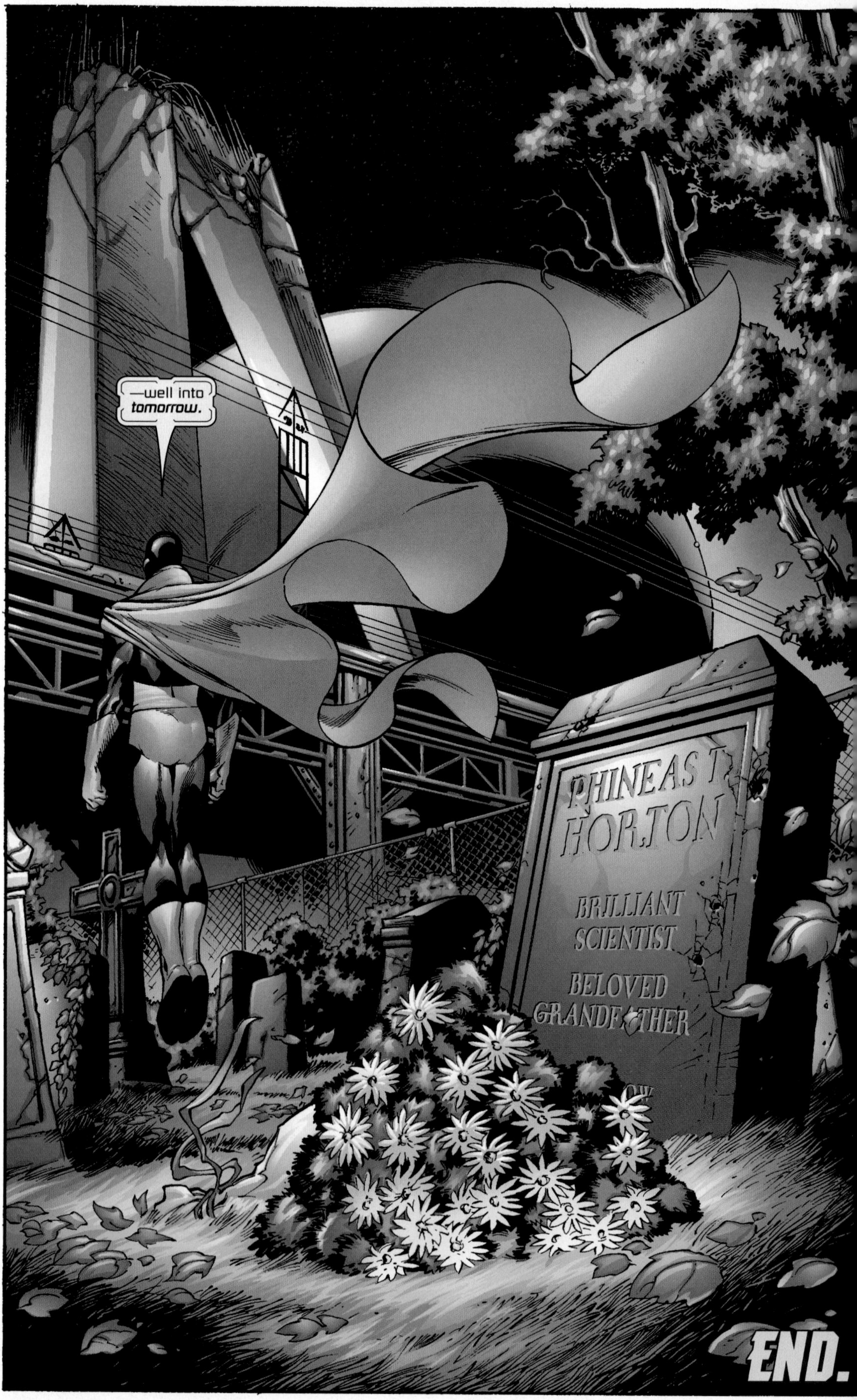
—well into *tomorrow*.
PHINEAS T. HORTON
BRILLIANT SCIENTIST
BELOVED GRANDFATHER
END.

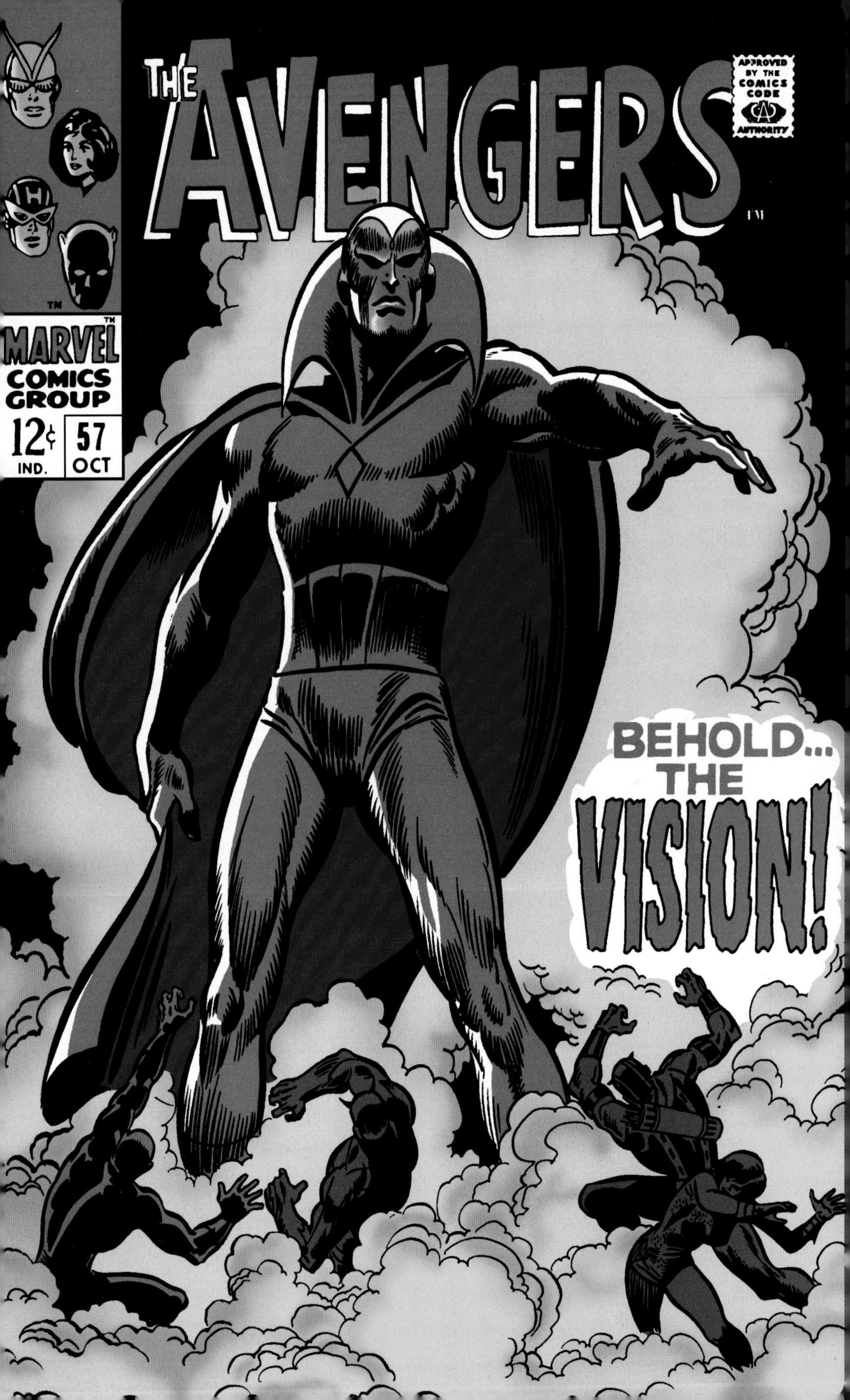

THE AVENGERS
APPROVED BY THE COMICS CODE AUTHORITY
MARVEL COMICS GROUP
12¢ IND.
57 OCT
BEHOLD... THE VISION!

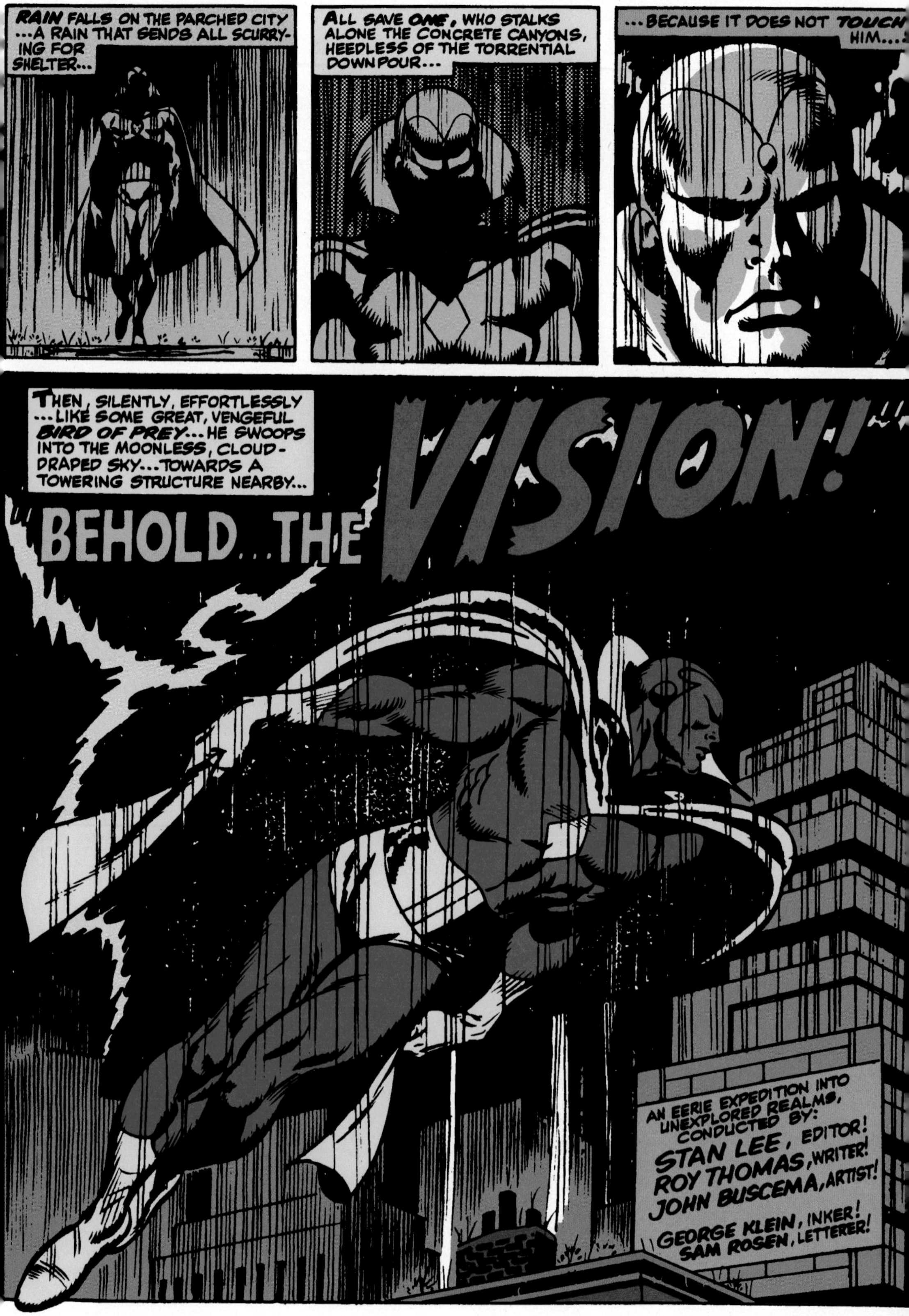
RAIN FALLS ON THE PARCHED CITY ...A RAIN THAT SENDS ALL SCURRYING FOR SHELTER...
ALL SAVE ONE, WHO STALKS ALONE THE CONCRETE CANYONS, HEEDLESS OF THE TORRENTIAL DOWNPOUR...
...BECAUSE IT DOES NOT TOUCH HIM...
THEN, SILENTLY, EFFORTLESSLY ...LIKE SOME GREAT, VENGEFUL BIRD OF PREY... HE SWOOPS INTO THE MOONLESS, CLOUD-DRAPED SKY...TOWARDS A TOWERING STRUCTURE NEARBY...
"BEHOLD... THE VISION!"
AN EERIE EXPEDITION INTO UNEXPLORED REALMS, CONDUCTED BY:
STAN LEE, EDITOR!
ROY THOMAS, WRITER!
JOHN BUSCEMA, ARTIST!
GEORGE KLEIN, INKER!
SAM ROSEN, LETTERER!

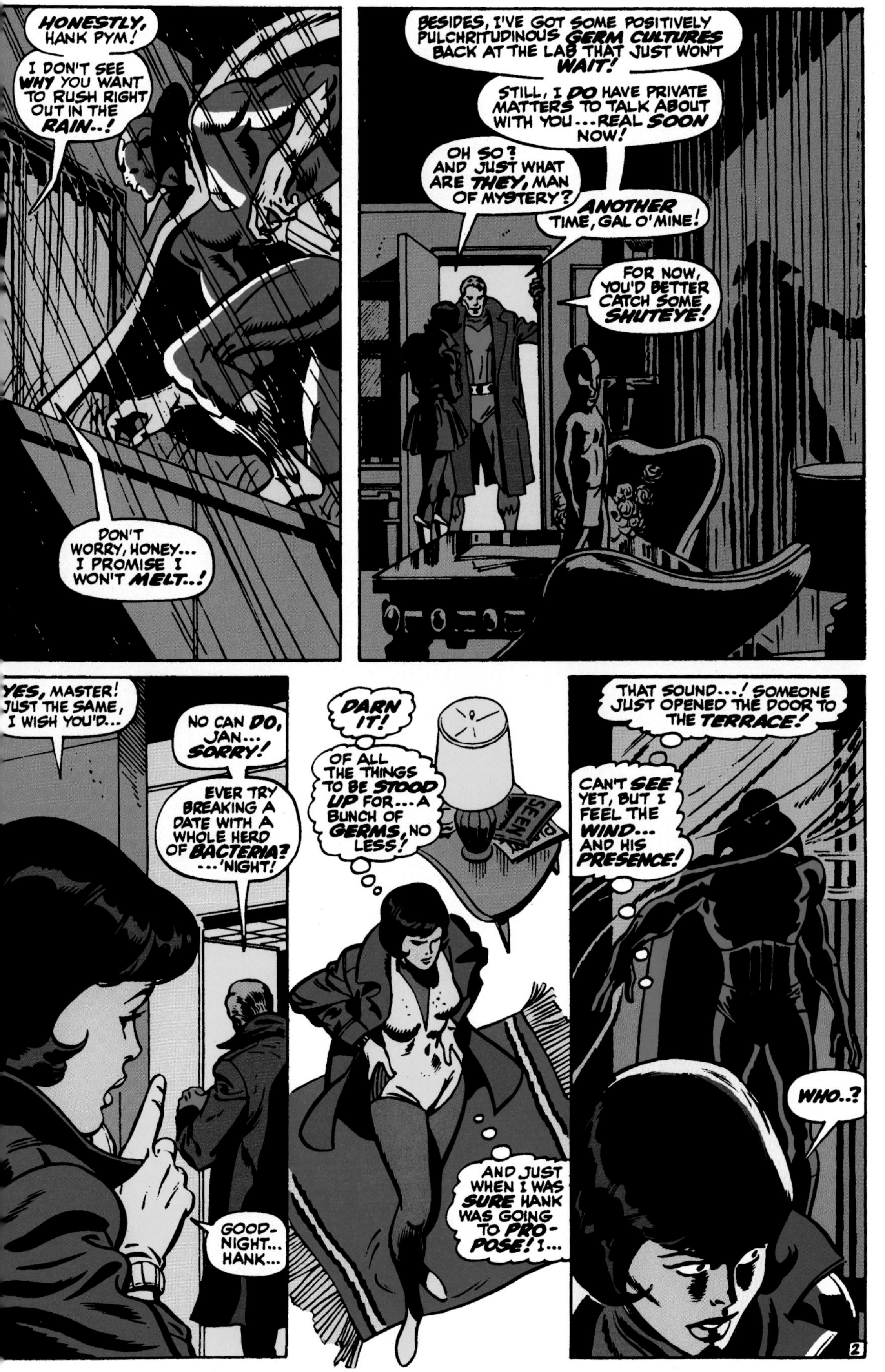

HONESTLY, HANK PYM!
I DON'T SEE WHY YOU WANT TO RUSH RIGHT OUT IN THE RAIN..!
DON'T WORRY, HONEY... I PROMISE I WON'T MELT..!
BESIDES, I'VE GOT SOME POSITIVELY PULCHRITUDINOUS GERM CULTURES BACK AT THE LAB THAT JUST WON'T WAIT!
STILL, I DO HAVE PRIVATE MATTERS TO TALK ABOUT WITH YOU... REAL SOON NOW!
OH SO? AND JUST WHAT ARE THEY, MAN OF MYSTERY?
ANOTHER TIME, GAL O'MINE!
FOR NOW, YOU'D BETTER CATCH SOME SHUTEYE!
YES, MASTER! JUST THE SAME, I WISH YOU'D...
NO CAN DO, JAN... SORRY!
EVER TRY BREAKING A DATE WITH A WHOLE HERD OF BACTERIA? ...'NIGHT!
GOOD-NIGHT... HANK...
DARN IT!
OF ALL THE THINGS TO BE STOOD UP FOR... A BUNCH OF GERMS, NO LESS!
AND JUST WHEN I WAS SURE HANK WAS GOING TO PRO-POSE! I...
THAT SOUND...! SOMEONE JUST OPENED THE DOOR TO THE TERRACE!
CAN'T SEE YET, BUT I FEEL THE WIND... AND HIS PRESENCE!
WHO..?
2

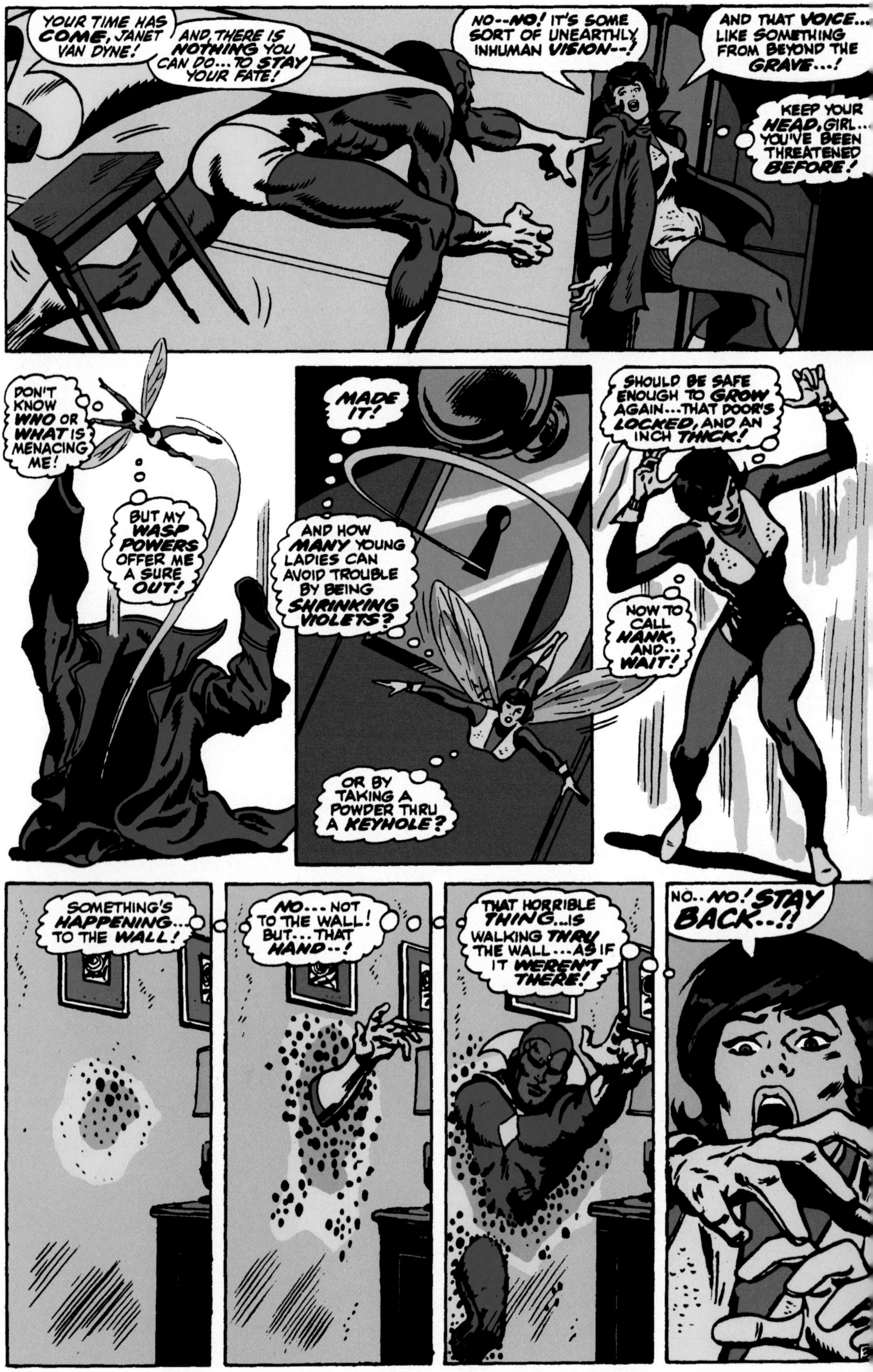
YOUR TIME HAS COME, JANET VAN DYNE!
AND THERE IS NOTHING YOU CAN DO... TO STAY YOUR FATE!
NO--NO! IT'S SOME SORT OF UNEARTHLY INHUMAN VISION--!
AND THAT VOICE... LIKE SOMETHING FROM BEYOND THE GRAVE...!
KEEP YOUR HEAD, GIRL... YOU'VE BEEN THREATENED BEFORE!
DON'T KNOW WHO OR WHAT IS MENACING ME!
BUT MY WASP POWERS OFFER ME A SURE OUT!
MADE IT!
AND HOW MANY YOUNG LADIES CAN AVOID TROUBLE BY BEING SHRINKING VIOLETS?
OR BY TAKING A POWDER THRU A KEYHOLE?
SHOULD BE SAFE ENOUGH TO GROW AGAIN...THAT DOOR'S LOCKED, AND AN INCH THICK!
NOW TO CALL HANK, AND... WAIT!
SOMETHING'S HAPPENING... TO THE WALL!
NO... NOT TO THE WALL! BUT... THAT HAND--!
THAT HORRIBLE THING...IS WALKING THRU THE WALL...AS IF IT WEREN'T THERE!
NO..NO! STAY BACK..!!

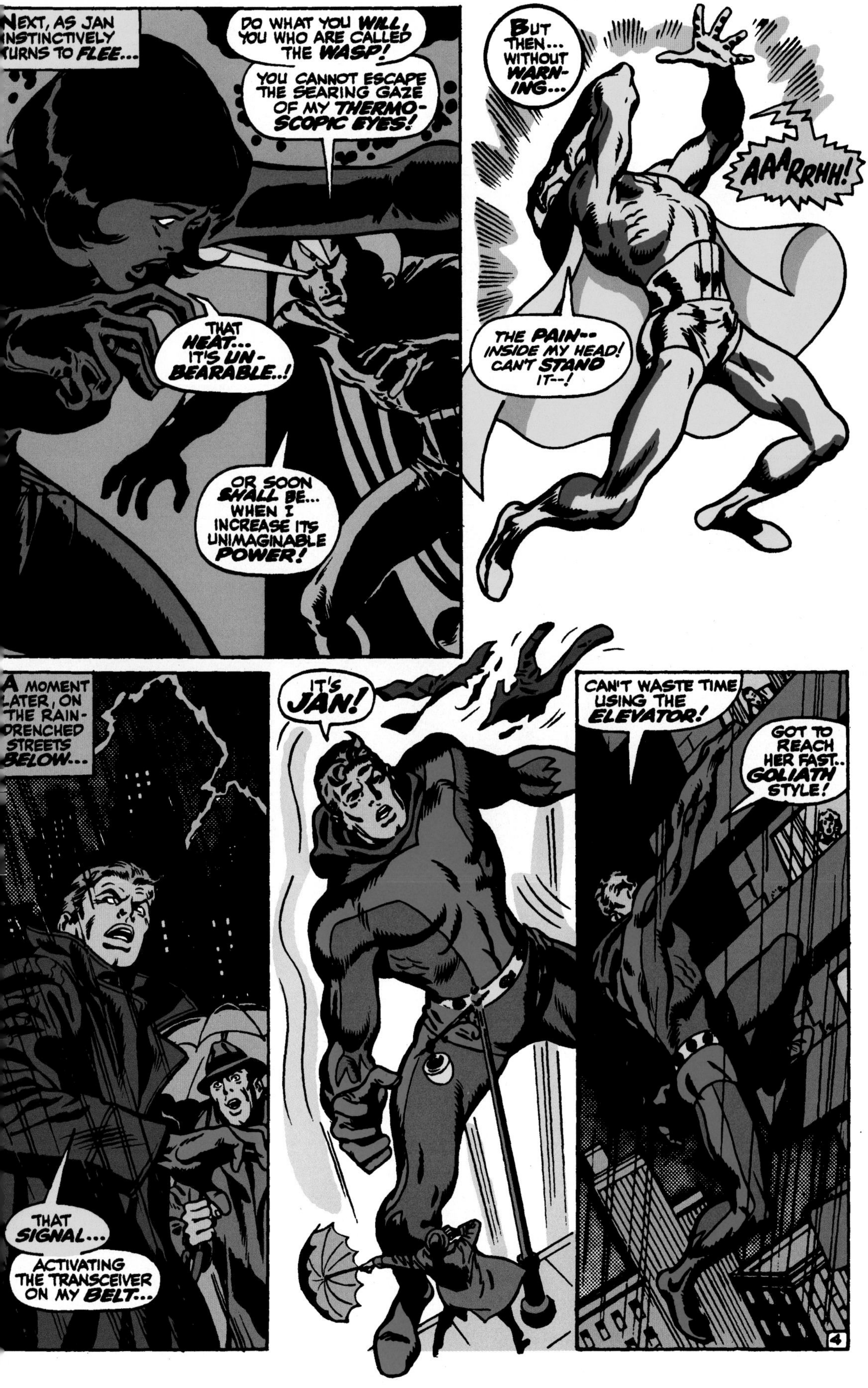
NEXT, AS JAN INSTINCTIVELY TURNS TO FLEE...
DO WHAT YOU WILL, YOU WHO ARE CALLED THE WASP!
YOU CANNOT ESCAPE THE SEARING GAZE OF MY THERMO-SCOPIC EYES!
THAT HEAT... IT'S UN-BEARABLE..!
OR SOON SHALL BE... WHEN I INCREASE ITS UNIMAGINABLE POWER!
BUT THEN... WITHOUT WARN-ING...
AAARRHH!
THE PAIN-- INSIDE MY HEAD! CAN'T STAND IT--!
A MOMENT LATER, ON THE RAIN-DRENCHED STREETS BELOW...
THAT SIGNAL...
ACTIVATING THE TRANSCEIVER ON MY BELT...
IT'S JAN!
CAN'T WASTE TIME USING THE ELEVATOR!
GOT TO REACH HER FAST.. GOLIATH STYLE!
4

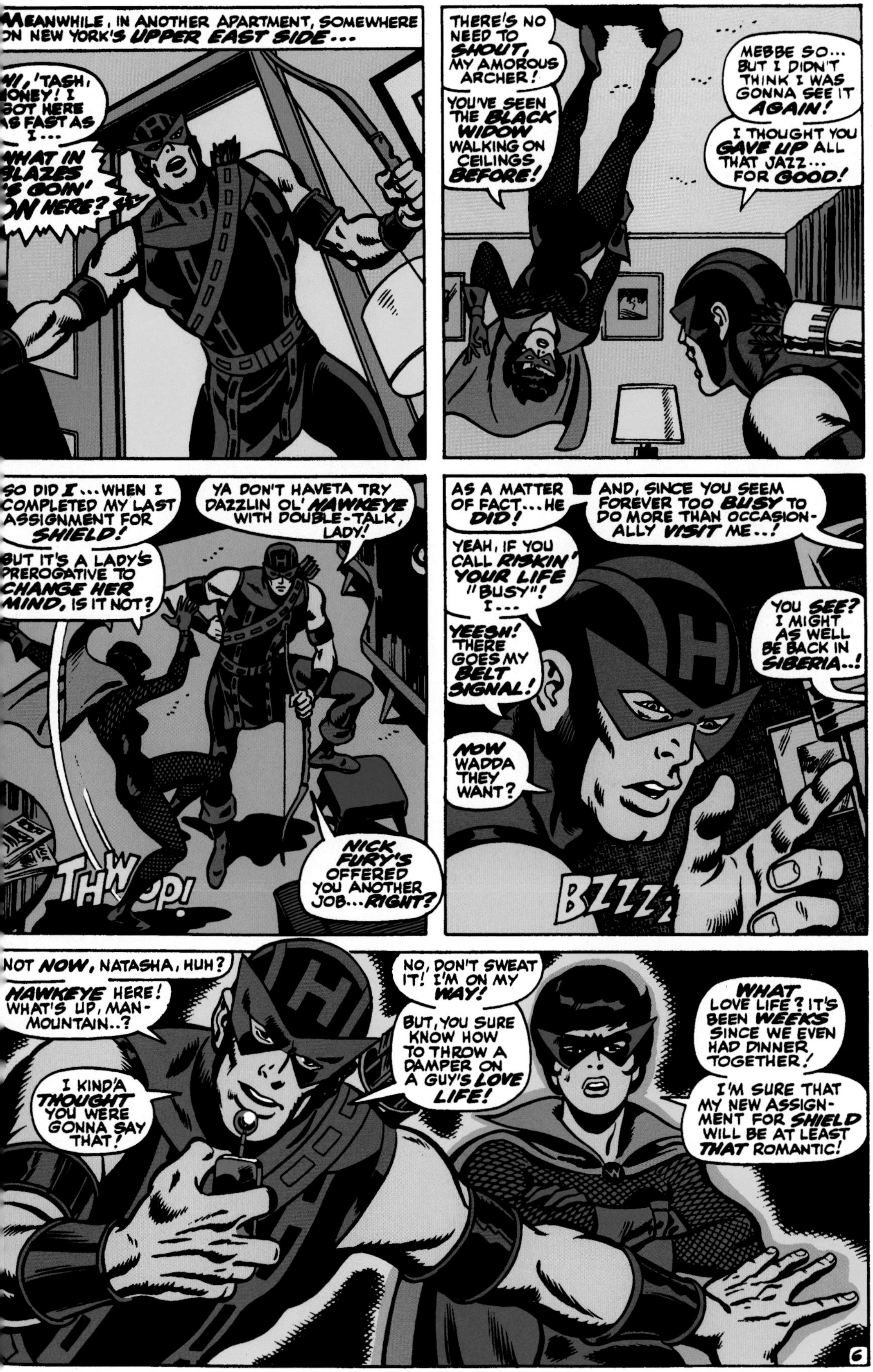
MEANWHILE, IN ANOTHER APARTMENT, SOMEWHERE ON NEW YORK'S UPPER EAST SIDE...
'TASH, ONEY! I OT HERE S FAST AS I...
WHAT IN LAZES 'S GOIN' ON HERE?
THERE'S NO NEED TO SHOUT, MY AMOROUS ARCHER!
YOU'VE SEEN THE BLACK WIDOW WALKING ON CEILINGS BEFORE!
MEBBE SO... BUT I DIDN'T THINK I WAS GONNA SEE IT AGAIN!
I THOUGHT YOU GAVE UP ALL THAT JAZZ... FOR GOOD!
SO DID I... WHEN I COMPLETED MY LAST ASSIGNMENT FOR SHIELD!
BUT IT'S A LADY'S PREROGATIVE TO CHANGE HER MIND, IS IT NOT?
YA DON'T HAVETA TRY DAZZLIN OL' HAWKEYE WITH DOUBLE-TALK, LADY!
THWOP!
NICK FURY'S OFFERED YOU ANOTHER JOB... RIGHT?
AS A MATTER OF FACT... HE DID!
AND, SINCE YOU SEEM FOREVER TOO BUSY TO DO MORE THAN OCCASIONALLY VISIT ME..!
YEAH, IF YOU CALL RISKIN' YOUR LIFE "BUSY"! I...
YOU SEE? I MIGHT AS WELL BE BACK IN SIBERIA..!
YEESH! THERE GOES MY BELT SIGNAL!
NOW WADDA THEY WANT?
BZZZZ
NOT NOW, NATASHA, HUH?
HAWKEYE HERE! WHAT'S UP, MAN-MOUNTAIN..?
I KIND'A THOUGHT YOU WERE GONNA SAY THAT!
NO, DON'T SWEAT IT! I'M ON MY WAY!
BUT, YOU SURE KNOW HOW TO THROW A DAMPER ON A GUY'S LOVE LIFE!
WHAT LOVE LIFE? IT'S BEEN WEEKS SINCE WE EVEN HAD DINNER TOGETHER!
I'M SURE THAT MY NEW ASSIGNMENT FOR SHIELD WILL BE AT LEAST THAT ROMANTIC!
6

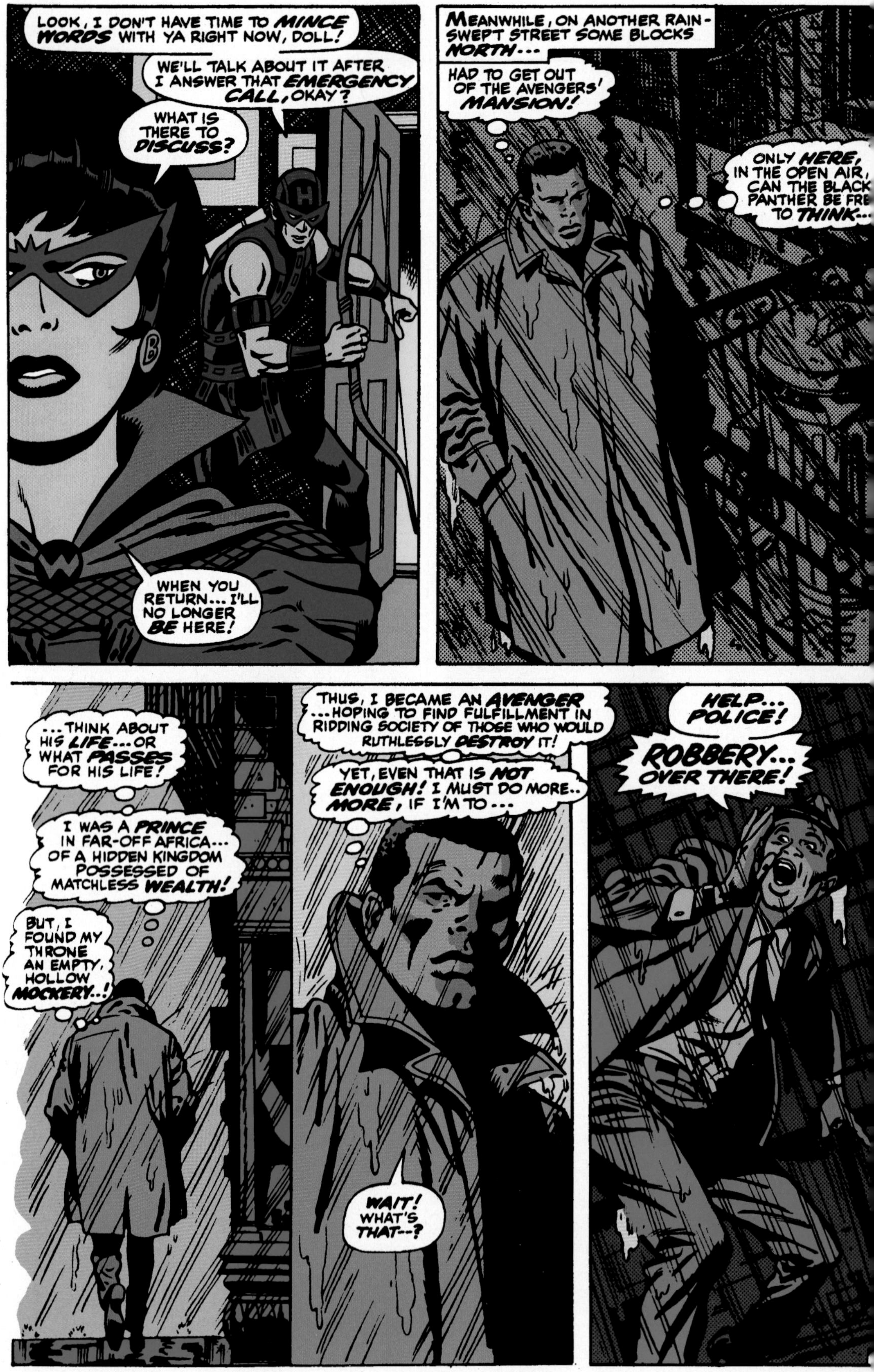
LOOK, I DON'T HAVE TIME TO MINCE WORDS WITH YA RIGHT NOW, DOLL!
WE'LL TALK ABOUT IT AFTER I ANSWER THAT EMERGENCY CALL, OKAY?
WHAT IS THERE TO DISCUSS?
WHEN YOU RETURN... I'LL NO LONGER BE HERE!
MEANWHILE, ON ANOTHER RAIN-SWEPT STREET SOME BLOCKS NORTH...
HAD TO GET OUT OF THE AVENGERS' MANSION!
ONLY HERE, IN THE OPEN AIR, CAN THE BLACK PANTHER BE FRE TO THINK...
...THINK ABOUT HIS LIFE... OR WHAT PASSES FOR HIS LIFE!
I WAS A PRINCE IN FAR-OFF AFRICA... OF A HIDDEN KINGDOM POSSESSED OF MATCHLESS WEALTH!
BUT, I FOUND MY THRONE AN EMPTY, HOLLOW MOCKERY..!
THUS, I BECAME AN AVENGER ...HOPING TO FIND FULFILLMENT IN RIDDING SOCIETY OF THOSE WHO WOULD RUTHLESSLY DESTROY IT!
YET, EVEN THAT IS NOT ENOUGH! I MUST DO MORE.. MORE, IF I'M TO...
WAIT! WHAT'S THAT--?
HELP... POLICE!
ROBBERY... OVER THERE!

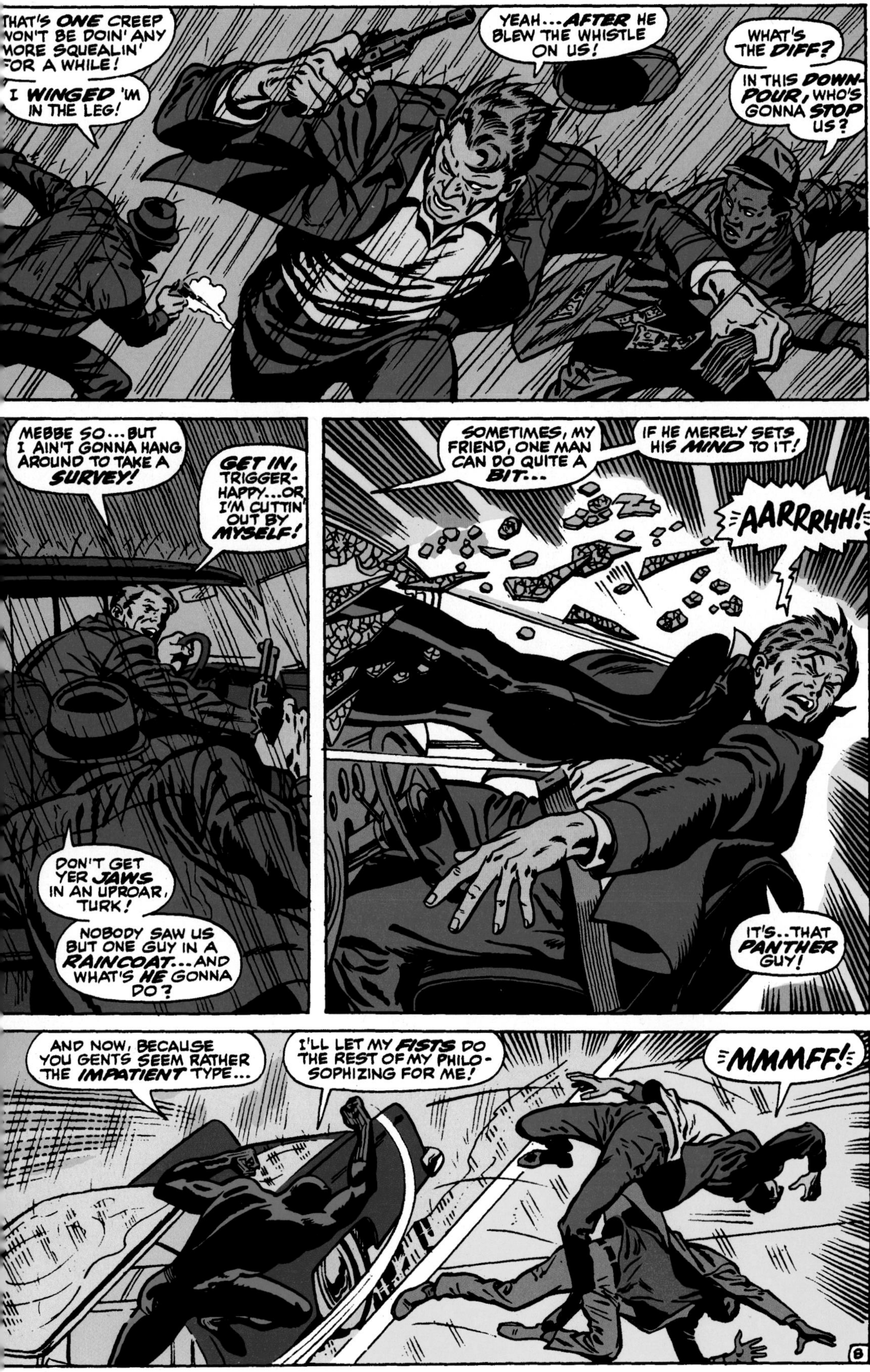
THAT'S ONE CREEP WON'T BE DOIN' ANY MORE SQUEALIN' FOR A WHILE!
I WINGED 'IM IN THE LEG!
YEAH...AFTER HE BLEW THE WHISTLE ON US!
WHAT'S THE DIFF?
IN THIS DOWN-POUR, WHO'S GONNA STOP US?
MEBBE SO...BUT I AIN'T GONNA HANG AROUND TO TAKE A SURVEY!
GET IN, TRIGGER-HAPPY...OR I'M CUTTIN' OUT BY MYSELF!
DON'T GET YER JAWS IN AN UPROAR, TURK!
NOBODY SAW US BUT ONE GUY IN A RAINCOAT...AND WHAT'S HE GONNA DO?
SOMETIMES, MY FRIEND, ONE MAN CAN DO QUITE A BIT...
IF HE MERELY SETS HIS MIND TO IT!
AARRRHH!
IT'S..THAT PANTHER GUY!
AND NOW, BECAUSE YOU GENTS SEEM RATHER THE IMPATIENT TYPE...
I'LL LET MY FISTS DO THE REST OF MY PHILO-SOPHIZING FOR ME!
MMMFF!
8

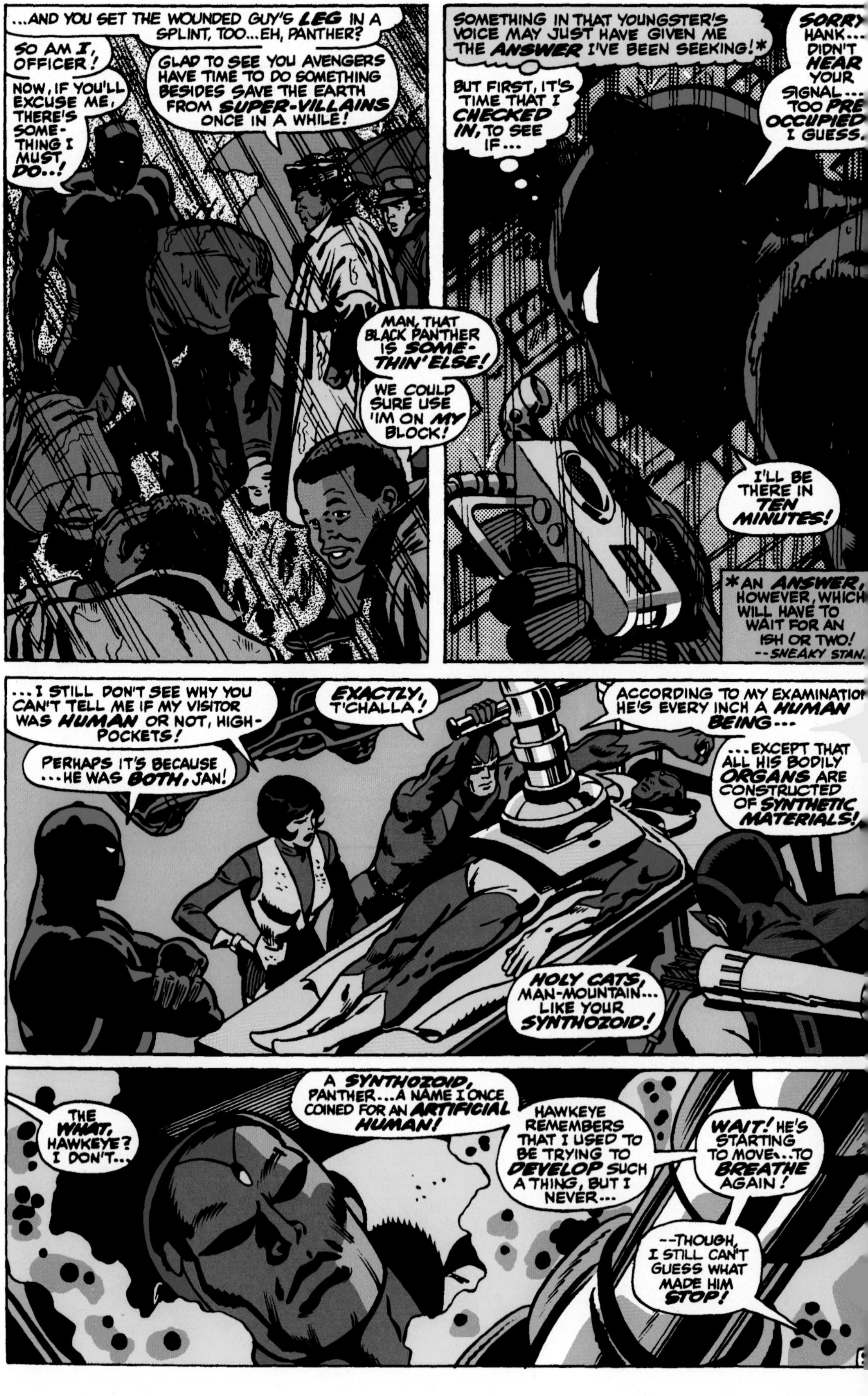
...AND YOU SET THE WOUNDED GUY'S LEG IN A SPLINT, TOO...EH, PANTHER?
SO AM I, OFFICER!
GLAD TO SEE YOU AVENGERS HAVE TIME TO DO SOMETHING BESIDES SAVE THE EARTH FROM SUPER-VILLAINS ONCE IN A WHILE!
NOW, IF YOU'LL EXCUSE ME, THERE'S SOME-THING I MUST DO..!
MAN, THAT BLACK PANTHER IS SOME-THIN' ELSE!
WE COULD SURE USE 'IM ON MY BLOCK!
SOMETHING IN THAT YOUNGSTER'S VOICE MAY JUST HAVE GIVEN ME THE ANSWER I'VE BEEN SEEKING!*
BUT FIRST, IT'S TIME THAT I CHECKED IN, TO SEE IF...
SORRY HANK... DIDN'T HEAR YOUR SIGNAL... TOO PRE OCCUPIED I GUESS.
I'LL BE THERE IN TEN MINUTES!
*AN ANSWER, HOWEVER, WHICH WILL HAVE TO WAIT FOR AN ISH OR TWO! --SNEAKY STAN.
...I STILL DON'T SEE WHY YOU CAN'T TELL ME IF MY VISITOR WAS HUMAN OR NOT, HIGH-POCKETS!
PERHAPS IT'S BECAUSE ...HE WAS BOTH, JAN!
EXACTLY, T'CHALLA!
ACCORDING TO MY EXAMINATION HE'S EVERY INCH A HUMAN BEING...
...EXCEPT THAT ALL HIS BODILY ORGANS ARE CONSTRUCTED OF SYNTHETIC MATERIALS!
HOLY CATS, MAN-MOUNTAIN... LIKE YOUR SYNTHOZOID!
THE WHAT, HAWKEYE? I DON'T...
A SYNTHOZOID, PANTHER...A NAME I ONCE COINED FOR AN ARTIFICIAL HUMAN!
HAWKEYE REMEMBERS THAT I USED TO BE TRYING TO DEVELOP SUCH A THING, BUT I NEVER...
WAIT! HE'S STARTING TO MOVE...TO BREATHE AGAIN!
--THOUGH, I STILL CAN'T GUESS WHAT MADE HIM STOP!

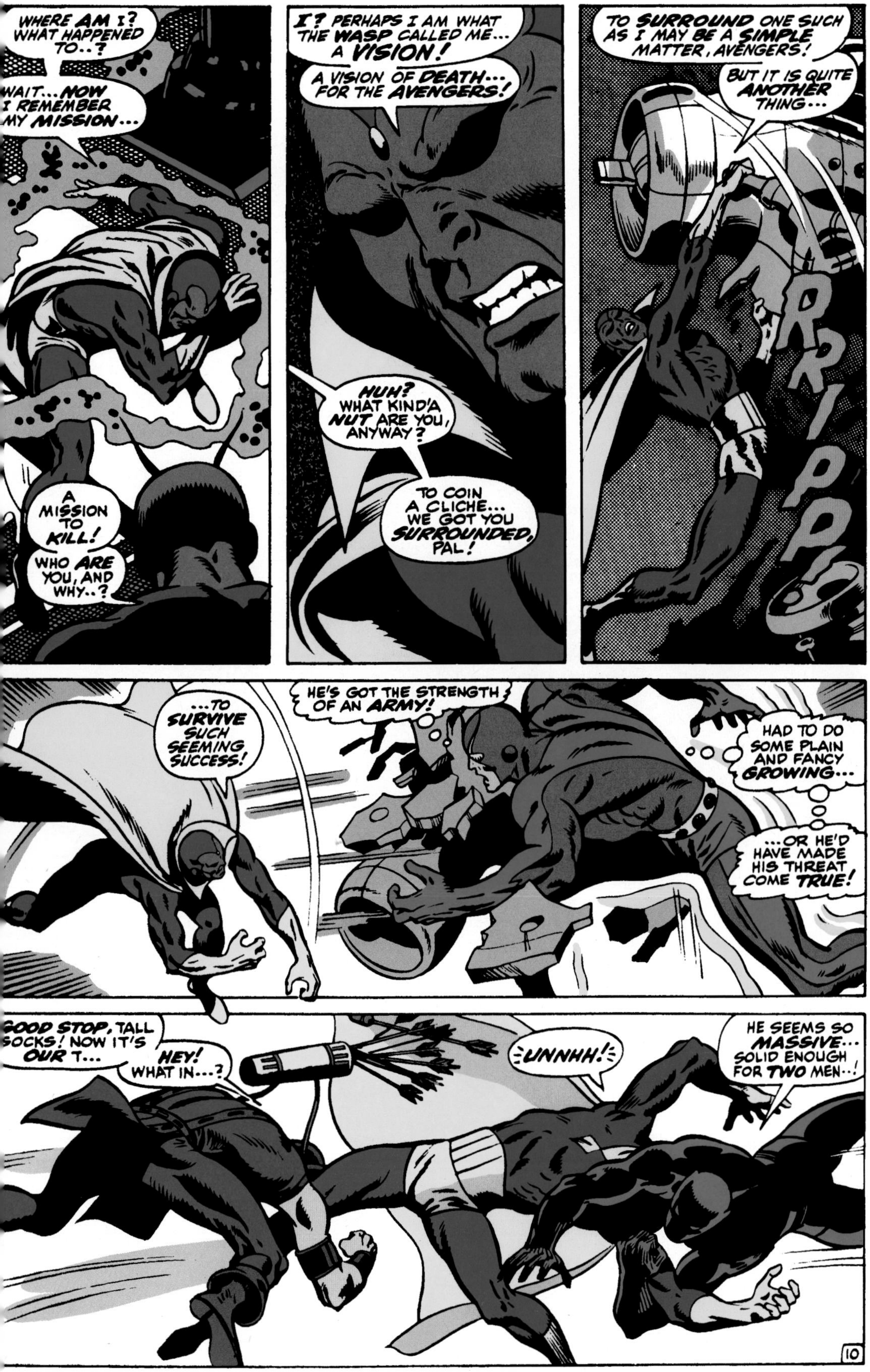
WHERE AM I? WHAT HAPPENED TO..?
WAIT...NOW I REMEMBER MY MISSION...
A MISSION TO KILL!
WHO ARE YOU, AND WHY..?
I? PERHAPS I AM WHAT THE WASP CALLED ME... A VISION!
A VISION OF DEATH... FOR THE AVENGERS!
HUH? WHAT KIND'A NUT ARE YOU, ANYWAY?
TO COIN A CLICHE... WE GOT YOU SURROUNDED, PAL!
TO SURROUND ONE SUCH AS I MAY BE A SIMPLE MATTER, AVENGERS!
BUT IT IS QUITE ANOTHER THING...
RRIPP!
...TO SURVIVE SUCH SEEMING SUCCESS!
HE'S GOT THE STRENGTH OF AN ARMY!
HAD TO DO SOME PLAIN AND FANCY GROWING...
...OR HE'D HAVE MADE HIS THREAT COME TRUE!
GOOD STOP, TALL SOCKS! NOW IT'S OUR T...
HEY! WHAT IN...?
UNNHH!
HE SEEMS SO MASSIVE... SOLID ENOUGH FOR TWO MEN..!

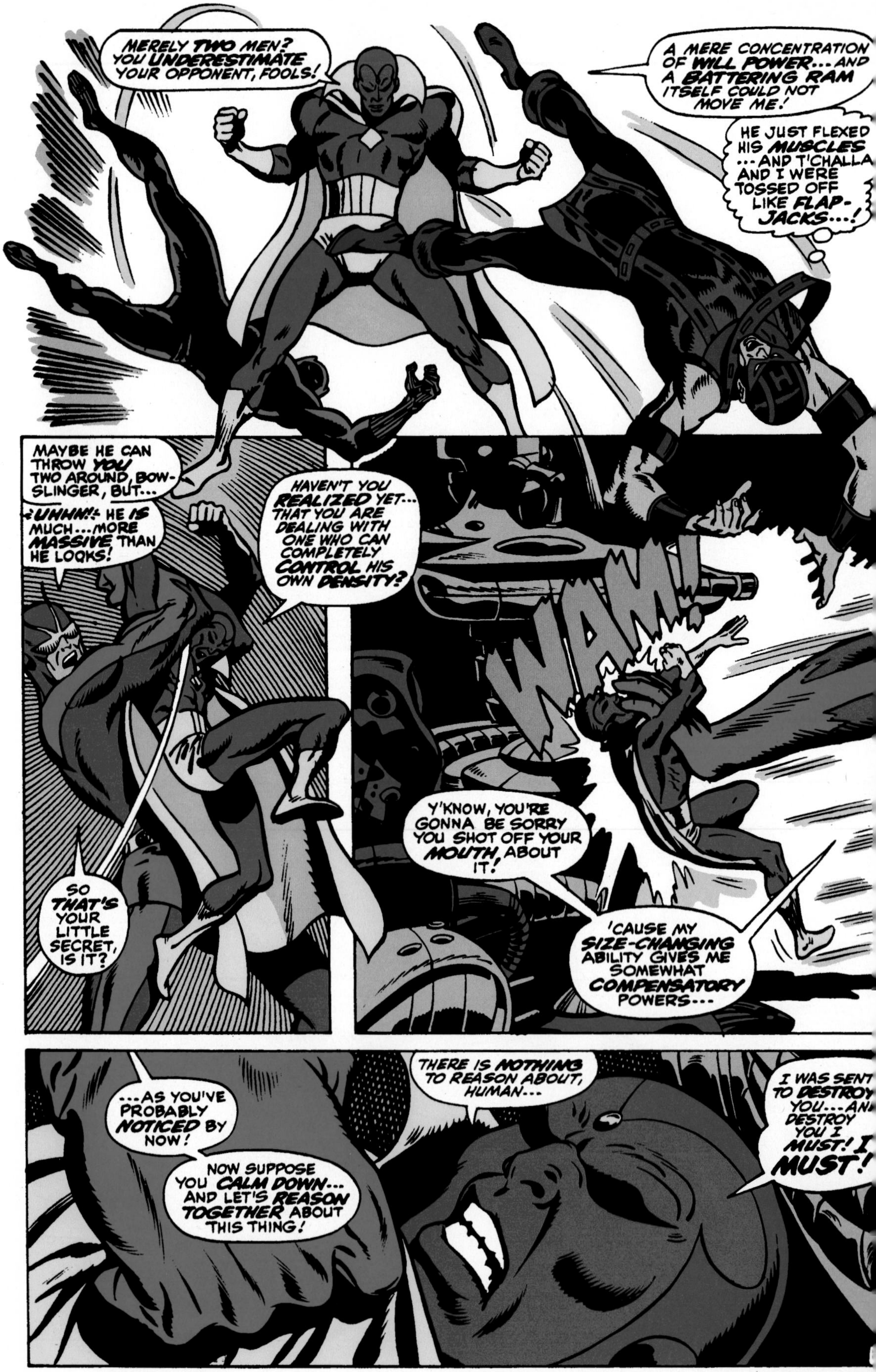
MERELY TWO MEN? YOU UNDERESTIMATE YOUR OPPONENT, FOOLS!
A MERE CONCENTRATION OF WILL POWER... AND A BATTERING RAM ITSELF COULD NOT MOVE ME!
HE JUST FLEXED HIS MUSCLES ... AND T'CHALLA AND I WERE TOSSED OFF LIKE FLAP-JACKS...!
MAYBE HE CAN THROW YOU TWO AROUND, BOW-SLINGER, BUT...
-UHHN!- HE IS MUCH... MORE MASSIVE THAN HE LOOKS!
HAVEN'T YOU REALIZED YET... THAT YOU ARE DEALING WITH ONE WHO CAN COMPLETELY CONTROL HIS OWN DENSITY?
SO THAT'S YOUR LITTLE SECRET, IS IT?
WAM!
Y'KNOW, YOU'RE GONNA BE SORRY YOU SHOT OFF YOUR MOUTH, ABOUT IT!
'CAUSE MY SIZE-CHANGING ABILITY GIVES ME SOMEWHAT COMPENSATORY POWERS...
...AS YOU'VE PROBABLY NOTICED BY NOW!
NOW SUPPOSE YOU CALM DOWN... AND LET'S REASON TOGETHER ABOUT THIS THING!
THERE IS NOTHING TO REASON ABOUT, HUMAN...
I WAS SENT TO DESTROY YOU... AND DESTROY YOU I MUST! I MUST!

IT IS *UNCANNY*... BUT, NOW THAT I HAVE *PLUMBED* MY DIM MEMORIES BACK AS FAR AS THEY WILL GO... I NO LONGER FEEL ANY DESIRE TO *ATTACK* YOU!

IN FACT, IF YOU *WISH*.. I'LL *LEAD* YOU TO HIM WHO... *CREATED* ME!

WE'VE BEEN *HUNTING* THAT METAL MANIAC FOR *WEEKS*!

SO, WE'VE GOT TO TAKE A *CHANCE* ON YOU!

STILL, JUST CASE THERE' SOME *TRICK* UP YOUR SLEEVE..

I'M KEEPIN' A *SHOCK ARRO* TRAINED RIGH ON YOUR SYNTHETIC *KISSER*!

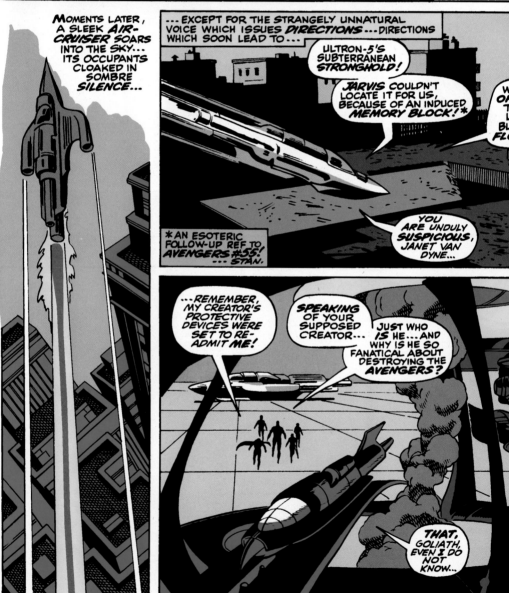

MOMENTS LATER, A SLEEK *AIR-CRUISER* SOARS INTO THE SKY... ITS OCCUPANTS CLOAKED IN SOMBRE SILENCE...

... EXCEPT FOR THE STRANGELY UNNATURAL VOICE WHICH ISSUES *DIRECTIONS* ... DIRECTIONS WHICH SOON LEAD TO...

ULTRON-5'S SUBTERRANEAN *STRONGHOLD*!

JARVIS COULDN'T LOCATE IT FOR US, BECAUSE OF AN INDUCED *MEMORY BLOCK*!*

WHY IS I' *OPENING* TO US... LIKE A BUDDING *FLOWER*

*AN ESOTERIC FOLLOW-UP REF TO *AVENGERS #55*! --- STAN.

YOU ARE UNDULY *SUSPICIOUS*, JANET VAN DYNE...

... REMEMBER, MY CREATOR'S PROTECTIVE DEVICES WERE SET TO RE-ADMIT *ME*!

SPEAKING OF YOUR *SUPPOSED* CREATOR...

JUST WHO *IS* HE... AND WHY IS HE SO FANATICAL ABOUT DESTROYING THE *AVENGERS*?

THAT, GOLIATH, EVEN *I* DO NOT KNOW...

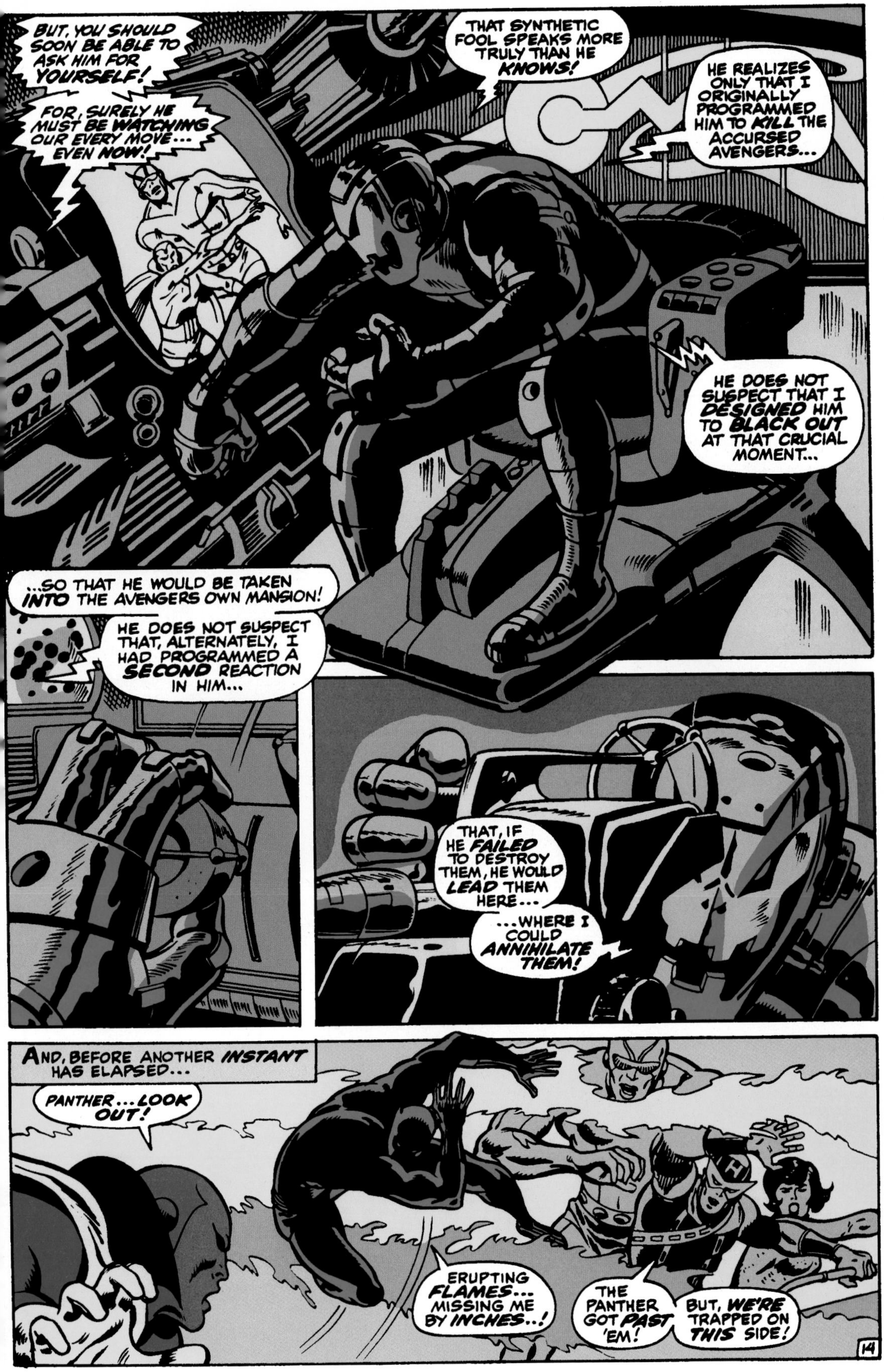
BUT, YOU SHOULD SOON BE ABLE TO ASK HIM FOR YOURSELF!
FOR, SURELY HE MUST BE WATCHING OUR EVERY MOVE... EVEN NOW!
THAT SYNTHETIC FOOL SPEAKS MORE TRULY THAN HE KNOWS!
HE REALIZES ONLY THAT I ORIGINALLY PROGRAMMED HIM TO KILL THE ACCURSED AVENGERS...
HE DOES NOT SUSPECT THAT I DESIGNED HIM TO BLACK OUT AT THAT CRUCIAL MOMENT...
...SO THAT HE WOULD BE TAKEN INTO THE AVENGERS OWN MANSION!
HE DOES NOT SUSPECT THAT, ALTERNATELY, I HAD PROGRAMMED A SECOND REACTION IN HIM...
THAT, IF HE FAILED TO DESTROY THEM, HE WOULD LEAD THEM HERE...
...WHERE I COULD ANNIHILATE THEM!
AND, BEFORE ANOTHER INSTANT HAS ELAPSED...
PANTHER... LOOK OUT!
ERUPTING FLAMES... MISSING ME BY INCHES...!
THE PANTHER GOT PAST 'EM!
BUT, WE'RE TRAPPED ON THIS SIDE!
14

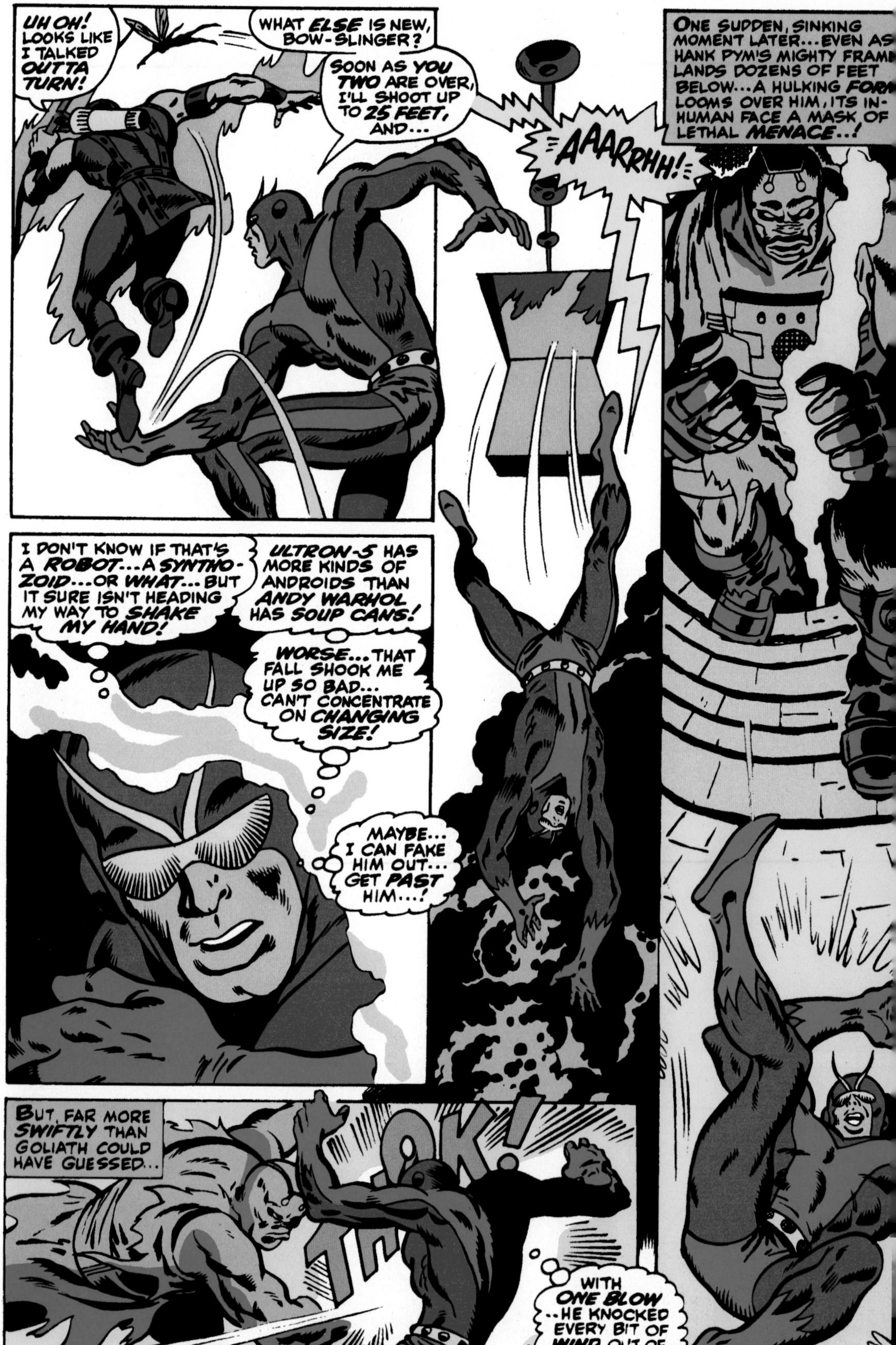

UH OH! LOOKS LIKE I TALKED OUTTA TURN!
WHAT ELSE IS NEW, BOW-SLINGER?
SOON AS YOU TWO ARE OVER, I'LL SHOOT UP TO 25 FEET, AND...
ONE SUDDEN, SINKING MOMENT LATER... EVEN AS HANK PYM'S MIGHTY FRAM LANDS DOZENS OF FEET BELOW... A HULKING FORM LOOMS OVER HIM, ITS IN-HUMAN FACE A MASK OF LETHAL MENACE..!
AAARRHH!
I DON'T KNOW IF THAT'S A ROBOT... A SYNTHO-ZOID... OR WHAT... BUT IT SURE ISN'T HEADING MY WAY TO SHAKE MY HAND!
ULTRON-5 HAS MORE KINDS OF ANDROIDS THAN ANDY WARHOL HAS SOUP CANS!
WORSE... THAT FALL SHOOK ME UP SO BAD... CAN'T CONCENTRATE ON CHANGING SIZE!
MAYBE... I CAN FAKE HIM OUT... GET PAST HIM...!
BUT, FAR MORE SWIFTLY THAN GOLIATH COULD HAVE GUESSED...
THOK!
WITH ONE BLOW ..HE KNOCKED EVERY BIT OF WIND OUT OF ME...!

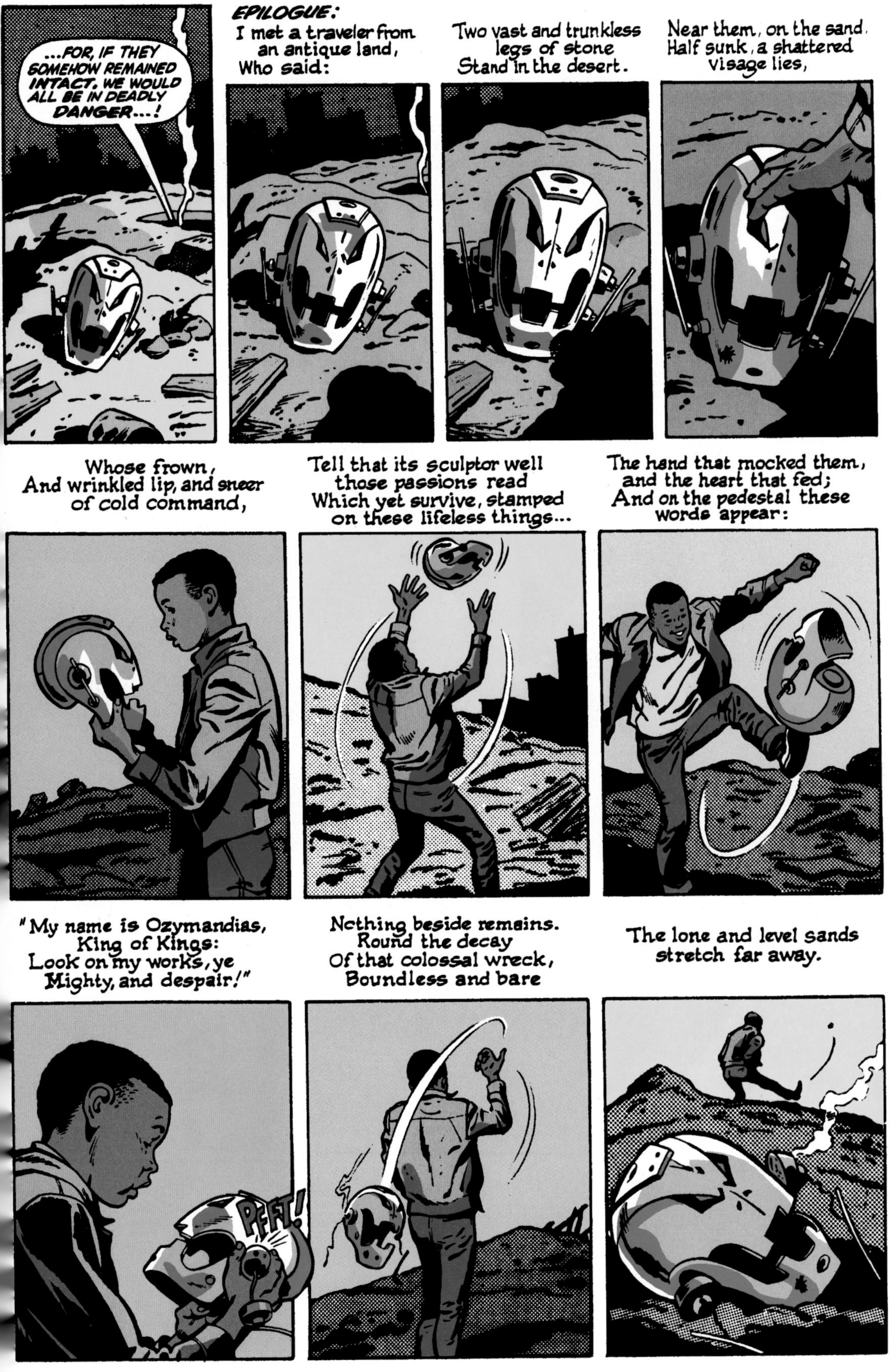

...FOR, IF THEY SOMEHOW REMAINED INTACT, WE WOULD ALL BE IN DEADLY DANGER...!
EPILOGUE:
I met a traveler from an antique land, Who said:
Two vast and trunkless legs of stone Stand in the desert.
Near them, on the sand, Half sunk, a shattered visage lies,
Whose frown, And wrinkled lip, and sneer of cold command,
Tell that its sculptor well those passions read Which yet survive, stamped on these lifeless things...
The hand that mocked them, and the heart that fed; And on the pedestal these words appear:
"My name is Ozymandias, King of Kings: Look on my works, ye Mighty, and despair!"
PFFT!
Nothing beside remains. Round the decay Of that colossal wreck, Boundless and bare
The lone and level sands stretch far away.

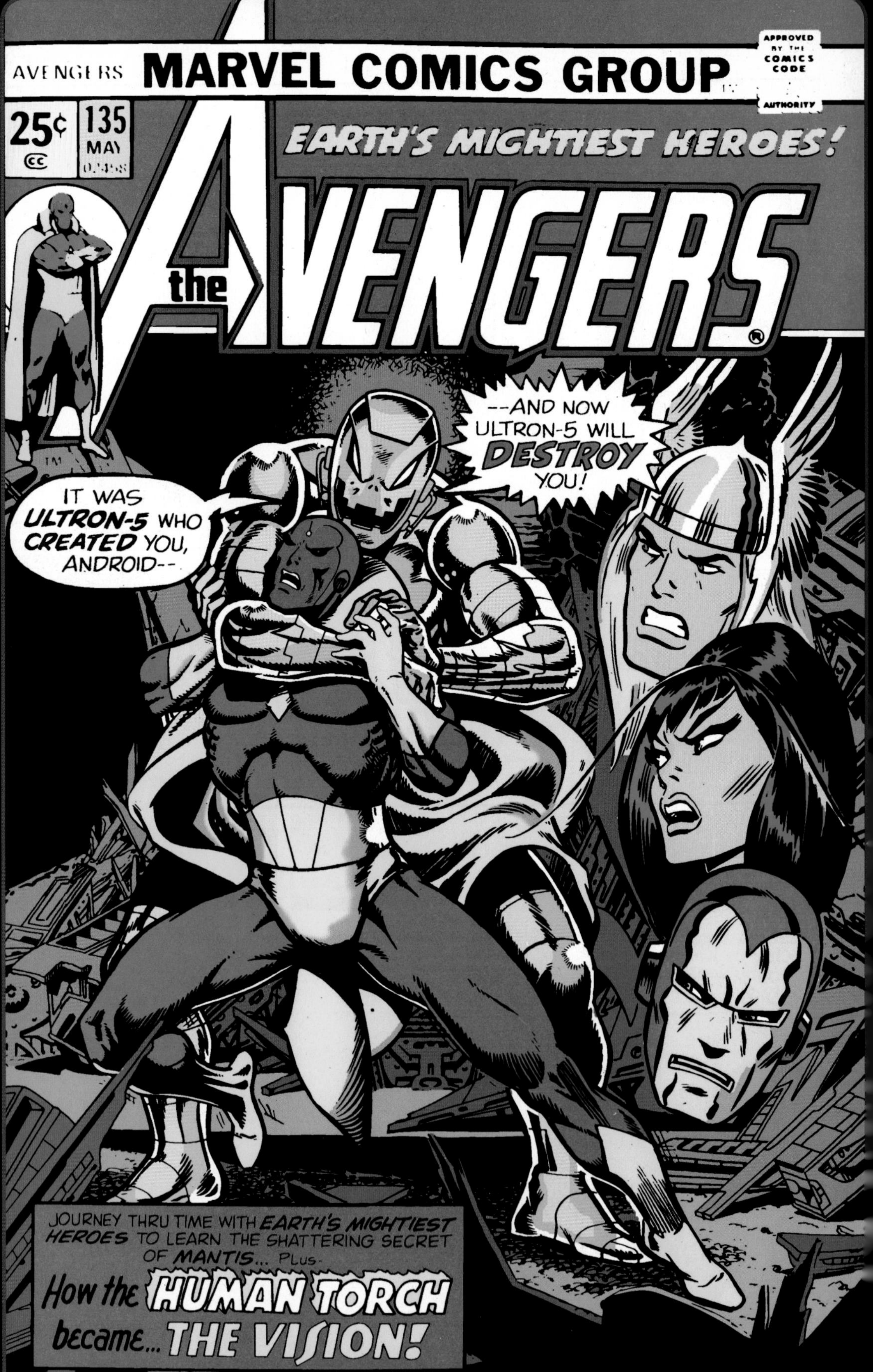
AVENGERS
MARVEL COMICS GROUP
APPROVED BY THE COMICS CODE AUTHORITY
25¢
135
MAY
EARTH'S MIGHTIEST HEROES!
the AVENGERS
IT WAS ULTRON-5 WHO CREATED YOU, ANDROID--
--AND NOW ULTRON-5 WILL DESTROY YOU!
JOURNEY THRU TIME WITH EARTH'S MIGHTIEST HEROES TO LEARN THE SHATTERING SECRET OF MANTIS... Plus-
How the HUMAN TORCH became... THE VISION!

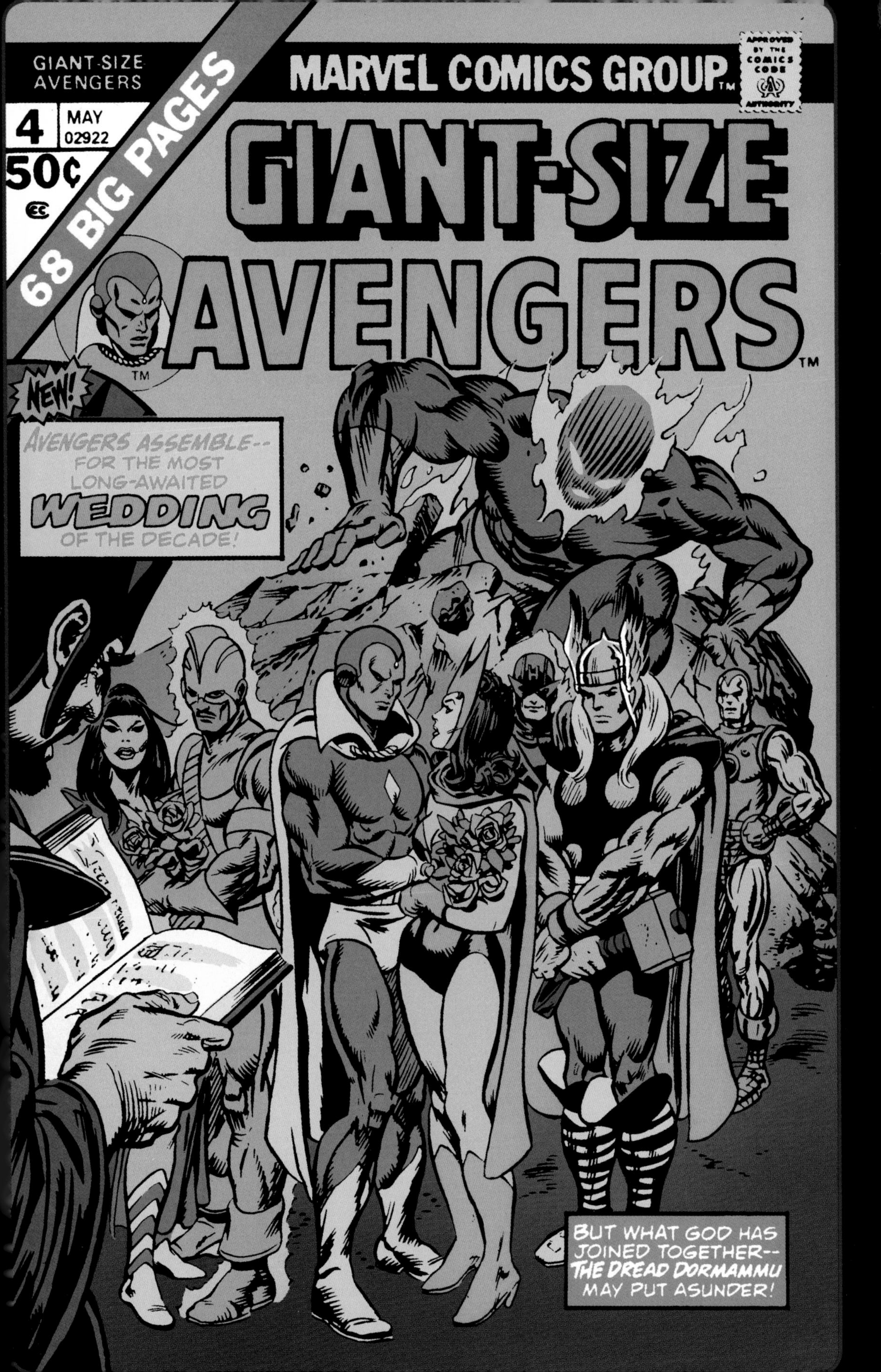
GIANT-SIZE AVENGERS
4
MAY
02922
50¢
68 BIG PAGES
MARVEL COMICS GROUP
APPROVED BY THE COMICS CODE AUTHORITY
GIANT-SIZE AVENGERS
NEW!
AVENGERS ASSEMBLE-- FOR THE MOST LONG-AWAITED WEDDING OF THE DECADE!
BUT WHAT GOD HAS JOINED TOGETHER-- THE DREAD DORMAMMU MAY PUT ASUNDER!

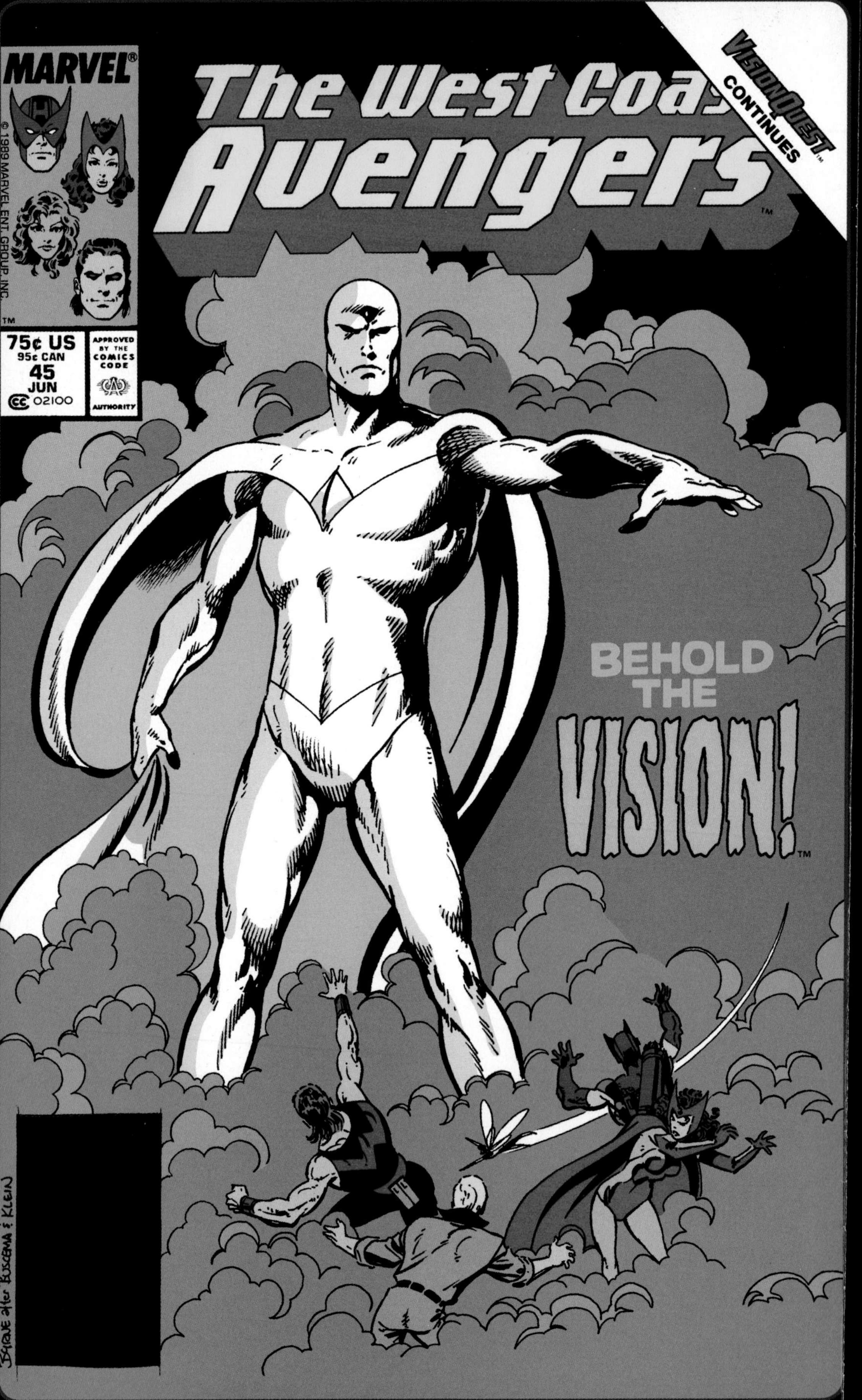

MARVEL®
The West Coas
Avengers™
VisionQuest™ CONTINUES
© 1989 MARVEL ENT. GROUP, INC.
75¢ US
95¢ CAN
45
JUN
02100
APPROVED BY THE COMICS CODE AUTHORITY
BEHOLD THE VISION!™